Black Performance and Cultural Criticism
Valerie Lee and E. Patrick Johnson, Series Editors

FATHERS, PREACHERS, REBELS, MEN

Black Masculinity in
U.S. History and Literature, 1820–1945

Edited By

TIMOTHY R. BUCKNER
and **PETER CASTER**

 THE OHIO STATE UNIVERSITY PRESS / COLUMBUS

Copyright © 2011 by The Ohio State University.
All rights reserved.

Library of Congress Cataloging-in-Publication Data
  Fathers, preachers, rebels, men : black masculinity in U.S. history and literature, 1820–1945 /
Edited by Timothy R. Buckner and Peter Caster.
    p. cm.—(Black performance and cultural criticism)
  Includes bibliographical references and index.
  ISBN 978-0-8142-1156-4 (cloth : alk. paper)—ISBN 978-0-8142-9255-6 (cd-rom)
  1. Masculinity in literature. 2. Masculinity—United States—History—19th century. 3. Masculinity—United States—History—20th century. 4. African American men in literature. I. Buckner, Timothy R., 1974– II. Caster, Peter, 1972– III. Series: Black performance and cultural criticism.
  PS374.M37F38 2011
  810.9'928608996073—dc22
                              2011006001

Cover design by Laurence J. Nozik
Text design by Juliet Williams
Type set in Adobe Bembo
Printed by Thomson-Shore, Inc.

∞ The paper used in this publication meets the minimum requirements of the American National Standard for Information Sciences—Permanence of Paper for Printed Library Materials.
ANSI Z39.48-1992.

9 8 7 6 5 4 3 2 1

Contents

Illustrations

Acknowledgments

This book has benefited from the help and encouragement of many institutions and individuals. We would like to thank our colleagues at Troy University's Department of History and the University of South Carolina Upstate's English Department for their collegiality and suggestions in the development of this project. USC Upstate's Office of Sponsored Awards and Research Support and the Center for Undergraduate Research and Scholarship provided funding for its completion. Riché Richardson and Jim Sidbury have shaped this collection in both direct and indirect ways, and we are grateful for their assistance, particularly Riché's eloquent postscript. The outside reviewers for The Ohio State University Press provided invaluable recommendations in shaping this book, and Sandy Crooms, Maggie Diehl, Malcolm Litchfield, and the entire staff of the Press remain the finest editors for which we could hope. Former USC Upstate undergraduate student Rachel McAllister provided important assistance in conducting the research for the introduction. Parts of chapter 1 were previously published in the *Journal of Southern History*. The University of North Carolina Chapel Hill Libraries provided permission to reprint images, while the Wofford College Sandor Teszler Library made other resources available. We are both indebted to the Buckner family, who has endured our shared obsession with national history and race for years. Most importantly, we thank the contributors to this book, whose essays shaped our understanding of race in history and imagination and constitute the book itself. Any errors are the responsibility of the editors alone.

Introduction

TIMOTHY R. BUCKNER and PETER CASTER

On August 19, 1864, President Abraham Lincoln met with Indian Affairs Commissioner William Dole, Wisconsin judge Joseph T. Mills, and Postmaster General Alexander Randall to discuss the upcoming presidential election and the need for a Republican victory to ensure sustained emancipation. Lincoln's demeanor became heated when he asserted he could never "return to slavery the black warriors" who saw directed combat with the U.S. Army. Later in the conversation, Lincoln related what he seemed to intend as a humorous episode from his 1858 debates with Stephen Douglas in which a black man he described as "a Sambo" declared, "I would vote for Massa Lincoln." Judge Mills then recalled his arrival at the White House when he met Frederick Douglass, and while at the time Mills recognized him, in conversation with Lincoln, Dole, and Randall, he describes in jest mistaking Douglass for the president.[1] This brief account of these white men's conversation depicts competing versions of black manhood as violently heroic, subservient, and presidential—though what humor Mills sought in fictionalizing his encounter with the famous abolitionist may have been lost on Douglass himself, who was nominated as a fringe candidate for vice president at the Syracuse National Nominating Convention in 1856, but was not chosen given the need to establish a more viable (white) candidate.[2] Here we see competing stereotypes, the conflation of history and fiction, Douglass and Lincoln as the titans of the mid-nineteenth-century color line, and the dubious viability of a black man for national office.

ALMOST A CENTURY and a half later, the 2008 presidential campaign offered a national political stage for the sustained and vexed challenges of racial difference in the United States. In terms of race history, the election of a black man as president of the United States functions as a symbolic act that does not end racism or resolve long-held implications of race with class in the color of poverty. For the twenty-first century, like those before, there remains the problem of the color line, though its racial calculus of division has become increasingly complicated in the recognition of other powerful demarcations of difference, particularly gender, class, ethnicity, sexuality, and disability.

President Barack Obama's most prominent articulation of these cultural schisms occurred in what has become known as the then-candidate's "race speech," a March 18, 2008, address hotly anticipated to acknowledge and perhaps resolve the controversy that emerged in response to inflammatory remarks made by his former pastor Reverend Jeremiah Wright in 2003 and replayed during the campaign. Its title, "A More Perfect Union," and initial delivery at the Philadelphia Constitution Center rhetorically join the birthplace of independence and the Preamble of the Constitution, echoing the titular line's prior use in Abraham Lincoln's "First Inaugural Address," as well as the title of a 2001 book by Jesse Jackson Jr., the co-chair of the Obama national campaign, Illinois congressional representative, and son of civil rights activist Reverend Jesse Jackson Sr.[3] The speech provides one presentist vantage point from which to begin an interdisciplinary study of the history and literature of black manliness in the nineteenth- and early-twentieth-century United States, because a black man whose election makes him at once exceptional and representative emphasizes some of the common threads uniting the essays in this collection: black stereotypes fostering fear and shame, the legacy of slavery, expectations and realities of criminality and poverty, and the imbrications of autobiography with national history.

Obama derided how Wright's invective taken out of context "conformed to the caricatures being peddled by some commentators," though he distanced himself from the anger and what he described as the lack of hope in the minister's rhetoric. He offered his own family as an American story of racial difference and patriotic commitment; his wife "carries within her the blood of slaves and slave owners," while his white Kansas grandmother "once confessed her fear of black men who passed by her on the street" and used "racial or ethnic stereotypes that made [him] cringe." Obama listed some of the sources of his former pastor's despair, particularly the "lack of economic opportunity among black men, and the shame and frustration that came from not being able to provide for one's family," silent resentments that "find voice in the barbershop or around the kitchen table." The presumptive patriarchy in a black man's responsibility to provide economically for his family produces the dishonor in being unable to do so, feelings vented in the masculine and public place of the "barbershop" and shared in the feminine, domestic, and private space of the "kitchen table." Those commonly raced but separately gendered spheres join in the call-and-response of the "voice in the church" that had prompted the controversy for which the presidential candidate then answered, but he pointed out that the history of inequity long precedes Wright's 2003 remarks. After a comment on the Confederate flag's persistence, Obama paraphrased a passage from William Faulkner's *Requiem for a Nun* (1951): "The past isn't dead and buried. In fact, it isn't even past," at once yoking past with present and fiction with history.[4] The speech concluded with an anecdote drawn from the campaign trail describing an older black man's commitment to political volunteering rooted in his response to a young white woman's promise to fight poverty on behalf of all families, a "single moment of recognition between that young white girl and that old black man."[5] In this campaign speech, mutual resolve across differences of race and gender (and age) provided a starting point toward that more perfect union.

Such an address offers an important textual case in merging history and imagination, as political speeches present documents that record the tenor of their time even as they chart its change, while incorporating literary devices for rhetorical effect. Response to the speech varied widely, and pertinent to the disciplinary approaches of this collection, historian Garry Wills positively compares it with Abraham Lincoln's "Cooper Union address," while renowned African American literary scholar Houston A. Baker Jr. describes it as "mimicry, aping Martin Luther King Jr."[6] Baker's response is characteristic of his occasionally iconoclastic skepticism regarding supposedly progressive turns in racial relations.[7] Here, he invokes minstrelsy and animal imagery, the mimic and the ape, and thereby self-consciously employs some of the widely held racist stereotypes with which black masculinity contends.[8] Paradoxically, Baker's critique itself incorporates the terms and tropes that are part of the history of racism in order to accuse Obama of demonstrating an insufficient commitment to the problems of African Americans, precisely the debate of whether he is "'too black' or 'not black enough,'" which the candidate addressed in the very speech.

Encoded in the oratory and this trace of academic response, then, we see the critical points of analysis in black masculinity studies crucial to this book: the lasting power of racial caricatures; their co-optation in minstrelsy as a largely white imagination of blackness; the relationship of individual experience with a larger history; the dependence of the present on the past and the need to reinterpret that past in order to open opportunities for the future; and even a gesture to the truth of fiction— tellingly, to an American novelist best known for complex narratives intertwining black and white characters. We are not yet done with the past, nor is it done with us. It is in attention to historical evidence and the literary record that we can recognize how completely the negative stereotypes of black masculinity—poverty, lack of intelligence, physicality, lawlessness, lying, capacity for violence, rapaciousness—were the justifi- cations for slavery that contributed to, on one hand, subsequent structural inequalities, and on the other, the fearful imaginations projected onto black men, masks with which they have had to contend. Baker's gam- bit casts Obama as a minstrel, in object and method raising longstand- ing questions regarding a black man's authenticity and in what capacity blackness and masculinity might be performatively embodied, particu- larly in the focus on the individual or the broader collective, whether personal achievement or alliances for the social and economic gain of the disenfranchised. Finally, Baker and Wills look backward to the familiar figures of Lincoln and King as the primary touchstones for the record of racial conflict in the United States, though the presence of African American men in national history is both longer and more crowded.

The History of Black Masculinity— and Its Subsequent Historiography

Venture Smith's 1737 account of his arrival in Rhode Island presented one of the earliest documented black masculinities, and his physical strength, resistance, emphasis on family, and struggle to earn his free- dom and that of his wife and children initiated the continuing conver- sation of what it means to be a black man in America. Smith's 1798 memoir, *A Narrative of the Life and Adventures of Venture, a Native of Africa, but Resident above Sixty Years in the United States of America, Related by Himself,* describes the trials by which his physical strength, "once equal if not superior to any man whom [he had] ever seen," has abandoned him in age, though he retains his freedom, wife, property, and character of "truth and *integrity.*"[9] Such narratives challenged the presumption that such self-determination in the nation's infancy was exclusively the right of white men, a privilege of race as well as gender. In the Revolutionary period, the movement of the British North American colonies toward independence featured highly gendered rhetoric on both sides of the Atlantic, leading white American men to suggest Parliament sought to take authority away from them, placing them in the role of dependents: women, children, or slaves.[10] At the same time, these white American men over decades had constructed a legal system that removed African American men from inclusion in conventional masculinity, taking away its foundations in the ability to control the fruits of one's labor and independence, as well as denying them meaningful roles as husbands and fathers. Famously, revisions to the Declaration of Independence suppressed the metaphoric power of enslavement given its actual practice, while the U.S. Constitution equated property and personhood to appease the Southern states. Such nation-making documents consolidated the paradox of a nation reliant on slavery yet defining itself by liberty.

Enslavement proved the most significant cultural force shaping black masculinity in the first century of the United States, particularly in obviating self-ownership, challenging the fundamental integrities of male and female kinship bonds, divorcing labor from production, transforming the body into a machine, and limiting both native language use and English literacy. For black men, slavery included emasculatory rituals and the failure of the white power structure to recognize individual identity, in part through the pronouncement of new names or the lack of a name, reducing black men to gendered diminutives "boy" and "uncle." The blanket erasure of African kinship bonds in effect invented blackness as an overarching identity in America, subsuming prior filial, tribal, linguistic, and religious identities under the mark of racial enslavement.[11]

White slave owners both did and did not see their manhood reflected in these bondsmen. However much a white master might assume as holy writ his superiority as a man to what he imagined as less than human, the position of master relied upon a slave's recognition of the other's superiority. At the same time, slave owners recognized in their bondsmen the potential of revolt, especially given the vast labor fostered in plantation slavery and the thereby disparate populations, with black often outnumbering white. Though slave insurrections in the United States were relatively few, never successful for more than a brief period, and resulted in far more deaths among blacks than whites, many slave owners lived in constant fear of a revolution such as that of Toussaint L'Ouverture in Haiti and Nathaniel Turner and Gabriel, each in Virginia. In addition to brutal physical and psychological assault that only worsened in the years leading to the Civil War, slave owners employed other means to prevent such rebellion. They fostered the spread of a strand of Christianity that demanded obedience to a heavenly Father in a fashion that dovetailed with slavery's paternalism, and it promised that a fulfilling afterlife would mitigate the pain of daily oppression, forestalling resistance. Another means involved resisting education, especially literacy, because knowledgeable black men and women would undermine the presumption of white supremacy, and literate slaves might read of slave rebellions, Northern abolitionists, and the evangelism of the Second Great Awakening, which linked Christian doctrine not to submission but to the antislavery movement.

A shift from orality to literacy, testimony of slavery's injustice, and narratives of religious conversion generally shaped the often autobiographical writing of late-eighteenth- and early-nineteenth-century African American authors Smith, Quobna Ottobah Cugoano, Olaudah Equiano (or Gustavus Vassa), Ignatius Sancho, Phyllis Wheatley, and others.[12] Much of their writing provided the basis for the genre of the slave narrative especially popular in the mid-nineteenth-century North, and the conventions of autobiography, sentimentalism, and detailed descriptions of slavery's brutality and injustice met the imperatives of Northern editors seeking to represent the experiences of formerly enslaved writers for their abolitionist purposes. For black male writers in particular, the gendered modes of description in suffering and sentimentality eroded further already threatened masculine expectations of strength, rationality, and autonomy. Nevertheless, slave narratives laid the basis for stories of self to serve as the dominant mode of African American literary production, but they were from the beginning a suturing of fact and fiction for specific rhetorical effect. That uneasy alliance of authorship, editorship, facticity, and purpose led to publications including authentication by white editors and featuring subtitles such as Smith's *Related by Himself* and protestations like Harriet Jacobs's "Reader, be assured this narrative is no fiction," even as later critics and historians demonstrated the lack of absolute veracity in some of these accounts.[13] For black writers, male and female, reliance on white editors challenged their authorial independence, and exaggeration or wholesale fiction threatened the "truth and *integrity*" Smith indicated as specifically definitive of manhood.

The best-known slave narratives were those of William Wells Brown, Douglass, and Jacobs, though others also would provide the basis for popular fictional narratives of slavery, most notably Harriet Beecher Stowe relying on Josiah Henson's narrative for *Uncle Tom's Cabin; or, Life Among the Lowly* (1852) and Brown's fictionalization of mythic history in *Clotel; or, the President's Daughter: A Narrative of Slave Life in the United States* (1853).[14] Brown also authored a history of black soldiers in the American Revolution, initiating an effort to recuperate obscured historical contributions by African Americans later carried on by Charles Chesnutt, W. E. B. Du Bois, and much later, Henry Louis Gates Jr. and many others. In *The Black Man, His Antecedents, His Genius, and His Achievements* (1863), Brown describes Douglass's reputation as "more widely known than that of any other living colored man" on the basis of his autobiographies and oratory.[15] Douglass's three autobiographies published in 1845, 1855, and 1881 (the last revised in 1892) recapitulate the ideals of American masculinity for both enslaved and freed black men, emphasizing literacy, righteous violence, and sociopolitical engagement as strategies of self-ownership. In his first autobiography, it is not writing but fighting that marks his self-assertion, as he declares of his physical defeat of a white slave-breaker that he regained "a sense of [his] own manhood," implicating him within a culture of violence bound inextricably to honor in the nineteenth-century South. The three autobiographies regularly revise the author's relationship to violence as a strategy of self-formation, suggesting a shift from physical to rhetorical engagement as a means of social transformation.[16]

Through the first half of the nineteenth century, abolitionist oratory and slave narratives rendered indivisible a rhetoric of dissent and an imperative to truth shaped by political expediency within journalistic and literary forms, and the national debate over slavery laid the basis for postbellum American regulations of blackness. These included jim crow laws dismantling the Fourteenth and Fifteenth Amendments, enacting widespread segregation. The frequent practice of lynching African Americans, particularly black men accused of desiring white women, proved the most spectacular, violent, and public of social systems dedicated to the control (and often the destruction) of black male bodies. Also, the Thirteenth Amendment's guarantee of emancipation did not prevent "slavery nor involuntary servitude" in the case of "punishment for a crime," and violations as hazily defined as mischief or as minor as petty thievery produced prison sentences of contract labor, especially in the South, as unscrupulous officials and businessmen conspired to exploit the labor of black and white men to personal profit. A South Carolina prison official in 1888 falsely claimed that Lincoln effectively invented the prison: "After the emancipation of the colored people, whose idea of freedom from bondage was freedom from work and license to pillage, we had to establish means for their control. Hence came the penitentiary."[17] If white officials were to treat a fictional past as a present fact, black authors had little choice but to offer in fiction only thinly veiled accounts of actual events. In *The Marrow of Tradition* (1901), Chesnutt turned his literary attention from his previous tragicomic post-plantation tales to rioting whites in the 1898 racial massacre of Wilmington, North Carolina. That novel's villain of Captain McBane, a notorious contractor of prison labor, saw revision and expansion in the character of William Fetters in the author's 1905 novel *The Colonel's Dream,* and Du Bois described the 1901 novel as among the finest sociological analyses of 1898 massacre he had read.[18]

The merging of generic forms can be seen not only in the literature but in the historiography of the period, as Du Bois's *The Souls of Black Folk* (1903) famously structures its social, cultural, and political analysis with fragments of lyrics and music of spirituals—and the later *Darkwater* (1920) extends that work of hybridity. The magisterial *Souls of Black Folk* effectively initiated U.S. cultural historiography; it also contested Booker T. Washington's "counsels of submission" in explicitly gendered terms, pointing out that the latter "overlooked certain elements of true manhood," as "manly self-respect is worth more than lands and houses."[19] Du Bois challenged Washington's leadership in terms that questioned the masculinity not so much of his opponent as of the people they sought to lead. Male suffrage effectively established the boundaries of political power, a tenuous right for black men of the time and one that Du Bois, unlike Washington, was unwilling to compromise. However, political agency and economic opportunity were more readily available in the North than in the South, and the "New Negro Movement" Du Bois helped shepherd in the second and third decades of the twentieth century proved at once a social migration and cultural shift, culminating in vibrant African American communities established in New York and elsewhere. The literary production of the writers of the Harlem Renaissance joined the cultural prominence of black jazz musicians, two cosmopolitan coalitions privileging blackness and reinterpreting conventions of African American masculinity.[20] Those geographic and aesthetic movements occurred immediately prior to other means of expanding the national visibility and recognition of African American accomplishment, often in the then strictly gendered and racially segregated worlds of sports and military service, contributing to the postwar acceleration of the civil rights movement. The gendering of social and political power in the first half of the twentieth century laid the basis for the struggles of the second, but remained tightly bound to expectations of black masculinity that had developed and transformed through the eighteenth- and nineteenth-century United States.[21]

For scholars of history and literature, black masculinity presents a set of distinct challenges, in part because the justifications for slavery were predicated upon racist imaginings of blackness that shaped not only the historical and literary records but their subsequent interpretation and revision. Though the cultural, economic, and social circumstances of black men in the United States changed, many twentieth-century historical and sociological constructions of black manhood remained rooted in eighteenth- and nineteenth-century justifications for American slavery. In *American Negro Slavery* (1918), Ulrich B. Phillips argued that slavery was benign to the intellectually substandard enslaved and maintained by paternalistic slaveholders despite its lack of profitability, a position that largely defined slavery in academia from its publication through the 1950s. E. Franklin Frazier's *The Negro Family in the United States* (1939) presumed that contemporary problems among black communities stemmed from the destruction of the black family, as the female-headed household replaced the patriarchal order. The erosion of the traditional male role led generations of studies to contend that gender identities among black men developed pathologically, creating a sense of social impotence both inside and outside of the family.[22]

Challenges to slavery as a relatively benign paternalism did not overturn fundamental understandings of racial difference, and Kenneth Stampp and others continued to study the "peculiar institution" by focusing on slave owners, not the enslaved. That object of study shifted with Stanley Elkins's *Slavery: A Problem in American Institutional and Intellectual Life* (1959), yet in arguing for slavery's total brutality and subjugation, the historian reinforced the sense of black male inferiority, albeit as an effect rather than natural state. That historiography influenced public policy, shaping Senator Patrick Moynihan's infamous 1965 report, "The Negro Family: The Case for National Action," which perpetuated the logic of black male subjugation. Indeed, the first scholarly attention since Du Bois at the turn of the century to black experience not exclusively determined by the white power structure took place in the 1960s and thereafter. The shift to social and cultural history incorporated tools from economics, sociology, and anthropology, and John Blassingame's *Slave Community* (1972), Eugene Genovese's *Roll, Jordan, Roll* (1976), and Herbert Gutman's *The Black Family in Slavery and Freedom, 1750–1925* (1976) demonstrated the vitality and self-creation of black culture. Early-twentieth-century literary critics had already paved the way with a project demonstrating how African American literature was defined by enslavement but characterized by folklore and resistance. From 1929 to 1938, V. F. Calverton, Alain Locke, and Vernon Loggins described the "Negro soul," "the New Negro," and "Negro Author," respectively, and efforts of literary recovery surged in the 1970s and 1980s, attentive to black writers whose popularity had faded in the intervening decades, while also committed to renewing interest in formerly widely read women authors since faded to obscurity.[23]

Current African American Gender Scholarship

Feminist historians and literary scholars since the 1970s focusing on African American experience rightly have rejected the masculine normative of a presumptive *homo universalis* and focused specifically on women. Elizabeth Fox-Genovese, Jacqueline Jones, Suzanne Lebsock, and Deborah Grey White, among many others, introduced the value of examining the experience of African Americans in terms of gender as well as race; correspondingly, literary scholars such as Frances Foster, Gates, Nellie Y. McKay, Hortense Spillers, and Mary Helen Washington have participated in the recuperative project of returning black women to U.S. literary history, recognizing their contributions to the imagination of the nation.[24] However, the gains created by scholarship focusing on black women only recently have had their parallel in a focus on black men *qua* men, as opposed to a synecdoche for all African Americans. As feminist scholars have noted, gender presents a polyvalent and multidimensional continuum of difference shaped not only by institutional discourses but also by community and individual notions. Based on such work, corresponding attention to black masculine identities has occurred since the 1990s. And indeed, though often denied equal participation in rites of manhood as constructed by whites, black men in slavery and in freedom found ways to assert their belonging in a masculine culture in public and private life. Of course, as many scholars of African American women's history and literature have pointed out, black men in the United States often have asserted themselves at the expense of black women, whether in claiming the right to work, a place in the pulpit, or domination at home. However, we can understand such efforts at marginalization as part of a reaction to the culture of white supremacy rather than exclusively demonstrating an inherent masculinist tendency, an effort that partially explains rather than wholly excuses the descriptions of early-twentieth-century black families offered by Du Bois, Frazier, and others.

Many scholars of history and literature have produced excellent work in the area of black masculinity, but more work remains to be done, especially in connecting antebellum black masculine culture through jim crow to the mid-twentieth century. E. Anthony Rotundo's *American Manhood: Transformations in Masculinity from the Revolution to the Modern Era* (1993) helped initiate masculinity studies in history, and many cultural studies entries thereafter emphasize the civil rights era and afterward, as do Marcellus Blount and George P. Cunningham's *Representing Black Men* (1996), Harry Stecopoulos and Michael Uebel's *Race and the Subject of Masculinities* (1997), bell hooks's *We Real Cool: Black Men and Masculinity* (2003), Ronald L. Jackson's *Scripting the Black Masculine Body: Identity, Discourse, and Racial Politics in the Popular Media* (2006), and Roland Murray's *Our Living Manhood: Literature, Black Power, and Masculine Ideology* (2007). Other works extend a longer historical reach to the early twentieth century, such as Phillip Brian Harper's *Are We Not Men? Masculine Anxiety and the Problem of African-American Identity* (1996) and William F. Pinar's *The Gender of Racial Politics and Violence in America: Lynching, Prison Rape, & the Crisis of Masculinity* (2001), which pair the history of now with early-twentieth-century events and further refine their objects in emphasizing sexuality. Among strictly historical studies, Darlene Clark Hine and Earnestine Jenkins's two-volume reader, *A Question of Manhood: A Reader in U.S. Black Men's History and Masculinity* (1999, 2001), is magisterial in its breadth, but understanding black masculinity can also engage the imaginative discourse crucial to recognizing the fantasies and fears that have a part in producing it.[25]

Other excellent entries focus more narrowly in era and region. Gail Bederman's *Manliness and Civilization: A Cultural History of Gender and Race in the United States, 1880–1917* (1995), Marlon B. Ross's *Manning the Race: Reforming Black Men in the Jim Crow Era* (2004), and Martin Anthony Summers's *Manliness and its Discontents: The Black Middle Class and the Transformation of Masculinity, 1900–1930* (2004) offer elegant accounts, as does Riché Richardson's *Black Masculinity and the U.S. South* (2007).[26]

This collection brings together scholars of history and literature focused on the discursive performances and lived experience of black men, not to re-center African American identity as male, but to demarcate the specifically masculine character of cultural practices as they have developed historically.[27] While some essays are in and of themselves interdisciplinary, others are situated more fully in one discipline or another, and their combination demonstrates the mutual implications of individual and social, evidenced and imaginative, in the broad, rich, and diverse texture of black masculinity, which presents a complex song of many, many voices. The song must be sung because the imagination of the black man as a threat, whether to personal security or national identity, maintains a lasting power. From the 2009 arrest of African American scholar Henry Louis Gates Jr. at his Cambridge home to the racial slurs of 2010 Tea Party rallies, white anxiety and hatred foster fear and anger among themselves and in the targets of their abuse. The perceived threat posed by black masculinity to the nation's unity and vitality remains an arresting one in the cultural imagination, and such a singularity proposes a set of contradictions in part definitive of black masculinity: an often mistaken threat of violence, belief in its legitimacy, and the rhetorical union of truth and fiction surrounding slavery, segregation, resistance, and self-determination. These characterizations are embodied in and challenged by the men and movements studied in the essays of this collection, which balances new accounts of well-known figures such as Chesnutt and Du Bois with the less familiar but critically important William Johnson and Nat Love.

Moreover, while singular black men typify important movements, trends, and contradictions of black masculinity, historical study of a broader texture provides valuable insight as well into the development of such formative forces as the emergence of a Northern black middle class and the African Methodist Episcopal ministry. Geographical breadth joins the historical range of these essays because black masculinity is neither limited to the American South nor embodied only in slavery and its resistance. From Los Angeles to Haiti, from Mississippi to New York, black men have defined themselves as husbands, fathers, preachers, rebels, brothers, teachers, sons, scholars, and more—the myriad ways they protested racism and claimed public rights of citizenship. These essays tellingly focus on black men at work, from the forced labor of slavery to working-class laborers to middle-class and scholarly professionals. However, these authors avoid the longstanding expectations of black men as entertainers, whether in sports or show business, performing for largely white audiences. Furthermore, these essays in their aggregate recognize the turn of the twentieth century as a vital center of gravity, the post-bellum, pre-Harlem period as an essential era of historical tension and literary production. Finally, a number of these essays extend beyond the privilege of print text in historical and literary studies, incorporating visual images and their analysis. The purpose of the collection is not to provide a historical corrective to imaginative work, to demonstrate what actual events were adapted in fictional accounts or otherwise shaped their production; instead, it is to demonstrate how history and literature operate dynamically in the formation and revision of national imaginations of black masculinity. The myth of the black male rapist as a rationalization for lynching is the most obvious and tragic example, but national conceptions of black men as liars, thieves, poor, and poor fathers ignored the history of domination, slavery, and segregation. Lying, stealing, poverty, and shame thereby can be understood more accurately not as causes, but as consequences of racism. Jeffrey B. Leak concludes in *Racial Myths and Masculinity in African American Literature* (2005) that "scholars need not romanticize or demonize black male subjectivity,"[28] and though the scholars of this collection respond to the legacy of such demonization, these essays are populated by African Americans who sought to be understood not as heroes or villains, but men.

CHAPTERS 1 AND 2 elaborate how black men in the antebellum South incorporated the demonstrations of white honor and masculinity into their own lived practices, while they negotiated their sense of self-hood directly with the dominant racial class. Historian Jeff Forret resists Orlando Patterson's famous characterization of a slave as a "person without honor," drawing from Southern antebellum magisterial court records to demonstrate that, in contrast with most current understandings, enslaved black men fought what amounted to physical and verbal duels on the basis of honor as a performance of character. While elite Southern white men might mock slave pretensions of respect and reputation, Southern white and enslaved black men shared a common culture of honor in the Old South. Black men were threatened with murder, torture, or other injury if they engaged in such challenges with white men, but subaltern black masculinity was produced in contest with other black men. Historian Timothy R. Buckner demonstrates that while slavery may have been the dominant condition of black men in the South before the Civil War, it was not an exclusive state, and black barber William Johnson interacted with black and white communities. He exemplifies an African American masculinity performed and imperfectly transferred generationally through relationships of trade and property, both within and across boundaries of race and class. Johnson presents a complex figure—free man, entrepreneur, slave owner, community leader—whose life provides a sense of the variability of race and manhood in the antebellum South.

Chapters 3 and 4 continue the emphasis on careerism as a crucible for black male identity, demonstrating how roles of business professional, preacher, and other means of social performance produced black masculinity in mid- and late-nineteenth-century America. American studies scholar Erica L. Ball shows how immorality was not bound within Southern religious confines but was part of a broader class definition of respectability for Northern black professional men. Not only ministers but editors and orators linked young black men's morality directly to combating white prejudice for racial advancement. By the 1840s, representing oneself as a virtuous "citizen father" or a "heroic son" became a hallmark of the emerging black middle class, as black masculinity was affirmed in public professional roles distinct from both women and feminine domestic space. Religious studies scholar Julius H. Bailey establishes how at a crucial movement in the development of the nineteenth-century AME Church, both men and women offered sermons and led congregations, but male ministers consolidated their authority in raising educational requirements to map the boundaries of gender rules more rigidly. The AME Church offered one of the few public spaces for African American men to demonstrate leadership in the face of their fears of falling short of what they perceived as the standards of masculinity embodied by their forerunners. Facing few professional opportunities outside of preaching and teaching, the educated black men of the ministry enhanced their professional position at the expense of black female church leaders through defining the ministry by conflating bodily strength and social authority.

Chapters 5 and 6 turn from black male self-presentation in print for largely African American readership to popular white illustrators' imaginations of black masculinity. These chapters build upon those prior in demonstrating how the efforts of black men to define themselves in terms of advancement, professionalization, and middle-class respectability faced the challenge of broadly distributed caricatures fostering images of black masculinity as impoverished and dependent. Historian Fiona Deans Halloran points out that the nation's top illustrator of the 1860s and 1870s, Thomas Nast, proved deeply ambivalent regarding the ability of black men to contribute to a public social sphere. For Nast—and by extension, his *Harper's Weekly* readers—soldiering, citizenship, and the integrity of families produced black manliness, but the possibilities of that masculinity remained limited by widespread expectations of black cultural inferiority. Literary scholar Peter Caster points out how in the wake of Reconstruction, regional reconciliation in part depended on genial depictions of Southern racial relations in publications such as *Harper's Weekly*, and while that magazine's articles remained critical of Southern racism in the 1870s and 1880s, its illustrations remained bound to antebellum racist caricatures. Black masculinity self-assertion faced massive challenges in those widespread stereotypes, and rather than ignore or deny them, African American author Charles Chesnutt subverted and then overturned them in his fiction in a manner that cost him his reading audience and thereby his full-time profession of author.

Chapters 7 and 8 focus on Nat Love, whose 1907 memoir offers a point of both arrival and departure for a black man who embodied diverse turn-of-the-century understandings of manhood, including cowboy, train porter, middle-class homeowner, and family man. Literary scholar Simone Drake focuses less on the text of the autobiography than the photos included and the records of Love's residences at the turn of the century, determining the specific ways Love refused a narrow definition of blackness and insists on transcending racial geographies. Black masculinity, like much human identity, is produced in ownerships of property, community, and self, however fictive the narratives of that self. In a complementary approach, historian Charity Fox reads the memoir *The Life and Adventures of Nat Love* against the grain of autobiography, suggesting instead that the generic conventions of his truth-telling blur to profound effect. His assertion that he is the real-life inspiration for Deadwood Dick, the popular dime novel character of the late 1800s, is one self-representation among many in which he negotiated barriers of race and class. Black masculinity, when produced at a regional frontier, creates new possibilities for economic necessities to trump racist values and foster at least some type of equality.

The final two chapters and the postscript elaborate the complex ways in which twentieth-century black masculinity responded to, appropriated, reinterpreted, or rejected imaginations of race and gender in the nineteenth century. Literary scholar Colleen C. O'Brien turns to Du Bois's little-examined 1909 biography of John Brown to demonstrate that the insurrectionary tradition of U.S. literature bound revolution to race from the start. Black masculinity thereby proves nation making even as it is racially fluid, embodied in cosmopolitanism, and bound to the landscape, rejecting both strict racial difference and racist white nationalism. Historian Malinda Alaine Lindquist reinterprets how black social scientists such as Du Bois and Frazier confronted racist expectations through engaging their reverse, the actual and the ideal of black family life. Specifically for Frazier, African American manhood was affirmed through social determinations whose enabling opportunities need not be bound to the challenges of attaining and maintaining middle-class status; black masculinity could include positive understandings of working-class fatherhood, self-concept, and authority. In her postscript, Riché Richardson points how understandings of black masculinity in the twenty-first century must engage meaningfully the complex history of black male experience and representation without being bound to its past or ignoring the transnational and cross-gender contexts of racial and gender identities.

The interdisciplinary nature of this collection recognizes that textual evidence and its interpretation provide the basis for both historical and literary study, contributing to the interdependence of the fields as well as their mutual uneasiness, and the cross-disciplinary nature of this collection results from the intersecting paths of history and literary study. In the 1980s, historians faced increasing challenges regarding the degree to which their practices of compiling and understanding historical records were shaped by narrativization and the interpretive strategies of reading itself. At the same time, canons of literature destabilized due to the recognition that aesthetic valuation did not take place outside of ideology, and literary critics and theorists turned to history and cultural difference as powerful bases of organization. Both humanities disciplines shifted from a foundation of *homo universalis* to social categorizations organized along fault lines of difference, most notably race and gender but also including class, ethnicity, and sexuality. Therefore, the line between historiographic and literary methodologies has blurred even as their shared bedrock has shifted.

Literary scholarship generally has proven more welcome to historiography in critical movements first described as new historicism and later naturalized to become merely good scholarship. Still, many critics of literature relegate historical documentation to evidence of context, an order secondary to the primary interpretive claims. Historians have been less willing to make wide use of imaginative texts beyond ornamental gestures to literary figures (Faulkner remains a favorite for historians of the South), as the emphasis on evidence over interpretation precluded, or at least limited, the relevance of fiction. The destabilizing intellectual shifts of the recent decades—the interpretative emphasis in history and the empiricism of historical documentation for literature—brought history's linguistic turn and literature's historical turn, and the past decades have seen an increase in interdisciplinary inquiry exciting in its impulses but uneven in its execution. This collection brings together historians and literary scholars in a fashion that demonstrates their shared roles while emphasizing their different strengths, and at the same time provides a contribution to race and gender scholarship, necessary precisely because of the tremendous shifts that have shaped that scholarly production. In their aggregate, these essays both join the growing body of work in history and literature attentive to gender, and they offer a response to Brown's 1863 call in *The Black Man, His Antecedents, His Genius, and His Achievements.* Just as Brown made literary narrative and the writing of history his dual methods in telling the stories of African Americans too large and complex to be contained entirely in either form, so too do these historians and critics attend to both discursive modes in the production not of the singular "Black Man," but the plural and contradictory depictions of black masculinity, those who have been fathers, preachers, rebels, and men.

Notes

1. *Abraham Lincoln Complete Works, Comprising His Speeches, Letters, State Papers, and Miscellaneous Writings, vol. 2,* John G. Nicolay and John Hay, eds. (New York: Century Co., 1894), 562; Matthew Pinsker, *Lincoln's Sanctuary: Abraham Lincoln and the Soldiers' Home* (New York: Oxford University Press, 2003), 159–61; William S. McFeely, *Frederick Douglass* (New York: W. W. Norton, 1991), 232.

2. John Stauffer, *The Black Hearts of Men: Radical Abolitionists and the Transformation of Race* (Cambridge, MA: Harvard University Press, 2004), 20. Douglass also was nominated for vice president in 1872 representing the Equal Rights Party.

3. Jesse Jackson Jr. with Frank E. Watkins, *A More Perfect Union: Advancing New American Rights* (New York: Welcome Rain Publishers, 2001); Barack Obama, "A More Perfect Union" (18 March 2008), accessed 16 February 2009, http://www.cnn.com/2008/POLITICS/03/18/obama.transcript/.

4. The actual line reads, "The past is never dead. It's not even past." William Faulkner, *Faulkner: Novels 1942–1954* (New York: The Library of America, 1994), 535.

5. Obama, "A More Perfect Union" (18 March 2008), accessed 16 February 2009, http://www.cnn.com /2008/POLITICS/03/18/obama.transcript/.

6. Garry Wills, "Two Speeches on Race," *The New York Review of Books* (1 May 2008), accessed 19 October 2010, http://www.nybooks.com/articles/21290. Houston

A. Baker Jr.'s remarks are included in a panel titled "What Should Obama Do about Rev. Jeremiah Wright?" *Salon* (29 April 2008), 2, accessed 19 October 2010, http://www.salon.com/opinion/feature/2008/04/29/obama_wright/index1.html.

7. See Houston A. Baker Jr., *Betrayal: How Black Intellectuals Have Abandoned the Ideals of the Civil Rights Era* (New York: Columbia University Press, 2008).

8. For stereotypes as a justification of slavery, see George M. Frederickson, *The Black Image in the White Mind: The Debate on Afro-American Character and Destiny, 1817–1914* (New York: Harper & Row, 1971); John W. Blassingame, *The Slave Community: Plantation Life in the Antebellum South* (New York: Oxford University Press, 1972); Joseph Boskin, *Sambo: The Rise and Demise of an American Jester* (New York: Oxford University Press, 1986), 4; James F. Davis, *Who Is Black? One Nation's Definition* (University Park: Pennsylvania State University Press, 1991); Jan Nederveen Pieterse, *White on Black: Images of Africa and Blacks in Western Popular Culture* (New Haven, CT: Yale University Press, 1995); Sarah Meer, *Uncle Tom Mania: Slavery, Minstrelsy, and Transatlantic Culture in the 1850s* (Athens: University of Georgia Press, 2005). For historical accounts of the simulacra of minstrelsy, see Eric Lott, *Love and Theft: Blackface Minstrelsy and the American Working Class* (New York: Oxford University Press: 1995); Annamarie Bean, James V. Hatch, and Brooks McNamara, eds., *Inside the Minstrel Mask: Readings in Nineteenth-Century Blackface Minstrelsy* (Middletown, CT: Wesleyan, 1996); William J. Mahar, *Behind the Burnt Cork Mask: Early Blackface Minstrelsy and Antebellum American Popular Culture* (Urbana: University of Illinois Press, 1998).

9. Venture Smith, *A Narrative of the Life and Adventures of Venture, a Native of Africa, but Resident above Sixty Years in the United States of America* (Whitefish, MT: Kessinger, 2004), 23.

10. Republican philosophy dictated that men alone were to become citizens, and conceptions dependence and independence were cast in gendered language or in terms of slavery. The Lockean sense of patriarchy suggested that Adam was made dominant and hence all men were superior to women; John Locke, *Two Treatises of Civil Government,* Thomas Hollis, ed. (London: A. Milar et al., 1794). George Washington, often described as the "father" of the American republic, declared that "the crisis is arrived when we must assert our rights, or submit to every imposition that can be heaped upon us, till custom and use shall make us as tame and abject slaves, as the blacks we rule over with such arbitrary sway"; reprinted in Michael P. Johnson, ed., *Reading the American Past: Selected Historical Documents,* vol. 1 (Boston: Bedford/St. Martin's, 2005), 109. See also Winthop D. Jordan, *White Over Black: American Attitudes Toward the Negro, 1550–1812* (Williamsburg, VA: Published for the Institute of Early American History and Culture by the University of North Carolina Press, 1968); Edmund S. Morgan, *American Slavery, American Freedom: The Ordeal of Colonial Virginia* (New York: W. W. Norton, 1975); Sylvia Frey, *Water From the Rock: Black Resistance in a Revolutionary Age* (Princeton, NJ: Princeton University Press, 1991); Kathleen Brown, *Good Wives, Nasty Wenches, and Anxious Patriarchs: Gender, Race, and Power in Colonial Virginia* (Williamsburg, VA: Published for the Institute of Early American History and Culture by the University of North Carolina Press, 1996); Ruth Bloch, "The Construction of Gender in a Republican World," in Jack P. Greene and Jack Richon Pole, eds., *A Companion to the American Revolution* (Hoboken, NJ: Wiley & Blackwell, 2000), 605–9; Clare Lyons, *Sex among the Rabble: An Intimate History of Gender & Power in the*

Age of Revolution, Philadelphia 1730–1830 (Chapel Hill: University of North Carolina Press, 2006).

11. For an analysis of the shift from African kinship bonds to a common identity of blackness in early African American writing, see James Sidbury, *Becoming African in America: Race and Nation in the Early Black Atlantic* (New York: Oxford University Press, 2007). See also Francis Smith Foster, *Witnessing Slavery: The Development of Ante-Bellum Slave Narratives* (Westport, CT: Greenwood Press, 1979), and Henry Louis Gates Jr. and William Andrews, eds., *Pioneers of the Black Atlantic: Five Slave Narratives* (New York: Basic Civitas Books, 1998).

12. Smith; Quobna Ottobah Cugoano, *Thoughts and Sentiments on the Evil of Slavery* (New York, Penguin, 1999); Olaudah Equiano. *The Interesting Narrative of the Life of Olaudah Equiano Or Gustavus Vassa, The African, Written by Himself,* vol. 1 (Whitefish, MT: Kessinger, 2004); Ignatius Sancho, *Letters of the Late Ignatius Sancho, an African,* Joseph Jekyll, ed. (London: No. 20 Charles Street, Westminster, 1802); Phillis Wheatley, *Poems on Various Subjects, Religious and Moral* (New York: Cosimo Classics, 2005).

13. Harriet Jacobs, *Incidents in the Life of a Slave Girl* (New York: Oxford University Press, 1988), 5. Henry Louis Gates Jr. has brought attention to African American literature in general and to slave narratives and early fiction in particular, largely through editing dozens of such works. See especially Gates's *Figures in Black: Words, Signs, and the "Racial" Self* (New York: Oxford University Press, 1987).

14. William Wells Brown, *Narrative of William Wells Brown, a Fugitive Slave. Written by Himself* (Boston: The Anti-Slavery Office, 1847); Frederick Douglass, *Narrative of the Life of Frederick Douglass* (San Diego: ICON Classics, 2005) and *My Bondage and My Freedom* (Chicago: Johnson Pub. Co., 1970); Jacobs; Harriet Beecher Stowe, *Uncle Tom's Cabin; or, Life Among the Lowly* (Boston: John P. Jewett & Co, 1852); Brown, *Clotel; or, the President's Daughter: A Narrative of Slave Life in the United States* (London: Partridge & Oakey, Paternoster Row, 1853). For her characterization of Uncle Tom, Stowe is understood to have relied on Josiah Henson's *The Life of Josiah Henson, Formerly a Slave, Now an Inhabitant of Canada, as Narrated by Himself* (Boston: Arthur D. Phelps, 1849).

15. Brown, *The Black Man, His Antecedents, His Genius, and His Achievements* (New York: Thomas Hamilton, 1863), 180.

16. Douglass, *Narrative; My Bondage; The Life and Times of Frederick Douglass* (London: Christian Age Office, 1882). For descriptions of rituals of manhood and honor, see Kenneth S. Greenberg, *Honor & Slavery* (Princeton, NJ: Princeton University Press, 1996); Craig Thompson Friend and Lorri Glover, *Southern Manhood: Perspectives on Masculinity in the Old South* (Athens: University of Georgia Press, 2004).

17. U.S. Constitution, amend. 13, sec. 1. Norton W. Brooker, "[Address]," *Proceedings of the Annual Congress, 1888* (Chicago: Knight & Leonard, 1888), 70. In *The Philadelphia Negro: A Social Study* (Boston: Ginn & Co., 1899), W. E. B. Du Bois identifies that crimes committed by African Americans did increase after the end of the Civil War, but due to a dramatic environmental shift rather than any natural predisposition, 3, 240. David M. Oshinsky demonstrates the perpetuation of antebellum practices of racial control in jim crow–era incarceration in *"Worse than Slavery": Parchman Farm and the Ordeal of Jim Crow Justice* (New York: Free Press Paperbacks, 1997). H. Bruce Franklin is the literary scholar who has done the most to draw attention to the histor-

ical relationship between the plantation and the prison in *Prison Literature in America: The Victim as Criminal and Artist* (New York: Oxford University Press, 1989) and *Prison Writing in 20th-Century America* (New York: Penguin, 1998). See also Peter Caster, *Prisons, Race, and Masculinity in Twentieth-Century U.S. Literature and Film* (Columbus: The Ohio State University Press, 2008), and Tara T. Green, ed., *From Plantation to the Prison: African American Confinement Literature* (Macon, GA: Mercer University Press, 2007).

18. Chesnutt, *The Marrow of Tradition* (Ann Arbor: University of Michigan Press, 1990) and *The Colonel's Dream* (Miami: Mnemosyne, 1969). For descriptions of Du Bois's response to Chesnutt, see Joseph R. McElrath's introduction to *Critical Essays on Charles Chesnutt* (New York: G. K. Hall & Co., 1999), 8–9.

19. W. E. B. Du Bois, *The Souls of Black Folk* (Chicago: A. C. McClurg & Co., 1903), 44, 50.

20. Martin Anthony Summers offers a fine account of the emergence of competing Northern black masculinities in *Manliness and Its Discontents: The Black Middle Class and the Transformation of Masculinity, 1900–1930* (Chapel Hill: University of North Carolina Press, 2004). The popularity of jazz and its celebrity center in Harlem's Cotton Club bears a debt to Jack Johnson, one epitome of black masculinity and the boxer who dominated heavyweight fighting in the early years of the twentieth century; however, he was forced to wait until 1908 for a white champion willing to meet him in order to officially win the title. In 1920, he opened the Cotton Club.

21. Eric Foner, *Reconstruction: America's Unfinished Revolution, 1863–1877* (New York: Harper & Row, 1988); Tera W. Hunter, *To 'Joy My Freedom: Southern Black Women's Lives and Labors after the Civil War* (Cambridge, MA: Harvard University Press, 1997); Leon F. Litwack, *Been in the Storm So Long: The Aftermath of Slavery* (New York: Alfred A. Knopf, 1979); Louis R. Harlan, *Booker T. Washington: The Wizard of Tuskegee, 1901–1915* (New York: Oxford University Press, 1983); David Levering Lewis, *W. E. B. Du Bois: Biography of a Race, 1868–1919* (New York: Henry Holt, 1993); James West Davidson, *'They Say': Ida B. Wells and the Reconstruction of Race* (New York: Oxford University Press, 2007); Eileen Southern, *The Music of Black Americans: A History,* 3rd ed. (New York: W. W. Norton, 1997); Barbara Foley, *Specters of 1919: Class and Nation in the Making of the New Negro* (Urbana: University of Illinois Press, 2003); Florette Henri, *Black Migration: Movement North, 1900–1920* (New York, Anchor/Doubleday, 1975); David Levering Lewis, *When Harlem Was in Vogue* (New York: Oxford University Press, 1982); David K. Wiggins and Patrick B. Miller, *The Unlevel Playing Field: A Documentary History of the African American Experience in Sport* (Urbana: University of Illinois Press, 2003).

22. Ulrich B. Phillips. *American Negro Slavery* (Charleston, SC: BiblioBazaar, 2006); E. Franklin Frazier, *The Negro Family in the United States* (Notre Dame, IN: University of Notre Dame Press, 2001).

23. Kenneth M. Stampp, *The Peculiar Institution: Slavery in the Ante-Bellum South* (New York: Vintage, 1989). Stanley Elkins, *Slavery: A Problem in American Institutional and Intellectual Life* (Chicago: University of Chicago Press, 1976); Patrick Moynihan, "The Negro Family: The Case For National Action" (Washington, DC: United States Department of Labor, Office of Policy Planning and Research, 1965), accessed 2 March 2009, http://www.dol.gov/oasam/programs/history/webid-meynihan.htm; John Blassingame, *Slave Community: Plantation Life in the Antebellum South* (New York:

Oxford University Press, 1972); Eugene Genovese, *Roll, Jordan, Roll: The World the Slaves Made* (New York: Vintage, 1976); Herbert Gutman, *The Black Family in Slavery and Freedom, 1750–1925* (New York: Random House, 1976); Victor Francis Calverton, *Anthology of American Negro Literature* (New York: The Modern Library, 1929); Alain Locke, *The New Negro* (New York: Albert and Charles Boni, 1925); and Vernon Loggins, *The Negro Author, His Development in America* (New York: Columbia University Press, 1931).

24. Any account of historical research focusing on the lives of black women would be incomplete, but particularly influential works include Suzanne Lebsock, *The Free Women of Petersburg: Status and Culture in a Southern Town, 1784–1860* (New York: W. W. Norton, 1984); Jacqueline Jones, *Labor of Love, Labor of Sorrow: Black Women, Work, and the Family from Slavery to the Present* (New York: Basic Books, 1985); Deborah Grey White, *Ar'n't I a Woman? Female Slaves in the Plantation South* (New York: W. W. Norton, 1985); Elizabeth Fox-Genovese, *Within the Plantation Household: Black and White Women of the Old South* (Chapel Hill: University of North Carolina Press, 1988). Critical early entries within literary studies include Foster, *Witnessing Slavery* and *Written by Herself: Literary Production by African American Women, 1746–1892* (Bloomington: Indiana University Press, 1993); Mary Helen Washington, *Invented Lives: Narratives of Black Women, 1860–1960* (New York: Doubleday, 1987); Hortense Spillers, *Comparative American Identities: Race, Sex, and Nationality in the Modern Text* (New York: Routledge, 1991); Gates's editing of the Schomburg Library of Nineteenth-Century Black Women Writers, 1988; and Nellie Y. McKay with Marcy Knopf, *The Sleeper Wakes: Harlem Renaissance Stories by Women* (New Brunswick, NJ: Rutgers University Press, 1993).

25. E. Anthony Rotundo, *American Manhood: Transformations in Masculinity from the Revolution to the Modern Era* (New York: Basic Books, 1993); Marcellus Blount and George P. Cunningham, *Representing Black Men* (New York: Routledge, 1996); Harry Stecopoulos and Michael Uebel, *Race and the Subject of Masculinities* (Durham, NC: Duke University Press, 1997); bell hooks, *We Real Cool: Black Men and Masculinity* (New York: Routledge, 2003); Ronald L. Jackson, *Scripting the Black Masculine Body: Identity, Discourse, and Racial Politics in the Popular Media* (Albany: State University of New York Press, 2006); Roland Murray, *Our Living Manhood: Literature, Black Power, and Masculine Ideology* (Philadelphia: University of Pennsylvania Press, 2007); Phillip Brian Harper, *Are We Not Men? Masculine Anxiety and the Problem of African-American Identity* (New York: Oxford University Press, 1996); William F. Pinar, *The Gender of Racial Politics and Violence in America: Lynching, Prison Rape, & the Crisis of Masculinity* (New York: Peter Lang, 2001); Darlene Clark Hine and Earnestine Jenkins, *A Question of Manhood: A Reader in U.S. Black Men's History and Masculinity, Vols. 1 and 2* (Bloomington: Indiana University Press, 1999, 2001).

26. Gail Bederman, *Manliness and Civilization: A Cultural History of Gender and Race in the United States, 1880–1917* (Chicago: University of Chicago Press, 1995); Marlon B. Ross, *Manning the Race: Reforming Black Men in the Jim Crow Era* (New York: New York University Press, 2004); Summers; Riché Richardson, *Black Masculinity and the U.S. South* (Athens: University of Georgia Press, 2007). Daniel P. Black's *Dismantling Black Manhood: An Historical and Literary Analysis of the Legacy of Slavery* (New York: Garland, 1997) and Maurice O. Wallace's *Constructing the Black Masculine: Identity and Ideality in African American Men's Literature and Culture, 1775–1995* (Durham, NC:

Duke University Press, 2002) are more admirable in intent than execution; the former works with too few sources and offers too cursory a survey, while the latter substitutes intensely theorized interpretations for historical evidence and broader contextualization. Few literary scholars focusing on black masculinity attend specifically to historical evidence beyond the literature itself—see James W. Coleman, *Black Male Fiction and the Legacy of Caliban* (Lexington: University Press of Kentucky, 2001); Jeffrey B. Leak, *Racial Myths and Masculinity in African American Literature* (Knoxville: University of Tennessee Press, 2005).

27. Bederman points out that "masculinity" is an invention of the late nineteenth century to describe characteristics of manliness distinct from "manhood," a much older term functionally synonymous with honor and delineating the positive attributes men sought to embody, 16–19. The essays of this collection use the term "masculinity" to describe traits characterizing manliness irrespective of positive or negative value as understood in their historical moment.

28. Leak, 139.

"He was no man attall"?

Slave Men, Honor, Violence, and Masculinity in the Antebellum South

JEFF FORRET

In antebellum Anderson District, South Carolina, Warren—a slave of Peter K. Norris—repeatedly threatened to kill Charles Barrett's bondman Dan. Although Warren and his wife had been "apart 12 months," he "accused Dan of being after" her and believed them altogether "too thick." Separated for a year, Warren still could not stomach the thought of his one-time spouse with another man. Protecting and defending women was one component of the masculine honor code in the Old South, and men asserted their manhood when they guarded wives and preserved reputations of self and family. However, Warren was a slave.[1] Scholars long have noted that a culture of honor flourished among Southern white men, but Bertram Wyatt-Brown excepted, Southern historians have been much slower than their counterparts studying Latin America to recognize honor among slaves.[2] Sociologist Orlando Patterson famously characterized the slave as, by definition, a "person without honor," and certainly Southern whites routinely dishonored slaves in their daily lives. They stripped bondpeople publicly for inspection at slave auctions and inflicted beatings in front of family and friends. Whippings provided the most enduring and visible bodily reminder of slaves' subordination; the lash left disfiguring scars on their backs that served as an indelible marker of their inferior position in Southern society. Absent an acute understanding of honor—and its inverse, shame—slaves would have experienced the tremendous physical pain of injury but not necessarily have felt the profound humiliation of a whipping so evident in their narratives and autobiographies.[3]

The degradation slaves suffered in white society only served to enhance their sense of honor among themselves. Antebellum Southern slaves descended from Africans for whom honor was not a foreign concept; one scholar has described honor as "the chief ideological motivation of African behaviour" not only among residents along North Africa's Mediterranean coast, but among those living in sub-Saharan Africa as well. Forms and definitions of honor differed from one culture to another, but many African peoples embraced it in some variation. For Africans forcibly transported via the Middle Passage to the American South before the formal termination of the transatlantic slave trade in 1808, relocation did not erase the significance of honor in their lives. Their white masters adhered to a code of honor too, though one from which blacks were excluded. In this context, Wyatt-Brown observes, "Male honor was richly prized in the slave quarters" of the antebellum South. Nevertheless, Southern whites could not explicitly acknowledge the honor of slaves, because to do so would recognize their manhood, undermining the fundamental premise that slaves were not men. They recognized only a narrower, vertical dimension of honor in which inferiors granted respect to those who outranked them in the social hierarchy. More than whites, slaves understood honor's horizontal component in which respect was distributed among equals. Consequently, as Wyatt-Brown noted, "[S]lave honor was confined to the slave quarters."[4]

Recovering the relationship among honor, masculinity, and violence for antebellum slave men is no simple task. The vast majority of violent episodes among slaves have gone unrecorded. If slaves belonging to the same master attacked one another, that master rarely had any legal recourse or justification for hauling the slave aggressor to court. Slaves, however, sometimes fought with bondpeople from nearby plantations. Masters might ignore such conflicts if any wounds inflicted were minor, and if they intervened at all, owners of the participants involved often handled such matters privately, without resorting to the court system. For trivial offenses, only the most litigious of masters utilized the court system for purposes of slave discipline. When slaves held by different masters severely injured, maimed, or murdered one another, though, slaveholders often pursued redress through formal legal channels, leaving a paper trail for scholars to follow.

In South Carolina, slaves accused of crimes appeared before the Courts of Magistrates and Freeholders. Extant records most thoroughly document the South Carolina upcountry districts of Anderson (including the former district of Pendleton), Laurens, Pickens, and Spartanburg. Episodes of slave-on-slave violence comprise only a small fraction of all documented slave crimes. Upcountry slaves proved far more likely to find themselves in court for assaulting not fellow bondpeople but neighborhood whites. This is not surprising, since slave codes across the South demonstrated a much stronger interest in prosecuting bondpeople for transgressions committed against whites and white property than against others in bondage. Virtually all slaves who physically assaulted a white person would face legal action, compared to only a small fraction who attacked another slave. Court of Magistrates and Freeholders records nevertheless document no fewer than seventy-five incidents of violence among slaves in antebellum South Carolina serious enough to warrant litigation. Although this figure is paltry compared to the prevalence of cases involving exclusively white combatants, when these documents are combined with scattered supporting evidence from courts in other states, the Court of Magistrates and Freeholders accounts of slave-on-slave violence offer a glimpse into an ethic of honor among slave men shared with white men in the Old South.

Slave men occasionally lashed out at whites in violent resistance, but even more frequently inflicted violence upon their counterparts in bondage. They came to blows over the possession of property, the issue of theft in the quarters, and the repayment of debts they owed to one another. Slave men also used violence to exercise dominance in the slave cabin, defend their wives from enslaved interlopers, and take vengeance upon male slaves who successfully violated their sexual claims.[5] An analysis of the circumstances prompting violent encounters among slave men, the words they uttered during confrontations, and the fighting techniques they utilized reveals that the ethic of honor so prevalent in Southern white society was ingrained in masculine slave culture as well. For some slave men, violence in the quarters afforded one means to construct a masculine identity within the context of a white society that routinely denied their manhood.

When male slaves behaved in the ways informed by and consistent with their honor code, they behaved as men. Bondage, many scholars have observed, directly challenged male slaves' manhood. The master exercised the final authority over the slave family. Without legal sanction of slave marriages, slaveholders retained the power to break up the enslaved family unit at any time, and enslaved husbands could not protect their wives from the physical or sexual abuse of the owner without risking great bodily harm. When masters whipped slave men in front of their families, they undercut male slaves' pretense of authority over their wives and children. Moreover, despite the efforts of enslaved men to provide necessities and material comforts for their families, they typically did not supply the bulk of the family's essential needs. All of these factors restricted the power male slaves maintained in their day-to-day lives. For masters, the ideal slave man was the perpetual "boy," the childlike, dependent, and submissive Sambo. As fugitive Lewis Clarke lamented, "A SLAVE CAN'T BE A MAN!"[6]

Despite Clarke's pronouncement, slave men successfully overcame the obstacles they faced to construct masculine identities. Their domination by masters certainly contributed to Southern white men's sense of mastery, but enslaved men also actively created their own paradigms of masculinity.[7] In his work on the cotton frontier of the antebellum South, Edward E. Baptist has detected different models of slave manhood. Some enslaved men acted heroically, by running away, fighting masters or overseers, or otherwise defying white authority. Others served as caretakers for new families cobbled together from the shards of broken ones. Still others acted as atomized individuals, rejecting altogether ties to other slaves. Male slaves across the South also acted as men when they took the lead in courtship or engaged in competitive contests that showcased their physical prowess. Escape, violent resistance, subversion of authority, family stewardship, and autonomy all represented attempts to forge a masculine identity amid the chaos of forced migration.[8]

Darlene Clark Hine and Earnestine Jenkins have noted that enslaved men exercised a "resistant masculinity," but they caution against "becoming ensnared in the trap of equating manhood with violence." Violent, aggressive behaviors, however, were crucial to the construction of masculinity and the functioning of the honor code for Southern men, whether white or black.[9] Southern white gentlemen engaged in duels, while lower-class white men fought rough-and-tumble brawls and eye-gouging matches.[10] For slaves, too, violence marked one expression of manhood. Bondmen sometimes defied white authority figures through individual acts of confrontation, such as Frederick Douglass's epic fight with the slave breaker Covey. After the purported two-hour altercation, Douglass recorded, "My long-crushed spirit rose, cowardice departed, bold defiance took its place." Douglass found redemption through violence. "This battle with Mr. Covey was the turning point in my career as a slave," he reflected, and it "revived within me a sense of my own manhood."[11] More extreme still, slave rebels such as Nat Turner "came to be associated with manhood and masculinity" because their violent actions marked "an unequivocal challenge to white male authority."[12]

Boasts, Insults, and Reputation

The degree to which slave men struggled for status and reputation in violent contests suggests that they possessed their own keenly developed sense of honor. Like Southern white men, bondmen employed violence to redress grievances and defend wives, family, and friends from any slights or aspersions. In 1851, Spartanburg District slave Bassett struck Joseph with "a large stick" for "abusing his wife." In Pendleton District, the slave "Leu Give the first Challeng." He "Cursed Dianna," a bond-woman of Jonathan Fealding, "& Calld her a Damnd Bitch." Dianna's sibling Jack, another slave belonging to Fealding, immediately cried out, "Dont you abuse my sister," and Leu found himself on the receiving end of the brawl that followed. Aron Motes, a slave in Laurens District, complained that other bondpeople at a corn shucking "were trying to run over Perry," another Motes family slave, "and he would not allow it." When the loyal "Aron said they should not impose on Perry or he would bust their heads," he rallied in support of a fellow bondman. As with Southern whites, slaves might invoke the concept of honor to jus-tify violence or the threat of it. At least some bondmen demonstrated the manifestations of a code of honor shared with the slave-owning class.[13]

In slaveholding locations as diverse as the border state of Delaware and Deep South Alabama, bondmen regularly voiced a willingness to defend their reputations and uphold the perceptions others held of them. When Delaware slaves Anderson and Emory quarreled at a camp meet-ing in 1858, Anderson assured Emory "that if he would follow him off the camp ground he would give him satisfaction." "Satisfaction" appears here as the operative word, the product of an encounter to determine the better man. A former Alabama slave put it more plainly: "It used to be that one man would walk up to another and say, 'You ain't no good.' And the other would say, 'All right, le's see.' And they would rassle." The resulting wrestling match helped determine rank among slave men.[14]

Slave men vocalized their readiness to protect themselves and their loved ones with violence, and their assertions and threats not only provided a warning to an adversary but announced to enslaved audiences or anyone within earshot that they would not submit meekly to another slave's insult or challenge. Threats preceded violence among slaves by mere moments or as long as weeks before a violent confrontation occurred. In Anderson District, Hew Wilson's slave "Charles said that he would knock Moses head off" before they in fact "attempted to kill Each other contrary to the lawes of this state." Also in Anderson District, Jake informed Baylis that "he could whip him." He then violated Baylis's physical space by shoving "his fist in Baylis' face." Baylis instructed him to desist, but defiantly, "Jake said he would put his hand on him as he pleased," and proceeded to "[p]ut his hands on his shoulders." After one more warning to "keep his hands off of him," Baylis gave Jake a sharp kick. In another episode, a Spartanburg District slave named Jason approached the bondman Larken, reporting the rumor that the latter had said he could "whip" Jason. Larken replied, "Goddamn you if you will follow me to the end of the lane I can do it." Not merely rhetorical devices, such pronouncements sometimes portended danger or death. In Mississippi, the slave Norvall mocked Simon "for his awkward plowing." A seething Simon, humiliated by Norvall's "laughing," retorted that "if he did not quit it, he would be damned if he didn't put his head under the dirt." A week later, Norvall was dead.[15]

Male slaves' ritual boasts and challenges reverberated throughout the quarters. Although not as elaborate or fanciful in their inflated words as the bragging of the "half horse, half alligator" Mike Fink and other semi-legendary or wholly fictional characters in the Southwestern humor genre, slaves nevertheless employed the exaggeration and masculine boasting reminiscent of the tall tales of the Old Southwest. At a Laurens District corn shucking, a dispute erupted in which "Aron boasted of his manhood" and crowed that "he was the best man there." Pendleton District slave Leu similarly declared himself "the best man of the Turff," right before other bondpeople deflated his ego by beating him into submission. In Anderson District, Toney announced that "he would whip Dick or any other negro that accused him of stealing leather" or "talked about him," because "he had as many wepons as any one els." One Saturday night, the bondman Lewis averred that Jackson Wilson's "Ben nor no other man should curse him." When Ben, reluctant to yield, dared to say "he would curse him or any other man," Lewis shoved him. Ben responded by stabbing him with a knife. On the way back from a

Christmas ball, the slave Ed also engaged in loud talk, bragging that he "could whip any man in the crowd except freinds." He "jumped up[,] slaped his hands together[,] and said . . . I dont fear no man." For good reason: Ed "drew a pistol" and warned his fellow slave revelers to "stand back Gentlemen." When one voice in the crowd, perhaps not believing his eyes, questioned if Ed really did have a gun, the armed slave snapped "that he did not tell no damned nigger what he had." The possession of a firearm enhanced Ed's self-esteem and, as he believed, commanded the respect of all his fellow slaves, whom he degraded as beneath himself in dismissing them as "damned nigger[s]." Nero displayed similar bravado when he declared "that he was man a nuff" to draw his knife and stab Griffin Brazeale's slave Sam multiple times "for no Reson or caus what ever." Throughout these altercations, the bondmen explicitly linked their violence in word and deed to a presumed sense of what it meant to act as a man.[16]

Verbal assaults frequently served as a prelude to physically violent encounters among slaves, a braggadocio explicitly bound with conceptions of manliness shared within the culture of bondmen. Insults offer an unconventional pathway into the culture in which the offending words were uttered. Individual cultures betray certain patterns of insults reflective of those cultures' values. Insults function by way of a shared language and set of expectations regarding behavior. They make sense because they strike inversely at that which society deems proper, respectable, and desirable, thereby revealing, in the negative, the social values of a given culture. Analyzing insults is particularly useful in the study of subaltern peoples such as slaves, who leave relatively little written documentation of their own. Insults often provoke violence, and violent episodes can generate a paper trail of official records.

Although these records are filtered through the minds and words of white magistrates, reading the evidence of insults backwards exposes social tensions and the origins of disputes, laying bare the mutual cultural understandings of the parties involved. By their nature, insults show disrespect, attack honor, and damage reputation. Slanderous words impinged on one's social rank and status, elevating the slanderer and degrading the slandered. Collectively, slaves already occupied a debased position in Southern society, so insults spoken by the master, however personally hurtful, did not necessarily shape what bondmen thought of themselves and one another. However, when slaves spit verbal venom upon one another, it likely stung, for slaves were peers inhabiting the same social plane. If one's equal voiced the insult, it mattered: one slave was attempting to establish superiority or dominance over another and deny the second slave's expectation of treatment as an equal. Their relationship was no longer reciprocal, but imbalanced. With social identity challenged through insult, the target of the offensive language might resort to violence to reestablish the social equilibrium.[17]

Court of Magistrates and Freeholders records reveal a range of insults slaves hurled at one another. Students of African American culture have described creative verbal sparring and dueling among blacks—playing the dozens—as a ritual contest. The very structure of such contests instilled discipline and emotional control in the participants, precluding the eruption of violence. In contrast, the known insults upcountry South Carolina slaves employed lacked the oral agility and theatrical wordplay of the dozens; instead, their blunt, forceful, and offensive words provoked violence. Some trial papers document only that a slave used "sasey language," but at times the records are more explicit, alleging a verbatim transcript as recalled by the witnesses. Bondpeople adopted "bitch" when referring to enslaved women and "son of a bitch" to describe slave men, verbally locating their adversary both in terms of gender difference and on the subhuman level of dogs. In Anderson District, the slave Ed called William J. Duckworth's slave George a "damned son of a bitch" because George did allegedly "bed up with my wife every night," and bondman "Jeff said Emory was a reel footed sun of a bitch." Bondmen sometimes called male slaves "rascals" or "rogues" as well. E. G. DuBose's slave Henry called John "a dam raskel," and Jake complained that "Baylis had cursed him like a dammd rascal." When Anderson District slave Steve refused to hand over "what he owed him," the cheated bondman "Jess cald him a damned rogue." The terms "rascal" and "rogue" both refer to someone judged dishonest, unprincipled, or mischievous, suggesting that in the quarters, slaves respected honesty, fairness, and trustworthiness. By identifying the scoundrels among them, slaves hinted at the boundaries that excluded certain slaves from the social group for violating cultural expectations of approved behavior.[18]

Lying and Fighting

Entrenched in the honor of the quarters, slaves also bristled when other bondmen gave them the lie. "Giving the lie"—calling someone a liar, questioning his word, and hence divorcing him from the culture of honor—provoked countless battles in honor-bound Southern white society, but has been insufficiently addressed among the enslaved. Masters assumed that slaves chronically lied; bondpeople told falsehoods, feigned illness, broke or "lost" tools to avoid work, and stole with impunity. It was no accident that the law prohibited slave testimony against white defendants in Southern courtrooms. "Whites," Kenneth S. Greenberg writes, "assumed that slaves lied all the time—and that their lies were intimately connected to their position as slaves." Indeed they were, not because slaves lacked honor but because lying was a necessary part of slaves' performance, part of the mask they wore in the presence of whites.[19]

However, whereas slaves routinely lied to whites, they expected honesty and truthfulness among themselves, as suggested in three cases from Anderson District that demonstrate the umbrage they took when a fellow slave accused them of deceit. "[T]he dam lie passed" between Charles Irby's slave George and John S. Carter's Jim, the latter of whom admitted to carrying a pistol as he left a Christmas dance. A trio of slaves testified that they "heard Bas give Joe the Dam lie" as "they cursed one another a while," and Martin Hall's bondman Dandy "threw a stone and hit Jim," the property of T. W. West, "in the side & wounded him sever[e]ly" because Jim "give the God dam lye." The obsession with lies in Anderson District was not unique. Copiah County, Mississippi, slave Simon confessed to killing Norvall "because the deceased had told lies on him." In nearby Marion County, "the negroes Harry and Claiborne Faulk had a quarrel with [James Duncan's slave] Green at his house in which the 'damn lie' and other offensive epithets of like character" were passed. Only the intervention of a white man "prevent[ed] a more serious difficulty." If slaves possessed no sense of honor, as Southern whites claimed, it would not have mattered whether another bondperson had "given the lie." That slaves responded promptly and violently suggests a compelling need to defend the honor they knew they possessed.[20]

The derogatory "fighting words" anchored in the language of honor sparked conflicts involving fists, sticks, rocks, knives, and fence rails, but slave men also utilized the rough-and-tumble fighting techniques more common among lower-class white brawlers. Such fighting flourished in the Southern backwoods and upcountry regions not yet fully incorporated into the market economy. There, values of the market had yet to replace the rural values of a semi-subsistence agricultural society. In such close-knit localities, the ethic of honor bound neighbors together. Southern gentlemen scoffed at lower-class claims to honor, but the rough-and-tumbles characteristic of the upcountry showed that its white residents, though socioeconomically inferior to the Southern gentry, were no less men. They willingly sacrificed their bodies, exposing themselves to ear biting and eye gouging, in defense of honor, reputation, and community standing. Contests among slaves displayed some significant overlap with the fighting styles of lower-class whites. In Pendleton District, the slave "Jack bit off pt of one of Lue Ears," Pickens District bondman Jesse was charged with "Biting Wiley Right year off," and when William Duckworth's slave Ned attacked Steve in Anderson District, he "bit of a peace of his year." Archibald Nicholes's slave Elijah appeared in court in 1845, charged with "fighting and abusing Dick the property of Cannon Brazeale." Dick testified that Elijah "threw him twice Down on the ground struck with his fist gouged him and scrched him." For some slave men, as with lower-class whites, the ritual violence of ear biting and eye gouging represented a form of manly assertion in a society that denied their claims to honor. Male slaves who participated in rough-and-tumbles verified their manhood to themselves and to the enslaved spectators looking on.[21]

Slave men, then, protected the women they claimed, settled scores with enemy bondmen, issued threats, boasted of their manhood, brooked no insults, and entered into rough-and-tumbles designed to inflict permanent scars on the loser. Many of these hallmarks of enslaved masculinity were familiar to various peoples on the African continent, and generations of tradition may have informed the behavior of slave men in the Old South.[22] By the antebellum decades, though, most African American slaves had been born and reared in the United States. Blacks and whites culturally borrowed from one another freely and frequently in Southern society, and the environment in which slaves lived greatly conditioned the way honor manifested itself in the quarters. The parallels between enslaved masculinity and Southern white masculine culture, and specifically with lower-class white male behavior, were remarkable. It was no coincidence that, in the South Carolina upcountry and in other parts of the South, slave and white men, poor white men in particular, shared a common culture of honor and violence.

Through their routine contacts of drinking, gambling, socializing, and trading, slaves and poor whites engaged in a process of cultural exchange. Through these transactions, male slaves imbibed lower-class white definitions and expressions of honor. After the slave Jesse accused Wiley of stealing his tobacco, the white James P. Jenkins of Pickens District informed Wiley that if he "wold tak the like of that he was no man attall." Only after a white man reminded the slave of the rules of honor as he understood them did a brawl commence between the slaves—but was this prompt necessary? Perhaps Jenkins was simply picking a fight between two bondmen for his own amusement, but Jesse and Wiley may have been preparing to fight regardless of his urging, or they may have preferred to delay their confrontation until no whites were present. If so, Jenkins's remark only reinforced sentiments already present and authorized their violence in his presence without fear of reprisal.[23]

Slave men seemed to understand that their sense of honor had its limitations within the constraints of Southern white society. In Anderson District, for instance, the slave Lewis had jettisoned his hat and umbrella while frantically escaping the patrol. This earned notice in the quarters. Slave Aaron remarked "that he would have fought a duel before any body should have taken his hat from him that way," and that he was willing to "loose every drop of blood in him before he would give up his hat and umbrella" as Lewis had. "Six or Eight negroes" who heard this, however, "all busted out in a Laugh." What was so funny? Interpreting humor over time proves difficult because modern observers of the past must reconstruct the cultural context in which the humorous comment or situation occurred. At the most basic level, the slaves who overheard the conversation may have considered it ridiculous to risk one's life over a hat and umbrella, for the value of the property was not worth the potential harm to the body. More substantially, the comment may have evoked laughter because Aaron was asserting a foolish willingness to stand up to the patrol, or exhibiting an overblown sense of honor that exceeded reason, elevating himself socially to the level of the white patrollers. Perhaps the mention of "a duel" elicited the laughter. Duels were clearly the preserve of elite white gentlemen; lower-class Southern whites did not even participate in them, so the thought of a slave, at the bottom rung of Southern society, drawing a pistol in a duel might have struck the "Six or Eight negroes" as humorous. Duels were always fought among participants who considered themselves social equals. That Aaron's hypothetical duel would have pitted him on the grounds against a white opponent may have exacerbated the humor of the mental picture the amused slaves were drawing. Whatever the reason, Aaron got the joke, for he, too, "Joined in the laugh."[24]

One pair of South Carolina slaves did attempt to emulate a duel to resolve a dispute, but without much success. In 1817, the slave Paul accused John Adams's Solomon "of carrying a negro girl to some person in Camden, words took place which brought on an argument," and they resolved "to have a Civil fight." Paul "agreed to fight with Solomon," testimony revealed, "because the latter was always picking at him," and now Paul would respond like a man. As in a duel, the combatants each had "seconds." Solomon had three seconds—fellow slaves Kildare, Frank, and Buck—while Paul had seven, including bondmen Eben and Charles. Like any responsible second, Kildare and Frank "advised them to not fight" and "endeavoured to make peace." The pair also wanted to guarantee that "no injury should be done Solomon" after the fight, for they shared the same master, and as Kildare explained, he feared "his man should blame him if any thing happened." Paul's friend Eben, however, "went out with Paul to see [that he] had a fair fight." For insurance, Eben concealed "two bricks in his pockets."

The duel commenced "on the grounds"; however, in the absence of pistols, what resulted was a strange hybrid, a brawl initially shrouded in decorum. Paul knocked Solomon down, but Solomon soon gained the advantage. As Frank parted the opponents, Eben mistakenly believed Frank was joining the fray. Noting that "one was enough to fight another," Eben fell upon Solomon, and Charles, another of Paul's seconds, joined in, striking "Solomon on the leg with a stick." Eben also carried a makeshift sword Kildare described as "some three edged thing . . . with a cob stuck on the end of it for a handle," but no one realized it until after the fight. John Martin, a white man present during the entire episode, asked Eben to relinquish the weapon. Eben "replied he could not give it up any how and live," and instead tossed it on the ground near Charles, who retrieved it and fled the dueling grounds. John Martin played a mysterious role in this confrontation, almost acting as a judge. In the heat of the brawl, Eben threatened to hit Kildare, but "he asked permission of the white people who were there," who disallowed it. Martin and at least one other white refereed the conflict, perhaps part of the slaves' effort to add legitimacy to their duel. The duel likely resolved none of the slaves' differences, as they all appeared in court charged with a "riot."[25]

ALTHOUGH SOUTHERN whites mocked slave pretensions to honor, slave men's degradation in white society enhanced their sense of honor among enslaved peers. A confrontation on the plantation of Spartanburg District farmer David Golightly Harris resulted in a loss of honor for one defeated bondman. Like any master, Harris surely preferred his slaves not engage in violent scrapes and suffer harm. As former slave Henry Gladney explained, "My old marster no lak dat way one of his slaves was crippled up" by fighting on the plantation. Injured slaves might require time off work, not labor as quickly or efficiently, or lose monetary value if their wounds proved serious enough. But slaves did enter into violent conflicts. "York and Old Will had a fight," Harris's wife recorded, and the elder slave's defeat at the hands of the younger York humbled him. No longer comfortable remaining on the plantation where York cost him honor among his fellow slaves—and perhaps still menaced him—Old Will asked his mistress for permission to locate a new master. As Emily Liles Harris explained of her aged bondman, "York has given him a whipping and he wishes to leave the place." The elderly slave's request suggests the pride that bondpeople maintained in the face of bondage.[26]

Slave men confronted many challenges to their masculinity, but violence afforded one avenue for them to display their manhood in the quarters and avenge any loss of honor. That one slave affirmed at trial that the gun Anderson District bondman George had clutched in his hand was authentic "& not merely a representation made of wood" suggests that a few slaves even carried fake wooden pistols as a demonstration of their power and capacity for violence.[27] Although it risks reinforcing stereotypes of black deviance or criminality,[28] examining slave life through the lens of violence is useful in prying into the culture of enslaved men. Prior to the 1980s, scholars accepted the experiences of male slaves as normative and therefore functionally genderless. Since then, historians such as Deborah Gray White, Stephanie M. H. Camp, and many others have called attention to the gendered lives of enslaved women. Their work revealed that female slaves' lives differed in significant ways from those of male slaves. Few attempts have been made, however, to view the experiences of enslaved men from the same gendered perspective. Slave men had at their disposal many models of masculinity, but in the context of antebellum Southern society, it would have been surprising had violence not become enmeshed in their definitions of masculinity and honor.

Notes

1. Anderson District, Court of Magistrates and Freeholders, Trial Papers, microfilm reel C2775, case #394, South Carolina Department of Archives and History, Columbia, hereinafter cited as SCDAH.

2. On honor in the Old South, see Bertram Wyatt-Brown, *Southern Honor: Ethics and Behavior in the Old South* (New York: Oxford University Press, 1982); Edward L. Ayers, *Vengeance and Justice: Crime and Punishment in the 19th-Century American South* (New York: Oxford University Press, 1984); Kenneth S. Greenberg, *Honor & Slavery:*

Lies, Duels, Noses, Masks, Dressing as a Woman, Gifts, Strangers, Humanitarianism, Death, Slave Rebellions, the Proslavery Argument, Baseball, Hunting, and Gambling in the Old South (Princeton, NJ: Princeton University Press, 1996); and Bertram Wyatt-Brown, *The Shaping of Southern Culture: Honor, Grace, and War, 1760s–1880s* (Chapel Hill: University of North Carolina Press, 2001). On honor among slaves, see Bertram Wyatt-Brown, "The Mask of Obedience: Male Slave Psychology in the Old South," *American Historical Review* 93 (December 1988): 1228–52; Jeff Forret, "Slave-Poor White Violence in the Antebellum Carolinas," *North Carolina Historical Review* 81 (April 2004): 144–46; and the following works on Latin America: Sandra Lauderdale Graham, "Honor among Slaves," in Lyman L. Johnson and Sonya Lipsett-Rivera, eds., *The Faces of Honor: Sex, Shame, and Violence in Colonial Latin America* (Albuquerque: University of New Mexico Press, 1998), 201–228; Richard Boyer, "Honor among Plebeians," in *Faces of Honor,* 161–64; and Lyman L. Johnson, "Dangerous Words, Provocative Gestures, and Violent Acts," in *Faces of Honor,* 130, 141.

3. Orlando Patterson, *Slavery and Social Death: A Comparative Study* (Cambridge, MA: Harvard University Press, 1982), 12; Ariela J. Gross, *Double Character: Slavery and Mastery in the Antebellum Southern Courtroom* (Princeton, NJ: Princeton University Press, 2000), 51–52.

4. John Iliffe, *Honour in African History* (New York: Cambridge University Press, 2005), 1, 4; T. J. Desch Obi, *Fighting for Honor: The History of African Martial Arts Traditions in the Atlantic World* (Columbia: University of South Carolina Press, 2008), 7, 111–21, 213; Wyatt-Brown, "Mask of Obedience," 1249. Under certain circumstances, white men could acknowledge that slave men had honor with respect to one another, but not relative to any white man. See Joshua D. Rothman, *Notorious in the Neighborhood: Sex and Families across the Color Line in Virginia, 1787–1861* (Chapel Hill: University of North Carolina Press, 2003), 161.

5. Lawrence T. McDonnell, "Money Knows No Master: Market Relations and the American Slave Community," in Winfred B. Moore Jr., Joseph F. Tripp, and Lyon G. Tyler Jr., eds., *Developing Dixie: Modernization in a Traditional Society* (Westport, CT: Greenwood Press, 1988), 31–44; Dylan C. Penningroth, *The Claims of Kinfolk: African American Property and Community in the Nineteenth-Century South* (Chapel Hill: University of North Carolina Press, 2003); Morris, "Within the Slave Cabin"; Jeff Forret, "Conflict and the 'Slave Community': Violence among Slaves in Upcountry South Carolina," *Journal of Southern History* 74 (August 2008): 551–88.

6. Eugene D. Genovese, *Roll, Jordan, Roll: The World the Slaves Made* (1974; New York: Vintage, 1976), 490–91, 494; John W. Blassingame, *The Slave Community: Plantation Life in the Antebellum South,* rev. ed. (New York: Oxford University Press, 1979), 164–65, 172; Elizabeth Fox-Genovese, *Within the Plantation Household: Black and White Women of the Old South* (Chapel Hill: University of North Carolina Press, 1988), 296–97, 326, 374; Brenda E. Stevenson, *Life in Black and White: Family and Community in the Slave South* (New York: Oxford University Press, 1996), 161, 240; Brenda Stevenson, "Distress and Discord in Virginia Slave Families, 1830–1860," in Carol Bleser, ed., *In Joy & in Sorrow: Women, Family, and Marriage in the Victorian South, 1830–1890* (New York: Oxford University Press, 1991), 108, 111–13, 120–21; Christopher Morris, "Within the Slave Cabin: Violence in Mississippi Slave Families," in Christine Daniels and Michael V. Kennedy, eds., *Over the Threshold: Intimate Violence in Early America*

(New York: Routledge, 1999), 271, 273; Emily West, "Tensions, Tempers, and Temptations: Marital Discord among Slaves in Antebellum South Carolina," *American Nineteenth Century History* 5 (Summer 2004): 4; Brenda E. Stevenson, "Gender Convention, Ideals, and Identity among Antebellum Virginia Slave Women," in David Barry Gaspar and Darlene Clark Hine, eds., *More Than Chattel: Black Women and Slavery in the Americas* (Bloomington: Indiana University Press, 1996), 180; Melton A. McLaurin, *Celia, a Slave: A True Story* (New York: Perennial, 2002), 139–40; Rothman, *Notorious in the Neighborhood,* 139. Clarke quoted in James Oliver Horton and Lois E. Horton, "Violence, Protest, and Identity: Black Manhood in Antebellum America," in Darlene Clark Hine and Earnestine Jenkins, eds., *A Question of Manhood: A Reader in U.S. Black Men's History and Masculinity,* vol. 1 (Bloomington: Indiana University Press, 1999), 384.

7. Drew Gilpin Faust, *James Henry Hammond and the Old South: A Design for Mastery* (Baton Rouge: Louisiana State University Press, 1982); Stephanie McCurry, *Masters of Small Worlds: Yeoman Households, Gender Relations, and the Political Culture of the Antebellum South Carolina Low Country* (New York: Oxford University Press, 1995).

8. Edward E. Baptist, "The Absent Subject: African American Masculinity and Forced Migration to the Antebellum Plantation Frontier," in Craig Thompson Friend and Lorri Glover, eds., *Southern Manhood: Perspectives on Masculinity in the Old South* (Athens: University of Georgia Press, 2004), 136–73; Rebecca J. Fraser, *Courtship and Love among the Enslaved in North Carolina* (Jackson: University Press of Mississippi, 2007); Fraser, "'Goin' Over There to See the Gals': The Performance of Masculinity amongst the Enslaved in the Upper South, 1830–1861," paper presented at the Masculinity in the American South History Postgraduate Symposium, University of Warwick, England, 7 June 2008; Sergio Lussana, "'A Robust and Vigorous Lad': Enslaved African American Masculinity in the Antebellum South," paper presented at the Masculinity in the American South Symposium. See also Hine and Jenkins, *A Question of Manhood.*

9. Hine and Jenkins, *A Question of Manhood,* 1, 30. As James Oliver Horton and Lois E. Horton stated, "Aggression, and sometimes sanctioned violence, was a common thread in American ideals of manhood." See Horton and Horton, "Violence, Protest, and Identity," 382.

10. On antebellum Southern violence, see W. J. Cash, *The Mind of the South* (1941; repr., New York: Vintage, 1991); John Hope Franklin, *The Militant South, 1800–1861* (Cambridge, MA: Belknap Press of Harvard University Press, 1956); Dickson D. Bruce Jr., *Violence and Culture in the Antebellum South* (Austin: University of Texas Press, 1979); Bertram Wyatt-Brown, *Southern Honor;* Ayers, *Vengeance and Justice;* Elliott J. Gorn, "'Gouge and Bite, Pull Hair and Scratch': The Social Significance of Fighting in the Southern Backcountry," *American Historical Review* 90 (February 1985): 18–43; Grady McWhiney, *Cracker Culture: Celtic Ways in the Old South* (Tuscaloosa: University of Alabama Press, 1988); Greenberg, *Honor & Slavery;* Edward E. Baptist, "'My Mind Is to Drown You and Leave You Behind': 'Omie Wise,' Intimate Violence, and Masculinity," in Christine Daniels and Michael V. Kennedy, eds., *Over the Threshold: Intimate Violence in Early America* (New York: Routledge, 1999), 94–110; and Loren Schweninger, "Slavery and Southern Violence: County Court Petitions and the South's Peculiar Institution," *Journal of Negro History* 85 (Winter–Spring 2000): 33–35.

11. David W. Blight, ed., *Narrative of the Life of Frederick Douglass, an American Slave, Written by Himself* (Boston: Bedford Books of St. Martin's Press, 1993), 79. Slave narratives faced challenges in dealing with violent acts committed by slaves. See Sarah N. Roth, "'How a Slave Was Made a Man': Negotiating Black Violence and Masculinity in Antebellum Slave Narratives," *Slavery & Abolition* 28:2 (2007): 255–75.

12. Hine and Jenkins, *A Question of Manhood,* 37.

13. Spartanburg District, Court of Magistrates and Freeholders, Trial Papers, microfilm reel C2920, case #128, SCDAH; Pendleton District, Court of Magistrates and Freeholders, Trial Papers, microfilm reel C2916, case #20, SCDAH; Laurens District, Court of Magistrates and Freeholders, Trial Papers, 1808–1865, Box 1, Folder 67, SC-DAH.

14. Helen Tunnicliff Catterall, ed., *Judicial Cases Concerning American Slavery and the Negro,* vol. 4 (Washington, DC: Carnegie Institution of Washington, 1926–37), 237; George P. Rawick, ed., *The American Slave: A Composite Autobiography,* vol. 9, pt. 4 (Westport, CT: Greenwood Publishing Company, 1972), 12.

15. Anderson District, Court of Magistrates and Freeholders, Trial Papers, microfilm reel C2919, case #371, SCDAH; Anderson District, Court of Magistrates and Freeholders, Trial Papers, microfilm reel C2917, case #160, SCDAH; Spartanburg District, Court of Magistrates and Freeholders, Trial Papers, microfilm reel C2920, case #117, SCDAH; *Simon, a slave v. the State of Mississippi* (1859), Box 5849, Case 8900, Mississippi Department of Archives and History, Jackson, hereinafter cited as MDAH.

16. Gorn, "Gouge and Bite," 28–31; Edward E. Baptist, "Accidental Ethnography in an Antebellum Southern Newspaper: Snell's Homecoming Festival," *Journal of American History* 84 (March 1998): 1355–83; Laurens District, Court of Magistrates and Freeholders, Trial Papers, 1808–1865, Box 1, Folder 67, SCDAH; Pendleton District, Court of Magistrates and Freeholders, Trial Papers, microfilm reel C2916, case #20, SCDAH; Anderson District, Court of Magistrates and Freeholders, Trial Papers, microfilm reel C2775, case #400, SCDAH; Anderson District, Court of Magistrates and Freeholders, microfilm reel C2917, case #195, SCDAH; Anderson District, Court of Magistrates and Freeholders, Trial Papers, microfilm reel C2919, case #292, SCDAH; Anderson District, Court of Magistrates and Freeholders, Trial Papers, microfilm reel C2917, case #189, SCDAH.

17. On insults providing clues to culture in the Americas, see Peter N. Moogk, "'Thieving Buggers' and 'Stupid Sluts': Insults and Popular Culture in New France," *William & Mary Quarterly,* 3d ser. 36 (October 1979): 524–47; Mary Beth Norton, "Gender and Defamation in Seventeenth-Century Maryland," *William & Mary Quarterly,* 3d ser. 44 (January 1987): 3–39; Cheryl English Martin, "Popular Speech and Social Order in Northern Mexico, 1650–1830," *Comparative Studies in Society and History* 32 (April 1990): 305–24; Kirsten Fischer, "'False, Feigned, and Scandalous Words': Sexual Slander and Racial Ideology among Whites in Colonial North Carolina," in Catherine Clinton and Michele Gillespie, eds., *The Devil's Lane: Sex and Race in the Early South* (New York: Oxford University Press, 1997), 139–53; Richard Boyer, "Respect and Identity: Horizontal and Vertical Reference Points in Speech Acts," *Americas* 54 (April 1998): 491–509.

18. Lawrence W. Levine, *Black Culture and Black Consciousness: Afro-American Folk Thought from Slavery to Freedom* (New York: Oxford University Press, 1977), 347–48,

358; Kershaw District, Court of Magistrates and Freeholders, Trial Papers, 1800–1861, Box 1, Folder 33, SCDAH; Anderson District, Court of Magistrates and Freeholders, Trial Papers, microfilm reel C2919, case #292, SCDAH; Anderson District, Court of Magistrates and Freeholders, Trial Papers, microfilm reel C2918, case #264, SCDAH; Clarendon District, Court of Magistrates and Freeholders, Trial Papers, 1863–1865, Folder 4, SCDAH; Anderson District, Court of Magistrates and Freeholders, Trial Papers, microfilm reel C2917, case #160, SCDAH; Anderson District, Court of Magistrates and Freeholders, Trial Papers, microfilm reel C2919, case #368, SCDAH. In North Carolina, Susannah Wilkins's slave Nelson murdered Benjamin Ward's bondman Gabriel. According to one report, "the death of Gabriel was sudden and entirely unpremeditated . . . provoked by a gross insult immediately resented by a blow stricken with a large piece of fence rail which happened to be at hand." See Governor's Papers, Gov. Edward B. Dudley, G.P. 90, folder October 1839, North Carolina Department of Archives and History, Raleigh.

19. Greenberg, *Honor & Slavery,* 8, 12, 40, 11 (quotation), 32

20. Anderson District, Court of Magistrates and Freeholders, Trial Papers, microfilm reel C2919, case #292, SCDAH; Anderson District, Court of Magistrates and Freeholders, Trial Papers, microfilm reel C2917, case #185, SCDAH; Anderson District, Court of Magistrates and Freeholders, Trial Papers, microfilm reel C2775, case #384, SCDAH; Catterall, *Judicial Cases,* vol. 3, 356; *Green, a slave v. the State of Mississippi* (1849), Box 5817, Case 2915, MDAH.

21. William B. Taylor, *Drinking, Homicide, and Rebellion in Colonial Mexican Villages* (Palo Alto, CA: Stanford University Press, 1979), 159; Gorn, "Gouge and Bite," 34, 21, 33, 41; Pendleton District, Court of Magistrates and Freeholders, Trial Papers, microfilm reel C2916, case #20, SCDAH; Pickens District, Court of Magistrates and Freeholders, Trial Papers, 1829–1862, Folder 11, SCDAH; Anderson District, Court of Magistrates and Freeholders, Trial Papers, microfilm reel C2918, case #261, SCDAH; Anderson District, Court of Magistrates and Freeholders, microfilm reel C2917, case #167, SCDAH. Jess and Wiley also appear in McDonnell, "Money Knows No Master," 38.

22. Iliffe, *Honour in African History.*

23. Pickens District, Court of Magistrates and Freeholders, Trial Papers, 1829–1862, Folder 11, SCDAH. On the range of slave–poor white contacts, see Jeff Forret, *Race Relations at the Margins: Slaves and Poor Whites in the Antebellum Southern Countryside* (Baton Rouge: Louisiana State University Press, 2006). Lawrence T. McDonnell perhaps underestimates the cultural interplay between black and white when he writes that slaves "emulated manly white behavior, boasting, carrying weapons, [. . .] parading a desperate, overblown, paper-thin honor." See McDonnell, "Money Knows No Master," 38.

24. Anderson District, Court of Magistrates and Freeholders, Trial Papers, microfilm reel C2917, case #185, SCDAH; Gorn, "Gouge and Bite," 41.

25. Kershaw District, Court of Magistrates and Freeholders, Trial Papers, 1800–1861, Box 1, Folder 24, SCDAH.

26. Rawick, *American Slave,* vol. 2, pt. 2, 129–30; Philip N. Racine, ed., *Piedmont Farmer: The Journals of David Golightly Harris, 1855–1870* (Knoxville: University of Tennessee Press, 1990), 354, 356; Genovese, *Roll, Jordan, Roll,* 485–86, 490, 492–93. Two of Spartanburg District master Henry Fergerson's slaves, Sam and Fed, came to

blows in 1864 in a dispute over how properly to construct a fence. Sam insisted Fed "had not built it right" and struck him with a fence rail. It was in the best interests of both slaves to build the fence correctly, and in that sense, Sam may have wanted it constructed to the satisfaction of the master so that the bondmen could avoid a whipping. Read another way, without necessarily internalizing the master's values, Sam may have felt a sense of pride in workmanship entirely independent of his desire to please the master and stay his hand. See Spartanburg District, Court of Magistrates and Freeholders, Trial Papers, microfilm reel C2922, case #270, SCDAH.

27. Anderson District, Court of Magistrates and Freeholders, Trial Papers, microfilm reel C2918, case #278, SCDAH.

28. David Wilson, *Inventing Black-on-Black Violence: Discourse, Space, and Representation* (Syracuse, NY: Syracuse University Press, 2005); Peter Caster, *Prisons, Race, and Masculinity in Twentieth-Century U.S. Literature and Film* (Columbus: The Ohio State University Press, 2008).

2

A Crucible of Masculinity

William Johnson's Barbershop and the Making of Free Black
Men in the Antebellum South

TIMOTHY R. BUCKNER

In November 1836, William Johnson recorded a strange account of a
fight that took place over a discussion of a duel: "[L]ast night [. . .] several gentlemen were in a conversation about a duel that was fought in
South Carolina. When Mr. Charles Stewart stated that those gentlemen
that fought actually fought with bullets, Mr. Dalhgreen said that they
must [have] fought with paper bullets." Stewart, obviously angered by
the suggestion that these duelists were only going through the motions
by not using deadly force, retorted that any man who claimed that
"paper bullets" were used was "a damned liar, a [damned] scoundrel and
a [damned] coward." Dalhgreen then slapped Stewart hard in the face
and let him know that they would decide the issue in the morning.
The confrontation the following morning began with a fight using sticks
and umbrellas, but then escalated to Bowie knives and pistols, ultimately
resulting in Stewart's death and severe injuries to Dalhgreen. Johnson
remarked that this was "one of the gamest fights we have ever had in our
city before."[1] While the fight Johnson described resulted in the death one
of the combatants, he did not view this as a tragedy or a murder; instead,
he wrote about this as a justified and entertaining struggle.

William Johnson was the famous "barber of Natchez," a free man of color in a region where the enslaved population vastly outnumbered the white and where only a few individuals were both black and free.[2] His analysis of this deadly confrontation would have been shared by most white men in the town and across the South, as this fight essentially offered a very public performance of masculinity. Elite white men in the antebellum South often engaged in rituals associated with a code of honor, which at its core was a public defense of a reputation for manliness, a complex code of often contradictory behaviors such as boasting, politeness, capacity for violence, the manifestation of integrity, imperatives of domination, generosity, competitiveness, and willingness to sacrifice. Southern honor was conceived of as the exclusionary domain of independent, adult white men, usually of the planter class, who expected dominance over dependents: women, children, and the enslaved.[3] The presence of free men of color disrupts these strict notions as, on one hand, free blacks had to be cautious and understood that it was crucial to maintain good relations with whites in order to preserve their independence and freedom, but on the other, they had to carve out lives for themselves, often without much assistance. William Johnson's life illustrates this tension. Johnson served a largely white clientele and, as such, his reputation was a part of his livelihood—but he also used his shop as a place to train young men of color, both free and slave, how to behave in a community of men.

Manliness in the Southwest frontier of the early-nineteenth-century United States was not built on restraint, submission, and knowing one's place; rather, it required boldness and independence. Slavery, of course, restricted most blacks from belonging in this category and thereby allowed whites a negative referent—a lack of manly qualities could define one as a slave. For the most part, antislavery activists of the nineteenth century and modern scholars have shared the notion that only violent resistance to white domination was an expression of masculinity. This understanding is rooted in the most famous black abolitionists from David Walker's *Appeal* advocating that men protect their wives and children via armed revolt in order to claim America as their own, as well as the frequent discussions of Frederick Douglass "becoming a man" as a result of his fight with Edward Covey. Free black men, though, complicated these ideas as they were restricted by racism but still capable of independence, and were able to protect themselves and their families without resorting to violence. Historians have often referred to free people of color as "slaves without masters"; however, such a description

negates the very real world that these men and women were able to create through their own efforts in the antebellum period.[4]

Free Men of Color and Masculinity

William Johnson has long been considered by scholars, beginning with
his biographers in 1954 and continuing through the most recent discussions, as a "class elitist" who "embraced the values of the white world
even as he aspired to be accepted into it." Just as often he has been
rejected for seeming to accept skin color prejudice; as a worker at the
Natchez Association for the Preservation of Afro-American Culture
remarked to the *New York Times* in 2004, "William Johnson is not high
on our agenda, because of the fact that he had slaves."[5] Johnson did in
fact own slaves and held slaves not in "nominal slavery," but rather for
the same reasons whites did: to generate profit by their labor.[6] However,
this does not mean that Johnson aspired to be a white man, nor does it
imply that he believed his roles as father, slave owner, and businessman
to signify the same ways that whites did. While scholars have chosen to
focus on diary entries as evidence that Johnson either internalized or
mimicked white values, a closer examination offers a much more complex look at how free black men conceived and performed masculinity.
Johnson clearly believed that there was a public component to being a
man that required boldness and the willingness to take risks, but he also
understood that black men in the antebellum South had to temper these
tendencies with restraint by choosing how and when they asserted their
manliness. Johnson's own actions demonstrate his complex understanding, his conceptions of how his free black friends, sons, apprentices, and
even slaves should behave, as well as their various acceptances and rejec-
tions of those ideas.

Johnson was born into bondage and released from slavery by his
father, also named William Johnson, with the permission of the Mississippi House of Representatives in 1820. William the elder contended that
emancipation would "give that Liberty to a human being which all are
entitled to as a Birthright, & extend the hand of humanity to a rational
creature, on whom unfortunately Complexion, Custom & even Law in
this Land of Freedom, has conspired to rivet the fetters of Slavery."[7]
Despite the kind wording of the petition emancipating him, it is unclear
what type of relationship father and son had, but what is known is that
the younger William Johnson's mentions of his father are rare within

his diary and are never substantial. The younger William Johnson was trained as a barber by his brother-in-law James Miller (another free man of color), who in addition to teaching the young man the art and mystery of the barber's trade also imparted the sense of how to succeed in a town and region built upon slavery and racial exclusivity. When Miller and his sister moved to New Orleans, a far more accommodating city for free blacks, Johnson purchased Miller's barbershop and continued both his predecessor's success in business and his practice of taking on apprentices, a crucially important move for young black men, as the only way to secure approval for freedom in Mississippi in the antebellum period was to possess a skill enabling self-support.

Restrictions on free blacks resulted from the town's economics and demographics. From the 1820s through the Civil War, Natchez and its surrounding area proved among the top cotton-producing regions in the United States and home to many of the nation's wealthiest slave owners. However, in many ways, the population more closely resembled sugar producing regions. By 1850, Adams County, of which Natchez was a part, was nearly 80 percent black and enslaved. Free men of color were viewed with suspicion throughout the Americas because these men almost always were suspected of fomenting slave rebellions, but unlike cities like Charleston or New Orleans, free blacks in Natchez had neither the customs of a large and entrenched community of free blacks nor the legal protection afforded to those of mixed race in places like Louisiana. The increasingly heated international debate over abolition coupled with the suspicion of revolt led Mississippi lawmakers and slave owners to be exceedingly cautious about releasing slaves from bondage.[8]

Despite the restrictions placed upon him because of his race, Johnson became a successful husband, father, and business man. As a young man, Johnson courted many women, but in 1835, at the age of twenty-six, married Ann Battles, the mulatto daughter of an enslaved woman, and the couple had ten children over the course of their sixteen-year marriage. The Johnson family lived in an impressive three-story building William owned in the center of Natchez, and he apparently spent lavishly to house, clothe, and feed his family. His children were educated by private tutors, and he taught his sons both the barber's trade and how to hunt, fish, ride horses, and other such activities helpful both as free blacks and men. Most importantly, Johnson offered his children his example and protection. In 1841, after six white men were killed in St. Louis by a group of free black men, state and local officials began to take more seriously the state law "requiring free persons of color to remove from the State.'"[9] Johnson had little to fear personally from this rule, as several of his white clients and acquaintances were willing to vouch for him so that his family could remain in spite of the law. Still, rather than rely exclusively on the goodwill of whites, Johnson sent his wife and several of their children to New Orleans in order to have them baptized at St. Louis Cathedral, creating both a second record of their freedom and also a safe haven outside of Natchez should public sentiment continue to turn against free blacks.[10]

While all free people of color had to contend with a legal and cultural milieu that in some situations barely tolerated their existence, Johnson frequently pushed the boundaries of these restrictions both in his business ventures and his personal life. The barbers' trade was a common profession for free black men in the South, and Johnson's commercial dealings went well beyond his shop in Natchez. In addition to opening another shop in the "under-the-hill" section of town, Johnson purchased real estate and became the landlord to multiple businesses from the 1830s through his death in 1851, including a coffee shop, a druggist, a boot maker, and a bowling alley. Each of these tenants were white men, and though it is not surprising that Johnson earned money from whites, by becoming a landlord Johnson essentially had authority over them, and at least in principle could remove them should they fail to live up to their side of the agreement. In reality, this may have been difficult. As a black man, Johnson could not take whites to court. Apparently, none of his renters chose to test his legal recourse, and they fulfilled their agreements.[11] In engaging in these ventures, Johnson was not only earning additional income but also expanding his own personal authority— essentially performing masculinity in ways usually reserved for white men. This could have placed him in financial danger, but Johnson viewed taking calculated (and sometimes not calculated) risks as part of what it meant to be a free man.

Johnson would push this sense of personal authority even further by taking up the town's highest profile occupation, cotton planter. In 1845, Johnson purchased a tract of land near Natchez, which he, ironically or not, called "Hardscrabble," and became a part-time farmer. As most of his interests were in the city, Johnson needed a capable labor force and a supervisor. To this end, Johnson wanted to select a white man who would serve as an overseer and a tenant as well as a full-time worker on the farm. In 1847, Johnson struck a deal with a white man named W. H. Stump to work the land in return for a third of "what is made on the ground" and a third of the profit made on timber sales. In the next

year, Johnson paid Stump $15 a month and provided housing for him
and for his wife. In terms of cash, Johnson was paying considerably less
for an overseer than other, larger planters in the area. William Minor
usually paid his overseers between $800 and $1,000 per year, whereas
Murden Harrison of Lowndes County paid $500 to $600.[12] Neither of
these planters offered portions of the crop to their overseers, as they
were much larger planters than Johnson. Perhaps Johnson believed tying
Stump's compensation to the productivity of the farm would lead to
better results from his overseer. If this was the case, Johnson surely was
disappointed. The color of his skin did not prevent Johnson from criticizing his white tenant, at least in his diary, or from high expectations of his
labor. In August 1847, Johnson noted that Stump was "on the Gallery as
usual and the hands at work cutting wood, They have made very Little
Head way indeed at wood cutting." However, he made no mention of
publicly confronting Stump about his poor job performance.[13]

Stump attempted to negotiate with the barber over his wages, but
found himself at a disadvantage. In late December 1847, Johnson traveled
to Hardscrabble to make Stump an offer to keep him on for the following year. Johnson wrote, "I offered him fifteen Dollars per month and
he Said that he Could not think of staying for Less than twenty Dollars
per month. So I told him that I could not give it, and remarked at the
same time that if he Could get more he was doing very wrong to stay."
Though it would appear that Stump would not stay at Hardscrabble, by
January 4 he had reconsidered and agreed to stay for another year for the
sum of fifteen dollars a month. Why Stump changed his mind is unclear.
Perhaps, as Johnson said, finding employment that would pay better was
difficult. Stump stayed on the farm until 1849, but the owner's criticism
would continue. In January 1849 Johnson complained, "I find that there
is Scarcly anything down thare done when I am not thare, I found Mr
Stump and Little Winn going down the Road when I Came down this
mor[n]ing." Stump would leave Hardscrabble the following year.[14]

Johnson could have turned the farm over to one of his workers or
possibly another free person of color, but like most Natchez farmers he
continued to hire white men to operate Hardscrabble. After hiring two
men as temporary help on the farm, Johnson found a permanent replace-
ment when H. Burke agreed to work for the same wage that Stump had,
along with housing and food for him and his wife. If anything, Johnson was less pleased with Burke than with Stump. Johnson lamented
the fact that Burke's avid hunting and fishing took time away from his
paid duties. Burke also enjoyed drinking, which led Johnson to chastise

him in his diary, if not in person. On one trip to Hardscrabble, Johnson found his overseer plowing the potato patch. This would not have been out of the ordinary except for the fact that Burke had reported that he had done this work the day before. Johnson approached Burke and found that he was drunk and apparently unconcerned about the presence of his employer, as Burke chose then to take a break.

Johnson decided that since his workers were not doing their work, he would do it himself. Johnson did not record an angry response to his overseer, but taking over the chores himself attests to his displeasure with Burke's behavior; it also shows that even though he was the one in power as the employer, he took no action against Burke. Johnson felt secure enough to hire white men to work for him, but he understood that it was beyond his legal right to subject them to the corporal punishment that his apprentices or those he enslaved had to endure. Despite local acceptance, Johnson understood that he was limited in how far he could push the color barrier, particularly in his dealings with his white employees, though as he routinely hired and fired these men he clearly established a sense of authority over them.[15] Johnson expected these men to perform their duties and clearly was displeased when they did not acquiesce to his demands. Regardless of the limitations placed upon him by skin color, Johnson was bold and crafty enough to place himself in positions of power over white men, traits that would have been considered masculine no matter the race of the subject.

Johnson and Personal Masculine Performance

Johnson's critique of his overseers' enjoyment of hunting, fishing, and drinking came from his anger that work was not being completed, not from a personal disdain for these behaviors. In fact, these recreational and competitive activities, not his various business ventures, often seem to have been his life's real passion. Johnson remarked that he was "always ready for anything," and perhaps more accurately should have added that he would put money on it. Throughout his life Johnson placed bets on his ability to shoot, his participation in card games, horse races, cock fights, toy boat races, elections, or his ability to outrun or outjump others. Outside of fighting, competition in these events was one of the most public ways that men could pit their abilities and even their masculinity against that of other men. The idiom "may the best man win" was not just an expression to William Johnson: he seems to have equated both the willingness to compete and the ability to win as crucially important to ranking himself and his competitors—usually his sons, friends, apprentices, and slaves, but sometimes whites as well. In fact, sometimes it seems as if his diary was written to prove his manliness to future readers via references to competitive activities; otherwise it is difficult to explain his line written after a hunt: "I always beat the crowd that I go with, make no mistake."[16]

Either the regions around Natchez were especially attractive to wild animals, providing fruitful opportunities for him to beat his "crowd," or he, like many, exaggerated his abilities to hunt and shoot. As an example, on the single day of November 17, 1843, he claimed to have shot and killed "2 teal and 3 wood ducks, 6 squirrels, 3 foxes and 1 wood cock" and seemed to have been disappointed to have had a late start on the day. He did admit to missing two other ducks. This type of abundance apparently persisted when he ventured out with others. On one excursion with two of his friends, he recorded that "we killed about thirty alligators between the three of us. Mr. Barland killed 4 ducks & one squirrel & Mc[Cary] killed two ducks and one loon and I killed one pelican, one large duck, & two black squirrels and a loon."[17] Nowhere does he mention what he did with all of the resultant corpses, and it seems unlikely that carrying thirty dead alligators from the swamp would not register a mention in his diary. As is a case with all hunters and fishermen, if there is no proof, it is difficult to confirm or refute a claim of prowess. Perhaps Johnson exaggerated his efforts in his diary to present to himself as the version of himself as he wished to be, or because he believed his family members, particularly the sons with whom he frequently hunted, would read entries like this and be impressed with their father's astounding abilities. Johnson often engaged his friends, sons, and slaves in competitions to prove his skills as well. He and his compatriots would shoot at targets and wager liquor, cigars, and at least once, a barrel of oysters. He was proud to outjump his apprentices and sons, but also seemed to enjoy it when the boys got the better of him on occasion. In 1847 he recorded that "the boys" beat "the old Shark at last" in a toy boat race.[18]

Like many other men in Natchez, Johnson enjoyed betting on animals as much has he did shooting them. Often the men who owned dogs, fighting cocks, or racehorses equated the performance of their animals with their own abilities. On a trip to buy supplies in 1837, Johnson spent five dollars on a "game cock," but afterward was disappointed when he "put him down in the yard and the Frizeling chicken whipped him

So I find he is not much." Apparently, after this experiment, he determined not to use the bird in an actual match, because not only would it be killed, but it would reflect poorly on himself. He does mention attending a cock fight in 1849, but wrote, "I wrode out this Evening To the Tract to See a fight of Chickens and I saw 3 fights and Lost 2.50 and it is a Sport that is to me Disgusting in the Exstream, I shall not go to see any more I promise."[19] There is no evidence that Johnson ever attended another, but it is telling that despite how disgusting he found the practice, he was willing to take part, both through betting and the attempt to raise a bird for fighting. The act of participating in the "sport" was an act of participation in a culture of manliness and one that apparently was open to men of all classes and for black and white alike.

Horseracing, unlike cockfighting, had been the exclusive domain of wealthy white Southern planters since the colonial period, but in nineteenth-century Natchez that changed. The opening of the Pharsalia Track to the non-elite, which planter and racing advocate William Minor complained of as a "desecration" of the track, allowed Johnson and other free men of color like William Winston to bet on races involving planter thoroughbreds. Over the course of four days in November 1847, Johnson made several bets with Winston and others, losing $105, but appears not to have been concerned over the amount.[20] Johnson also raced his own horses. In December 1835, Johnson mentions taking two of his horses out for a race, presumably at the quarter-track Under-the-Hill. He noted, "John rode the sorrel Horse and Bill Nix wrode the Bay horse, Paginini—They won two heats a piece." Just as other slave owners did, Johnson used enslaved jockeys rather than riding the horses himself. After the Pharsalia course opened to general participation, his horses ran there, as well in events that followed the higher-stake races involving horses of the elite. The purse for these lower-stake races remained below $50, but small purses did not lessen the opportunity for Johnson to compete with his white associates, as well as against other free men of color.[21] Gambling in its various forms offered men, white and black, a venue for competition that might have been less bloody than fighting—whether between themselves or in bouts staged with their animals but was not less meaningful in terms of asserting manliness. For free men of color like Johnson, these activities allowed them to test their skills against each other and against whites, and while the social distinctions of race and class might have remained once these contests were over, at least within the game, these differences could be leveled or at least mitigated.

Johnson's Barbershop:
A Crucible of Respectable Manhood

Outside of these games, social distinctions remained crucial, and free people of color like William Johnson were intimately aware of this, even as they actively tried to create spaces to succeed within this racist social structure. In addition to being the site of Johnson's primary business and the initial guarantor of his freedom, his barbershop became one of the few avenues for young black men to learn a trade and escape bondage. Free black parents as well white fathers of mixed race children asked Johnson to take on their sons as apprentices, but it was not uncommon for him to refuse. While many of these choices might have been based on business rather than personal circumstances, it is clear that Johnson viewed his role in these the education of these young men as going well beyond just training them to become barbers. Perhaps he turned some away because he did not need their labor, but there is evidence that he felt they did not have the right character or work habits. The apprentices that he did choose would be offered an education in Johnson's idea of manliness, though his ability to transmit these characteristics met with various degrees of success.

Johnson often praised his apprentices' abilities and business sense, but complained of their other choices. William Nix was one of Johnson's most successful apprentices and would later start his own barbershop in the nearby town of Rodney on Johnson's recommendation. Johnson never questioned Nix's skills and seemed pleased when he began attending the Catholic Church to learn how to sing or took French lessons. In personal matters, however, Johnson had serious problems with Nix's behavior. In one of the most often quoted lines in his diary, Johnson wrote, "Bill Nix is up to this Day a pure pure Negro at Heart and in action." Much to Johnson's dismay, Nix enjoyed the company of enslaved women, and the former criticized the younger man for this. While most historians have used this line as evidence of Johnson's sense of color prejudice—Nix was of light complexion—another reading is that Nix was being irresponsible. If the enslaved women that Nix had relations with had his children, they would legally be slaves owned by their masters, not by Nix. When Nix finally did marry a free woman of color, Johnson remarked that she had been "made use of" by a white man prior to their nuptials. Even if, as one historian has noted, "attitudes toward male fornication were permissive" and "male lust was simply a recognized fact of life" for men in the United States, slavery and slave codes altered what was considered permissible both for whites and blacks.[22] Moreover, the criticism of Nix's wife was really a criticism of Nix's manliness; whether the relationship between the woman and the white man was consensual or not, Johnson regarded Nix's choice of companion a poor one because it did not live up to example that he had tried to set for his apprentices. For Johnson, manliness was competitive, and despite his praise for Nix's other abilities, the apprentice had fallen short when it came to his relationship with women.

Johnson offered similar complaints when Nix and his other apprentices attended "darkey balls." These festivities were held frequently at the Mississippi Hotel's ballroom, regarded by most residents and travelers as one of the best inns in Natchez. These parties, and those held by free people of color in their own residences, clearly were popular among the town's black community, but Johnson never seemed to attend them. When Robert Lieper, the patriarch of a large free family of color, held a party, Johnson punished his free worker "French" William by refusing to let him attend. Given the popularity of these parties, French William no doubt considered this a substantial punishment.[23] Even when he permitted them to go, Johnson found reason to complain in his diary: "Bill [Nix] and Charles and Wellington all goes out to a party given by a servant of the Missis Evans out there at the residence—Butter, Butter will run in suitable weather."[24] The reference to "butter" here implies that Johnson believes these young men are soft by giving in to the desire to attend these parties. For Johnson, these parties likely had no appeal not because he would not consort with other people of color, free and enslaved, but rather because he was at a different stage in his life; given that he was married and was an older man, these parties likely did not hold the same appeal for him. What might have bothered Johnson about this is that these young men were not following his model of restraint and hence jeopardizing their futures.

When the young men within his household defied his attempts to impose restraint upon them by sneaking away at night without permission, Johnson could react violently. Occasionally, they would sneak away to "Mr. Parker's Kitchen," the name that the black community had given to the Mississippi Hotel, in order to meet women and carouse. Rather than punishing his slaves and apprentices on their return, Johnson enjoyed catching them in the act. In one instance, he found his apprentice William "at Mr. Parker's Kitchen" and whipped him for it. When his workers attracted the interest of the city's slave patrol for being out without permission or being drunk, Johnson had no qualms about supplementing the patrol's punishment with his own.[25] Though it is not surprising that any slaveholder would react to defiance with a whipping, Johnson apparently liked to catch both free and enslaved workers in the act, perhaps attempting to impose a sense of shame upon them in addition to physical pain.

Johnson did not simply treat free blacks one way and enslaved people another; in fact, he considered an enslaved man named Charles one of his best workers and eventually allowed him to operate one of his barbershops. Charles was sent by his owner to work with Johnson at the age of ten or eleven, and though the actual intentions of the bargain are not entirely clear, Johnson was to teach Charles "the trade" and "his books" and "to write also." It is unclear whether Charles was the son of his owner, but it seems likely, as his time with Johnson appears to have been a condition to attaining freedom. By the time Charles was a teenager, Johnson was paying his owner $150 a year more for the slave's services than the wages he paid to the free journeymen in his shop. Johnson steadily increased Charles's responsibilities in his shops and came to view him as his most capable barber. Still, Charles did not display restraint when it came to his personal life. Johnson complained in his diary, "Charles disgraced himself this morning by marrying Mrs. Little[']s Servant Girl Mary Known to the City as being a Buster"—in other words, a woman of dubious distinction. Based on Johnson's words, the disgrace was that Charles, a master barber, had married this girl of low reputation in the town; there is nothing explicit that indicates his problem was that she was enslaved. Again, one of his most promising young men had rejected Johnson's model. Of course, Charles was also a slave at this point, and his owner reported to Johnson that Charles "should have to give up that wife or remain a slave all of his life." Apparently Charles did give up his wife, and in 1851 his master arranged for him to be sent North to become free. He did not return to Natchez, and Johnson never recorded any reaction to Charles's departure.[26]

Other enslaved men rejected Johnson's example even more thoroughly and were much more severely punished. Along with criticizing their relationships with women, Johnson frequently complained that the enslaved boys and men within his household drank too frequently. Johnson did not have a problem with alcohol, given that liquor often was the prize when he gambled with his friends, but he clearly had a problem when his slaves and apprentices imbibed too much, risking his reputation as a slave owner and potentially his bottom line. They also rejected his example of restraint and jeopardized any chance they might have had of establishing themselves as independent. One slave referred to as "Old Middleton" was the property of Johnson's sister Adelia and was allowed to remain in Natchez after she and her family moved to New Orleans, with the caveat that that he would give a portion of his earnings to William, who would forward them on to his owner. In a letter to Adelia, William asked, "[W]hat must be done with Old Middleton—he is now lying [. . .] the old fellow has killed himself—drinking—he has not paid me a cent for I can't tell when [. . .] he says he [can't] work nor walk."[27] Among Southern white men, drinking was considered a way to assert manliness, not as a hindrance to it. Buying drinks for others was a display of hospitality, consuming drinks was a display of stamina, refusing purchased drinks from another could create a complicated scenario of insult or debt, but in no way was drinking considered out of the ordinary for an honorable man. Johnson's complaints about the tendency of his slaves to drink reveal that the free and enslaved men that he dealt with often held different ideas than he did about the role of alcohol. For slaves or free blacks a dependency on alcohol could either lead to sale away from family, a concern for Middleton who was married, or be a hindrance to freedom and independence. Neither of these fit with the masculine values of fatherhood and freedom that Johnson cherished and attempted to impart upon the young men within his household.

Old Middleton might have been an alcoholic, and clearly Johnson believed that this created a problem with his health, but the latter did not view all cases of excessive drinking in the same way. If Old Middleton's case was a depressing one for Johnson, his relationship with Steven, one of his slaves, proved to be much more vexing. Perhaps no one in his household rejected Johnson's example as thoroughly as Steven did: he frequently went about the city without permission, usually to drink and carouse, but sometimes to drink and avoid work. On March 19, 1838, Johnson complained that Steven "got drunk last night and was not here this morning," and then "he ran off 4 times in about three hours," presumably to drink more but also to keep from doing his prescribed tasks. Eventually, Johnson "gave him a pretty severe thrashing with the cowhide," and he remarked that "tis singular how much good it does some people to get whipped." Whatever good this was supposed to have done Steven, he ran away eight days later, and this time Johnson vowed to "hurt his feelings" should he be fortunate enough to catch him again. This is a curious line for a slaveholder. Obviously Johnson saw some promise within Steven, and the younger enslaved man must have professed some desire to change if Johnson believed their next confrontation would hurt the younger man's feelings. In the alternative, Johnson could have employed "hurt his feelings" as a euphemism for corporal punishment. Steven apparently sent word to Johnson that he would return and promised never to run away again if there would be no whipping, but he did not vow to stop drinking.

By 1843, Johnson once again had to confront Steven's issues with alcohol; however, by this point he clearly felt there was no more room for compromise with the young man and decided to sell him rather than continue to deal with the problem. In December of that year he wrote in his diary, "[A]nd what is the Cause of my parting with him, why it is nothing but Liquor, Liquor, His fondness for it. Nothing more, Poor Fellow. There are many worse fellows than poor Steven is, God Bless him. Tis his own fault."[28] On New Year's Eve, Johnson attempted to take Steven to the Mississippi River, where a boat would transport him to his new owner. This was an emotional parting, and Johnson admitted to his diary, "[T]oday has been to me a very sad day; many tears was in my eyes today on acct. of my selling poor Steven." Somehow they missed the boat, and Steven slipped away, managing to get drunk, whereafter Johnson "took him home & made him sleep in the garret and kept him safe." Finally, on the first day of 1844, Johnson managed to part with Steven, giving him several gifts and shaking his hand as he departed. Johnson wrote, "I would not have parted with him if he had only let liquor alone but he cannot do it I believe."[29]

As this long relationship with Steven illustrates, black men, both free and enslaved, adopted different positions when it came to masculinity. Johnson bought and sold slaves several times during his life, but only rarely recorded emotional reactions to these transactions. He respected much about Steven, and likely Steven felt the same way about Johnson—but Johnson, the slave owner, businessman, and patriarch, could not continue to deal with Steven's actions. It seems likely that Steven was an alcoholic, but if this is the case, he was a highly functional one, as Johnson found only his bouts with liquor to be the problem, not his work. On the other hand, Steven might have simply enjoyed the opportunities that the urban space of Natchez offered him. Steven was intelligent and crafty, and though charged with theft, he was able to convince a jury that, like all juries in antebellum Mississippi, was comprised exclusively of white men, that he was innocent based entirely on his own testimony.[30] It is possible that Steven rejected the way that Johnson lived and that Johnson, as often was the case, found this incomprehensible. Either way, Steven still was sold.

Johnson was more sympathetic to other free black men who also had problems with alcohol. Winslow Winn, often referred to in Johnson's diary as "Young Winn" or "Little Winn," was the son of a free man of color named George Winn, who, upon his death in 1831, left Winslow and his two sisters a cotton plantation of almost 1,200 acres as well as twenty-two slaves. Though Johnson has garnered more attention from historians, this inheritance made Winn the largest free black slaveholder in Mississippi. Winn often fished and hunted with Johnson and their mutual friend Robert McCary, but the older men did not view Winn as their peer. Like Steven and Old Middleton, Winn was a heavy drinker to such a degree that it seemed to adversely affect his health. In one instance, Winn stayed at the Johnson family's residence for several days in order to get over an "illness," but the diarist also wrote, "Poor creature, I Pitty him very much indeed—I am Sorry that he drink So much."[31] A similar penchant for drinking had led Johnson to sell Stephen, but Winn was brought into his household and nursed back to health. Winn drew Johnson's pity for what he clearly viewed to be a weakness. While Winn had the same level of independence and a similar level of wealth as Johnson, he could not live up to Johnson's example of self-control, and Johnson seems to have viewed Winn more like a younger brother.

Even those young men within Johnson's household who most closely modeled themselves after Johnson's example were not exempt from serving as examples for failing to meet their elder's code of conduct. Clearly, performance was important for Johnson's conception of masculinity, and his treatment of William Winston illustrates this. Winston, Johnson's favorite and most successful apprentice, entered into his contract while still enslaved by his father, Lieutenant Governor Fountain Winston, in 1836. Learning the trade enabled William Winston to demonstrate that he could support himself, and he legally attained his freedom by a special act of the legislature at the age of twenty-one, permitting him to remain in Natchez.[32] Not long after his arrival at Johnson's shop, Winston had a fight with the similarly named "Bill Wilson," and, as Johnson recorded in his diary, "Winston has the best of the fight." Despite what appeared to be a victory in the scuffle, Johnson "made a great deal of fun of Winston," apparently with the intention of egging him on into a new fight, which, not surprisingly, occurred. Johnson was no doubt pleased that "Winston whipped him fairly and [Wilson] hollowed [hollered?] to have Bill Winston taken off of him." This second fight was clearly staged by Johnson as a means of testing Winston's mettle and demonstrating that to the rest of the household. Johnson might have used the fight as a way to prove that Winston was worthy of being his favorite. Later in 1842, Johnson met with Winston's father and recorded that he was "a very smart boy" and "that I liked him very much indeed." Winston would continue working in the barbershop long after Johnson's death in 1851.[33]

Because of the slave society in which he lived, Johnson did not necessarily have to take on apprentices for their labor; he simply could have put his slaves to work, but it is clear that Johnson's interest in the boys and young men who worked for him both as slaves and apprentices was based on more than profit. By taking on apprentices, Johnson opened the door for these young men to secure their freedom and become men in the same ways that he had, but his expectations were exceedingly high. When they did not live up to or rejected his example, Johnson was not above giving up on them, in some cases, as was true with Winston, it seems that Johnson's ideals were transferred to the next generation.

JOHNSON'S SENSE of respectable manhood was formed by his experience as a young man of mixed race, by his efforts to provide for and protect his family, and by the public performance of masculine behaviors. Viewing Johnson as a class elitist or as a reflection of white values does not explain his complicated relationships with the boys and young men who lived within his household or with his other friends and acquaintances. Johnson's barbershop became a nexus of work and personal life for Johnson, and, ultimately, it became the site where he forged his own sense of paternalism focused on creating free black men who could form and protect their own families within a hostile environment. While Johnson himself frequently pushed the color barrier and even hired or served as a landlord to whites, he recognized that such risks could be taken only after establishing a reputation in town and that this could be precarious even for someone as well established as he. Arguably, his murder at the hands of one of his neighbors, a man of indeterminate racial identity, illustrates the dangers faced by free men of color. Though Johnson was free, successful, and operated within the law, his skin color could render him as vulnerable as a slave. His protégés sometimes accepted Johnson's teachings, but just as often rejected them due either to impatience or to adherence to an alternative conception of masculine behavior. When these young men fell away from his example, Johnson did not always respond like a slaveholder interested in correcting a disobedient bondsman; sometimes, even with his slaves, he reacted as a father might respond when his sons disobeyed or made poor choices. This is not to say that Johnson was never brutal to his slaves, as he willingly used physical punishment against or sale of his slaves as any other slave owner, but it is also the case that Johnson lamented it when these young men abandoned his example. His emotional responses are frequently recorded in his diary ranging from anger, to disappointment, to abject sadness when these men made what he considered bad decisions. The relationships that Johnson established with these men and boys belie the notion that he held himself aloof from other free people of color. Johnson was not outside of the free black community of Natchez—he was its center.

Notes

1. William Ransom Hogan and Edwin Adams Davis, *William Johnson's Natchez: The Antebellum Diary of a Free Negro* (Port Washington, NY: Kennikat Press, 1968), 149–50 (hereafter cited as *Diary*); Edwin Adams Davis and William Ransom Hogan, *The Barber of Natchez* (Baton Rouge: Louisiana State University Press, 1959), 157–59, quotations modified for readability.

2. The highest number of free people of color for the whole of Adams County was 283 in 1840 (205 lived in Natchez), with 4,910 whites and a slave population of 14,241. Census data available online, accessed 6 November 2010, http://mapserver.lib. virginia.edu/; Ronald L. F. Davis, *The Black Experience in Natchez, 1720–1880: Special History Study* (Denver: National Parks Service, 1993), 40.

3. Bertram Wyatt-Brown, *Southern Honor: Ethics and Behavior in the Old South* (New York: Oxford University Press, 1982); Craig Thompson Friend and Lorri Glover, *Southern Manhood: Perspectives on Masculinity in the Old South* (Athens: University of Georgia Press, 2004); Kenneth S. Greenberg, *Honor and Slavery: Lies, Duels, Noses, Masks, Dressing as a Woman, Gifts, Strangers, Humanitarianism, Death, Slave Rebellions, the Pro-Slavery Argument, Baseball, Hunting, and Gambling in the Old South* (Princeton, NJ: Princeton University Press, 1997).

4. Sean Wilentz, ed., *David Walker's Appeal, in Four Articles; Together with a Preamble, to the Coloured Citizens of the World, but in Particular, and Very Expressly, to Those of the United States of America, Written in Boston, State of Massachusetts, September 28, 1829* (New York: Hill & Wang, 1965); David W. Blight ed., *Narrative of the Life of Frederick Douglass: An American Slave, Written by Himself* (Boston: Bedford/St. Martin's, 1993); Edward E. Baptist, "The Absent Subject: African American Masculinity and Forced Migration to the Antebellum Plantation Frontier," in Friend and Glover eds., *Southern Manhood*, 136–73; Ira Berlin, *Slaves without Masters: The Free Negro in the Antebellum South* (New York: New Press, 1974).

5. Jack Davis, "A Struggle for Public History," 59; Davis and Hogan, *The Barber;* Patricia Leigh Brown, "New Signpost at Slavery's Crossroads," *New York Times,* 16 December 2004.

6. Michael P. Johnson and James L. Roark, *Black Masters: A Free Family of Color in the Old South* (New York: Norton, 1984); Larry Koger, *Black Slaveowners: Free Black*

Slave Masters in South Carolina, 1790–1860 (Columbia: University of South Carolina Press, 1985); Kimberly Hanger, *Bounded Lives, Bounded Places: Free Black Society in Colonial New Orleans* (Durham, NC: Duke University Press, 1997); Ira Berlin, *Slaves without Masters;* Charles S. Sydnor, "The Free Negro in Mississippi before the Civil War," *The American Historical Review* 32 (July 1927): 769–70; Davis, *The Black Experience in Natchez;* Suzanne Lebsock, *The Free Women of Petersburg: Status and Culture in a Southern Town, 1784–1860* (New York: Norton, 1985); Juliet E. K. Walker, "Racism, Slavery, and Free Enterprise: Black Entrepreneurship in the United States before the Civil War," *Business History Review* 60 (Autumn 1986): 343–82; Loren Schweninger, "Prosperous Blacks in the South, 1790–1880," *American Historical Review* 95 (February 1990): 31–56.

7. Race and Slavery Petitions Project at the University of North Carolina-Greensboro, accessed 3 April 2009, http://library.uncg.edu/slavery_petitions/SearchResults. asp?lbSubject=All&lbState=MS&lbFYStart=1819&lbFYEnd=1820&cbNoDate=true &Submit=Search+the+Database&offset=-1#.

8. Census data available online, accessed 6 November 2010, http://mapserver.lib. virginia.edu/; Charles Sydnor, *Slavery in Mississippi* (Baton Rouge: Louisiana State University Press, 1933); David Libby, *Slavery in Frontier Mississippi, 1720–1835* (Jackson: University Press of Mississippi, 2004).

9. *Trials and Confessions of Madison Henderson, Alias Blanchard, Alfred Amos Warrick and Others, Murderers of Jesse Baker and Jacob Weaver, as Given by Themselves* (St. Louis: Chambers and Knapp, 1841); Berlin, *Slaves without Masters,* 332; "Civis" published in the *Mississippi Free Trader,* 13 May 1841, reprinted in Sydnor, "The Free Negro," 776.

10. Virginia Meacham Gould, ed., *Chained to the Rock of Adversity: To Be Free, Black & Female in the Old South* (Athens: University of Georgia Press, 1998), xxxvi. The most complete exploration and usage of the role of the church for people of African heritage in Louisiana is available in Kevin D. Roberts, "Slaves and Slavery in Louisiana: The Evolution of Atlantic World Identities, 1791–1831" (PhD diss., University of Texas at Austin, 2003), especially chapter 3. See also letters written to Ann Johnson from New Orleans in Gould, 11, 13. Incidentally, Ann Johnson lied to the priests, claiming that her children had been born in Concordia Parish, across the river from Natchez, in order to qualify them for baptism at St. Louis Cathedral.

11. Davis and Hogan, *Barber,* 41–42.

12. J. Carlyle Sitterson, "The William J. Minor Plantations: A Study in Ante-Bellum Absentee Ownership," *Journal of Southern History* 9 (February 1943): 63; Sydnor, *Slavery in Mississippi,* 69.

13. *Diary,* 36–37, 580.

14. Ibid., 37, 600–601, 641.

15. Ibid., 37, 731.

16. Hogan and Davis, *Barber,* 69.

17. *Diary,* 66, 460.

18. Hogan and Davis, *Barber,* 76–77; *Diary,* 559–60.

19. Hogan and Davis, *Barber,* 74.

20. John M. Findlay, *People of Chance: Gambling in American from Jamestown to Las Vegas* (New York: Oxford University Press, 1986), 19–24; Davis and Hogan, *Barber,* 206;

D. Clayton James, *Antebellum Natchez* (Baton Rouge: Louisiana State University Press, 1968), 255; *Diary,* 592.

21. Davis and Hogan, *Barber,* 207.

22. Wyatt-Brown, *Southern Honor,* 295.

23. Frederick Law Olmstead, *Journey in the Seaboard States* (New York: Capricorn Books, 1959), 84–85. Hogan and Davis, *Barber,* 56–57; Ronald Davis, *The Black Experience in Natchez,* 53. French William or French William Johnson was a free black barber employed by the diarist between 1831 and 1839, and it is likely that the two were related, though how closely is up for speculation. *Diary,* 67.

24. Hogan and Davis, *Barber,* 56–57.

25. *Diary,* 73.

26. Ibid., 61–62.

27. Hogan and Davis, *Barber,* 64.

28. *Diary,* 469–70; Hogan and Davis, *Barber,* 64–66.

29. *Diary,* 470.

30. Hogan and Davis, *Barber,* 66.

31. Ibid., 247.

32. Ibid., 57–59.

33. Ibid., 59.

3

To Train Them for the Work

Manhood, Morality, and Free Black Conduct Discourse in Antebellum New York

ERICA L. BALL

In Samuel Ringgold Ward's 1855 narrative, *Autobiography of a Fugitive Negro,* the renowned public speaker and outspoken abolitionist activist interrupted the story of his family's escape from slavery in Maryland and his upbringing in New York to make an important point about how free Northern blacks could incorporate the fight against slavery and racism into their daily lives. After asking, "what is antislavery labour?" he argued that such work is done "not alone by lecturing, holding anti-slavery conventions, distributing anti-slavery tracts, maintaining anti-slavery societies, and editing anti-slavery journals . . ." but, in connexion with these labours . . . the cultivation of all the upward tendencies of the coloured man." As Ward saw it, antislavery principles were embodied in "the expert black cordwainer, blacksmith . . . mechanic or artisan, the teacher, the lawyer, the doctor, the farmer, or the divine." Thus, by simply succeeding "in his vocation from day to day, with his hoe, hammer, pen, tongue, or lancet," the free black man "is living down the base calumnies of his heartless adversaries—he is demonstrating his truth and their falsity."[1]

Brief as it is, Ward's declaration provides remarkable insight into an early sort of identity politics that helped give shape to an emerging black middle class in the antebellum North. In his statement, Ward suggests that by prospering and living the frugal, industrious, and independent life associated with the "respectable" occupations he mentions, free black men could refute and extinguish the period's increasingly popular pro-slavery nationalism that defined African Americans as naturally servile, dependent, thoroughly degraded, and unfit for freedom and incorporation into the body politic of the young republic. Ward was not the only black activist to make such claims in the period. By reversing what one scholar has called the process of "racial synecdoche"—whereby white Americans highlighted the "misdeeds of the few African Americans who "were thought to have affronted public morality," and characterized those behaviors as the innate racial traits of all African Americans—members of the free black leadership advocated a politics of respectability in the hopes that a visible, "elevated" black population might undercut the racism of the day, sway white public opinion in their favor, and bolster their campaign for the abolition of slavery and the acquisition of citizenship rights.[2]

Although scholars have done much to analyze the breadth, depth, and limits of this strategy, they have not engaged in a sustained effort to interrogate the roles that early-nineteenth-century gender ideals and practices played in this ideological formation.[3] Such an omission is surprising, for this brand of personal politics clearly centered on the gender ideals of the region's emerging middle class. The trades and professions Ward deemed "antislavery labours"—yeoman farmers; skilled mechanics and artisans; and teachers, lawyers, doctors, and ministers—all fell within the parameters of the period's most respectable independent male ideal.[4] And unlike the late nineteenth century, when African American activists fretted over the moral state of African American women, and characterized the policing of African women's sexual purity as essential for the social and political progress of the race,[5] African American activists like Ward framed male acquisition of these professions—with all their attendant implications of virtue and independence—as essential for the project of living an antislavery life.

This essay will examine this phenomenon by analyzing the widely disseminated didactic discourse on morality and training produced by African Americans in New York and Pennsylvania. In the process we will see that the antebellum politics of respectability advocated by spokesmen and women like Ward hinged upon the period's emerging middle-class ideals of manhood. Consequently, even as they offered a plethora of advice on training and education, black conduct writers expressed significant anxiety over the moral and educational state of young African American men. By interrogating the anxieties and the advice of these African American conduct writers, this essay further hopes to expand our understanding of the history of African American gender ideals in the early nineteenth century. Scholars have tended to limit their discussions of early-nineteenth-century African American ideals of manhood to a narrowly defined concept of masculinity,[6] one premised mainly on physical action and militant or violent resistance to oppression and slavery. In this formulation, Frederick Douglass's victory over the slave breaker Covey serves as an archetypal model for African American manhood, and the celebration of male physical resistance to oppression emerges as the basis for the rise of black abolitionism and nationalism. Meanwhile, those scholars who have emphasized the relationship between antebellum African American male identities and work habits have focused on working-class occupations and their accompanying cultural practices to the exclusion of those connected with the emerging black middle class in the free states of the North.[7] As Ward's comments suggest, however, these were not the only ideals of manhood available to antebellum free black men. African American conduct writers advocated training young black men for occupations that signified both the period's notions of manly respectability and older eighteenth-century republican ideals of virtue and independence, positions that they believed would enable young black men to personify a challenge to proslavery discourse in their daily lives. Black conduct writers argued that every African American success in these professions provided a living, breathing refutation of the antiblack discourse of proslavery theorists, and therefore, they urged parents to attend to the educations of their sons, to train their young men for these personal "anti-slavery labours," and prepare them for membership in an emerging black leadership class.

Middle-Class Morality, Anxiety, and African American Conduct Discourse

Conduct discourse emerged as a fixture of black print culture as early as 1827, when *Freedom's Journal* first began publication in New York City. Designed to give a voice to the free black community and facilitate the improvement of the manners and habits of aspiring free blacks, *Freedom's Journal* published a mixture of essays, stories, and letters on politics and personal advice.[8] Subsequent black newspapers like the *Colored Ameri-*

can and *Weekly Advocate* would follow suit, publishing conduct literature alongside strident critiques of slavery and calls for racial justice. Even the most well-known African American political organ, the *North Star,* continued this pattern, printing advice columns like Jane Swisshelm's "Letters to a Country Girl" and essays "On Elevation" along with its sustained verbal assault on the peculiar institution.[9]

The advice on conduct printed in these pages echoed the counsel disseminated in black-authored pamphlets; in the pulpits of black churches; in the meetings of African American literary societies, voluntary associations and temperance organizations; and in the debates and speeches of black political conventions. In these spaces, the leadership of the Northern free black population admonished men and women to adopt plain, frugal habits, and they extolled the virtues of education and fidelity to the principles of Protestant Christianity. Take, for example, the report issued on the "Condition of the Free People of Colour of the United States" during the first national black convention of 1831. After discussing the political rights owed to them by the Declaration of Independence and the Constitution, which "guarantees in letter and spirit to every freeman born in this country, all the rights and immunities of citizenship," the committee returned to a discussion of personal conduct and individual self-improvement, saying that, "in their opinion, *Education, Temperance* and *Economy,* are best calculated to promote the elevation of mankind to a proper rank and standing among men as they enable him to discharge all those duties enjoined on him by his Creator. We would therefore respectfully request an early attention to those virtues among our brethren, who have a desire to be useful."[10] Scholars have debated the political efficacy of these sentiments, but the intent of those who advocated attention to moral and educational self-improvement was clear. An 1837 editorial in the African American newspaper the *Colored American* crystallized the political goals that Northern blacks hoped to realize: "If our colored population desire to be useful and respected—If they would have their rights and attain their level, they must use the means, and adopt the measures of elevation and respectability." Furthermore, "When we speak of elevation," the piece continues, "we mean a perfect equality with the whites, in moral and mental character—in rights and in immunities—in usefulness and in honors." Anything short of this would be "ungodlike and ignoble."[11] Abolitionist William C. Nell put it this way in the *North Star:* "The elevation of a high standard of morality is an indispensable requisite for our advancement. We are living in a land, where, on the side of the oppressor there is power; and every dereliction on our part is trumpeted forth as a giant offence; it behoves us, therefore, to be careful in our morals, that at least, we may be conscious of being in the right."[12]

Although a casual overview of this discourse suggests that it is gender neutral, a more critical reading reveals that it is highly gendered. Indeed, one of the most striking features of this antebellum discourse of respectability is the urgency with which black conduct writers fretted over the moral state of young African American men, and their comparative silence on the subject of African American women.[13] Writing to the editor of the *Colored American* in 1839, a man using the pseudonym "Uncle Ben" complained about this discrepancy, noting:

> While our Editors and Divines are declaiming through the press and the pulpit, on the necessity of the moral and mental elevation of our young men, lamenting, in doleful strains, the apathy and indifference of our *hopeful youth,* shedding rivers of ink and oceans of briny tears, on the prevalence of vice and immorality among our men in embryo, they seem to have lost sight of "Heaven's last best gift to man" and either neglect to encourage them to cultivate their minds for the important place they are designed to fill in the domestic and social relations of life [. . .] or speak of them incidentally as though they were a disjointed part of creation.[14] (original emphasis)

While warnings about vain, intemperate, and talkative women were not unheard of in the black press, African American conduct writers in the years before the Civil War more frequently referred to women, both black and white, as innately pure.[15] Although they felt that women might fall from this exalted position or perhaps exhibit other faults, conduct writers consistently wrote as if respectable African American women were largely above moral reproach. In fact, the idea that any women would ever need to be elevated morally seemed preposterous to one *Freedom's Journal* contributor, who noted with derision a "society in Brazil for mending the morals and manners of young ladies! What next?" he asked. "Young ladies are admitted to be angelic; and really we consider them as patterns of all that is moral and mannerly. The men had better set about reforming themselves before they undertake to improve the ladies," he wrote.[16]

In contrast, many writers seemed to feel that young, urban, African American men were at significant risk of moral corruption. In his second published piece in a series entitled "Means of Elevation," the New Yorker "Cushing" complained of the "numerous porter-houses and low grog-shops that [...] are more or less frequented by youth and young men, on every day of the week, but more especially upon the Sabbath." The young men "who neglect their business and desecrate God's holy day, to congregate in these vicious places," did so "to the utter ruin of their prospects and their reputation."[17] New York was not an isolated Gotham, and Boston resident Maria Stewart, best known for her protofeminist public speeches, begged young men to avoid disreputable establishments in an 1833 address. "I would implore our men," she said, "and especially our rising youth, to flee from the gambling board and the dance-hall."[18] When discussing the need to improve the moral fiber of the free black population in general terms, "Augustine" grew quite specific when laying out a plan of action for young men. He specifically urged them "to cease to haunt [...] the corners of our streets" in Manhattan's lower Broadway, and instead to "crowd into the lecture room or library," and "read the newspaper" rather than "drinking grog or smoking tobacco."[19]

These persistent expressions of moral anxiety had more to do with the rough and tumble nature of city life than any measurable moral deficiencies in the free black population. In fact, in the decades leading up to the Civil War, several black and abolitionist organizations published statistical summaries and narratives emphasizing the virtue, morality, and growing prosperity of free black communities throughout the North. As far as they were concerned, key virtues such as temperance, education, frugality, cleanliness, and piety were threatened by the popular leisure activities of urban communities. In the cities where the majority of the Northern black population resided, the laboring man's free time revolved around raucous, masculine spaces such as theaters, taverns, and dance halls.[20] And as the leader of New York City's Vigilance Committee David Ruggles put it, it seemed that "many are in danger of being led into idle and licentious habits by the allurements of vice which surround them on every side."[21] Consequently, throughout the antebellum era, conduct writers characterized the most popular of entertainment venues, specifically the theater, the tavern, and the dance hall as vice-ridden, immoral, and illicit spaces respectable young men should avoid at all costs.

Black conduct writers agreed that theses spaces posed a particular threat to the earning potential and economic mobility of young black men. Maria Stewart, for example, put the issue in practical terms, suggesting that those young men who spent their earnings in the tavern, dance hall, or theater were undermining the larger attempt to raise the economic status of the Northern black population. "We are poor," Stewart reminded them, "and have no money to throw away." She lamented that "it is astonishing to me that our fine young men are so blind to their own interest and the future welfare of their children as to spend their hard earnings for this frivolous amusement."[22] This economic concern ultimately sharpened the gender-specific nature of black conduct writers' representations of moral and immoral behavior. More often than not, black conduct writers framed the economic dangers that they perceived were posed by urban leisure activities in explicitly masculine, economic, *and* moral terms. Thus, when African American conduct writers discussed the importance of "morality, or purity of conduct," and the eradication of "licentiousness" and "vice," they turned their attention toward those spaces where the young men of the race might be tempted to spend their hard earned wages, "the most fruitful sources of vice in this community [. . .] *the theatre, the gaming table,* and *the porter house,*" spaces frequented most often by men.[23] Here, they argued, young African American men could be led astray down the slippery slope of intemperance and Sabbath breaking to economic ruin and, ultimately, damnation.

In conflating male poverty with immorality so easily, black conduct writers were drawing upon the language used by the white reformers of the period. By the 1830s, many white middle-class Northerners considered poverty to be more of a character flaw and sign of dependence rather than simply an unfortunate economic state. For many of these reformers, poverty also could be interpreted as the result of an individual's dependence upon some form of vice. For example, reformers argued that drunkenness placed in question a man's ability to exhibit self-control, drained his economic resources, and imperiled his ability to support his wife and children and fulfill his obligations as head of the household.[24] Because of these close associations, male poverty, in and of itself, suggested intemperate, immoderate, and even immoral conduct to many reformers. Because it simultaneously signified dependence and immorality, male poverty held greater political implications for Northerners than the poverty of women, who were expected to be dependent upon the fathers, husbands, and brothers in their lives. Therefore, black conduct writers forcefully urged young men to avoid all spaces with the potential to inculcate moral weakness, and therefore, hasten economic dependency.

We can see this most clearly when African Americans discussed the dangers posed by the most popular form of entertainment of the day: the theater. Spokesmen and women for the Northern black population insisted that respectable young African American women, theoretically absent from such spaces, were less susceptible to these threats. Although

a few respectable young women might be tempted to enter the theater on occasion, where they might be drawn into "intrigue with a bold
and wily adventurer," conduct writers directed their warnings toward the
young men of the race who might become addicted to spending their
earnings on this entertainment, "one of the broadest avenues which lead
to destruction."[25] When denouncing the theater, black conduct writers
focused on the dangers faced by those vulnerable young men in attendance, sliding easily between economic and moral objections, often
blurring any distinction between the two critiques. They urged young
men to avoid theaters because "people of color" were "only allowed an
entrance in the galleries, where they must mingle with the very lowest
order of the white visitants."[26] They also worried about how the subject
matter of the plays staged in the theater might impact the young men of
the race. Just "think," wrote a contributor to the *Weekly Advocate,* of "a
young man" returning from the theater "at the hour of midnight," with
"his passions inflamed by every thing he has seen, and every thing he has
heard." As if that weren't enough, the anonymous writer offered a provocative description of the poor, defenseless young man "having to pass
through ranks of wretched creatures waiting to ensnare him and rob him
of his virtue. Does it not require extraordinary strength of principle to
resist the attack?"[27]

Virtue, Independence, and the African American Ideal

The economic disaster, poverty, and sexual corruption that conduct
writers saw looming over the young men who dared to spend an evening at the theater suggests far more about black middle-class anxieties
about male dependence than it reveals about the culture of the theater
or working-class African American behavior. In fact, the charge of male
dependency was fraught with considerable gendered social and political
meaning that many free blacks sought to avoid. In the early years of the
republic, male dependency carried with it a significant "social stigma."
The political culture of the period framed dependence, most notably
the dependence of women and children upon male heads of households,
as a state that clearly demonstrated one's incapacity to wield the full
privileges of citizenship. As Nancy Cott notes, "Participatory citizenship in the American political tradition required [. . .] *independence.*"[28]
Such understandings of masculinity defined by autonomy were not lim-

ited to the African American community, and in an effort to avoid any appearance of dependency, white servants insisted on being called "help" rather than "servants," and refused to call their employers "master."[29] In this context, the culture's distaste for evidence of male dependence put African Americans in a particularly difficult position. Due to the recent history of slavery in the Northern states, the growth of slavery in the Southern states, and the pseudoscientific arguments of proslavery theorists, many white Northerners associated blackness itself with a natural state of dependence.[30] Many poorer free blacks fought against this characterization by expressing their independence and freedom whenever possible. Working-class black New Yorkers, for example, organized parades to celebrate their own holidays, and daily would work, lounge, play, and promenade in the streets of Lower Manhattan. Rather than relying on the politics of respectability, New York's poor and laboring African Americans preferred to use informal demonstrations, expressive street culture, and parades to raise black consciousness and publicly object to the racial, economic, and political status quo.[31]

However, those conduct writers who offered advice for the aspiring classes of African Americans endorsed a slightly different method of asserting black male freedom and independence. Maintaining the popular tendency to conflate immorality, poverty, and dependence, conduct writers emphasized the importance of virtue, frugality, and independence in all their educational and occupational advice to young black men warning them that upward mobility, along with what they believed to be antislavery implications, required strict attention to personal virtues. Nowhere was this more apparent than in the discussion of agricultural pursuits. Spokesmen repeatedly urged young men to leave the limited occupational opportunities, and the filth, crime, and vice of the city behind, and establish new lives for themselves in the countryside.[32] Many believed that in the countryside, "a Colored farmer has just the same chance of getting along that a white one has." A contributor to the *Colored American* asserted that "in this department of industry, if in no other, he is on perfect equality. Nature has no prejudice in her heart."[33] Former slave Austin Steward made a similar point in his narrative, *Twenty-Two Years a Slave,* saying that while he resided in upstate New York: "I knew many colored farmers, all of whom are well respected in the neighborhood of their residence." Based on these observations, he argued that "it is a mistaken idea that there is more prejudice against color in the country. True, it exists everywhere, but I regard it less potent in the country, where a farmer can live less dependent on his oppressors."[34]

Scholars have rightly understood this tendency to be a reaction to the limited opportunities and racism free blacks faced in Northern cities, but it also had much to do with the prevailing ideals of manly independence and civic virtue. Conduct writers' frequent admonitions against moving to cities, where "our people [. . .] allow themselves to be made 'hewers of wood and drawers of water;' barbers and waiters," must be understood not only as cautionary warnings about the disadvantages and dangers of the city, but as evidence of a concern about the political implications of black male dependency on white employers.[35] Country life therefore offered the promise of a level of economic autonomy, and was assumed also to be more conducive than city life for the inculcation of virtue in the "young men in this community" whose "characters are forming for good and evil."[36]

Believing that land ownership provided the surest road to morality, prosperity, independence, and thus political equality, black conduct writers emphasized the importance of property accumulation—particularly through the agricultural pursuits—as critical for young black men.[37] In New York State, where back male suffrage was limited to those with $250 in property, the link between property ownership, independence, and the political rights of a male adult proved entirely clear.[38] However, the connection was not lost on free black spokesmen throughout the North, and they continued to give gender specificity, political significance, and urgency to their quest for respectability and elevation. "In our large cities," spokesmen pointed out, "we are passed by as not at all incorporated in the body politic." To remedy this situation, they argued that free black men should follow the example of those who "overcame all obstacles, conquered the soil, and finally became the independent masters of it," because only then would free blacks become "respectable" with "power" and "influence."[39] Such ideals of the yeoman citizen drew unmistakably on an older eighteenth-century republican vision of civic virtue, wherein an independent man best represented the interests of his family and community, which remained popular in the period.[40]

Training, Education, and Literary Societies

In addition to warning young men about the perils of immorality, and celebrating an African American agrarian ideal, there was also a consensus that training young black men for "stations of honor and respectability" would be essential in the fight for "political and civil elevation."[41]

Conduct writers argued that with formal training, a new generation of African American men would become virtuous artisans or professionals, placing themselves in a position to secure the respectable forms of employment that met the period's middle-class ideal of manhood. When "P." wrote to the *Colored American* to complain that too few free black boys were being apprenticed to mechanics, he declared that "a knowledge of the mechanic arts, and several good operative mechanics, would, in a great degree, assist in the elevation of our people." According to his letter, the "mechanic and the artizan are the wealth of the country; and it is an essential point that we should direct the attention of parents to this subject." The editor of the *Colored American* agreed and replied that "a virtuous life, a cultivated mind, industrious habits, and prudent conduct, with a share of the learned professions, the commercial business, the mechanical trades, and the agricultural pursuits of the country, are the means under God, on which we should depend for our political and civil elevation."[42] These sentiments were echoed in the African American conventions of the period. In the famous national convention of 1843, where delegates endorsed the Liberty Party and Henry Highland Garnet gave his famous "Address to the Slaves" for the first time, the delegates also resolved to "recommend and encourage agricultural pursuits among our people generally, as the surest and speediest road to wealth, influence and respectability," and to "recommend to our people the importance of aspiring to a knowledge of all the Mechanic arts of the age."[43]

A brief comparison with the discussion over women's education makes the political significance that conduct writers placed upon young men's education even more apparent. The members of the press certainly made it clear that like young men, young African American women and girls should receive an adequate education.[44] However, unlike calls for male education, discussions of female education remained infrequent and lacked the consistency that characterized discussions of male learning, training, and intellectual improvement. Matilda wrote to the *Freedom's Journal* to point out this discrepancy, declaring, "I don't know that in any of your papers, you have said sufficient upon the education of females. I hope you are not to be classed with those, who think that our mathematical knowledge should be limited to 'fathoming the dish-kettle,' and that we have acquired enough of history, if we know that our grandfather's father lived and died."[45] Ellen later wrote to the *Colored American* to point out, "The weight of female influence upon the literary and moral character of society is generally acknowledged; but I believe the full importance of it has never been felt nor appreciated; else why so few who appear to take an interest in the improvement of females, or whence the total apathy of your able and talented correspondents on a subject so nearly connected with our welfare?"[46]

When the editors of the *Colored American* published an article on "Female Education" in reply to "Uncle Ben," they began with the statement that "we are constrained to acknowledge our remissness, and the neglect with which we have hitherto treated" the subject. They pointed out that "in our general remarks on education we have always included (in intention) females as well as males," but agreed with those critics who suggested that "something more than a simple allusion is needed." They called for a "more liberal and enlightened policy," not only "in the education, but also [in] the general training of our females, their minds, habits, and their tastes." They laid out their expectations in that regard: "We expect our females to be educated and refined; to possess all the attributes which constitute the lady." Ideally, young African American women should "acquire an education which will fit them to become the wives of an enlightened mechanic, a store keeper, or a clerk"—wives suitable for "respectable," ideal men of the emerging black middle class.[47]

In contrast, conduct writers characterized the education of young black men as a political imperative for the entire race. When David Ruggles announced that he had opened a reading room for young African American men at the New York Committee of Vigilance, he discussed its importance to the young men of the race at length. He wrote, "[t]he prosperity and the existence of good society" depends specifically upon the "intelligence and virtue" and "the present and future prosperity of young men in this community."[48] The delegates to the National Convention of 1843 made a similar case:

> We cannot too earnestly recommend to our people the importance of the mechanic arts. In almost every age of the world, this has been a subject of deep importance to the people; and the nearer the mechanical arts have been carried to perfection, the higher have the people risen in wealth and intellect. It is a branch of industry which naturally expands the mind; and every country where proper attention is paid to education, the mechanics form a powerful and influential body. Many of the ablest statesmen, divines, and philanthropists of this country, and in other countries, have arisen from this class."[49]

Free black author and newspaper publisher William C. Nell put it this way: "A great responsibility devolves upon the young colored men of the present generation, who should duly prize the means now at their disposal, and . . . [prepare] themselves for stations of honor and respectability—gaining access to the various avenues for improvement in morals, science, and the mechanic arts, and through that medium, like valiant pioneers, affecting an opening for their brethren to the goal of human prosperity."[50] The delegate and publisher were not alone. "[I]f we wish our children," wrote a contributor to the *Colored American,* "to grow up efficient, strong minded, money making and money saving men: if we wish them to obtain those rights which are withheld from us [. . .] then we must *train* them for the work."[51]

The training they advocated included a moral component as well. Throughout the antebellum era, black conduct discourse continued to underscore the importance of cultivating and maintaining male virtue. In a reprint of a short essay by S. Rose called "To Young Men," the *Colored American* hoped young male readers would take note of their uniquely important and precarious situation in the world. For unlike "Woman," who is "sheltered by fond arms and loving counsel," the "young man" must stand "amid the temptations of the world like a self-balanced tower." Given that public role, "happy is he who seeks and gains the prop and shelter of morality."[52] When Robert Banks addressed the annual meeting of the Female Dorcas Society of Buffalo, he took time to rally the young men in attendance. "There must," he said, "young men, there *must* be a rousing up to action if we expect to keep pace with the times." Free black men "should gird on the armor of moral improvement, and take hold of the work with spirit and energy. A united effort, with such views, would have a powerful tendency to improve our moral, intellectual and political situation." He wondered, "shall it be said that the colored people alone are inactive? No, young men, let not this charge be brought against us; but let us be diligent, unite our efforts, and we shall eventually ascend the rugged steep to the temple of knowledge and respectability."[53]

To safeguard their own virtue and acquire the education that would place them in ideal occupations, young African American men created literary societies offering those previously unable to receive an education the opportunity to improve themselves. Unlike women's literary societies, which generally taught basic reading skills to those enrolled, young men's literary societies often functioned as valuable substitutes for college educations.[54] Young men's societies usually offered public lectures (sometimes to audiences of men and women), sponsored debates and scholarly presentations, and maintained their own libraries.[55] Though instruction was rarely formal, members would work together through cooperation and criticism to improve their body of knowledge and their writing, public speaking, and analytical skills.[56] In New York City, the men of the Phoenix Society maintained a reading room, and the Young Men's Society entertained the black public by demonstrating their debating and public speaking skills on a regular basis. Black Bostonians patronized the male-controlled Adelphic Union Library Association and the Young Men's Literary Society.[57] In Philadelphia, men developed and polished these skills in the Philadelphia Library Company of Colored Persons, the Rush Library Company and Debating Society, and the Demosthenian Institute.[58]

For the emerging free black elite, societies such as these offered an opportunity to educate those sons who were excluded from the American colleges of the Northeast, and lacked the funds or sponsorship to travel and be educated abroad or attend select American institutions like Oberlin College in Ohio. These literary societies, in turn, reinforced the link between intellectual elevation and moral elevation by limiting membership to those young men who were able to abstain from the consumption of alcohol and maintain a high moral standing in their community. For example, membership in the Young Men's Union Literary Association of Philadelphia was limited to young men "of a strict moral character" between the ages of eighteen and forty.[59] In April 1834, when Henry Highland Garnet joined other young black men in New York City to found the Garrisonian Literary and Benevolent Association for young men like themselves, they designed the organization to promote the "diffusion of knowledge" while encouraging the "moral and intellectual improvement" of its young members. Toward that end, the members passed resolutions against degraded displays of behavior including intemperance and "profane swearing."[60]

IN 1839, the editors of the *Colored American* reprinted a white-authored ode to young men that seemed to crystallize their own particular hopes and anxieties for the future of the race. In their introduction to the essay, the editors urged their "young brethren" to read the article very closely so that they could learn the importance of their role in society and their duties to their people. If those youthful readers continued on, they would have learned that the "condition of a young man" is of "peculiar interest" to society. For "not only is he the centre of all the ties of our common humanity, he clusters around him the utmost amount of the hopes and fears, the prophetic visions, the trembling contingencies of existence

[. . .]. He bears the visible proof of existing for nobler purposes." And "like the proudest ship in the fleet, [the young man] not only carries the richest freight, but the most numerous company down the rapid stream of time, to a boundless, unexplored eternity."[61]

As important as these sentiments may have been to the white middle-class readers of the period, the editors of the *Colored American* clearly felt that the advice contained in the piece was even more important for the young men of their community. For much of the antebellum era, African American conduct writers consistently emphasized the importance of improving young African American men. They also insisted that their young men were physical embodiments of all of the hopes and dreams for the future of the race. Given the larger American tendency to believe above all, morality, prosperity, and independence demonstrated fitness for inclusion in the body politic, African American conduct writers insisted that their own particular campaign to present living refutations of the charges of African American dependency made the creation of an independent class of free black middle-class manliness a political imperative. And the schools and literary societies created in Northern black communities offered the means to put this discourse into practice.

Indeed, in time, many of the young men who attended these institutions would grow to be extraordinary men, paragons of respectability who were committed to the abolitionist cause and ready to meet the political demands of the coming decades. As they fought to bring an end to the peculiar institution, they would embrace a variety of political perspectives. Some, like Henry Highland Garnet, would endorse armed resistance against slavery. Others, like Martin Delany, would advocate emigration to Africa. Samuel Ringgold Ward, meanwhile, would emigrate to Jamaica, become an independent farmer, and engage in his antislavery labors from abroad. Despite their differences, however, aspiring African Americans like these would always remain suspicious of dependence in any form, and they would continue to see morality and "virtuous," independent employment as the key components of idealized black male identity, and crucial to their fight against racism and slavery.[62] As they saw it, these were the most personal of antislavery labors, and they were essential for the project of living an antislavery life.

Notes

1. Samuel Ringgold Ward, *Autobiography of a Fugitive Negro: His Anti-Slavery Labours in the United States, Canada & England* (London, 1855; repr. New York: Arno, 1968), 42, 43.

2. For discussions of racial elevation, black abolitionist activism, and the politics of respectability in the early nineteenth century, see James Brewer Stewart, "Modernizing 'Difference': The Political Meanings of Color in the Free States, 1776–1840," *Journal of the Early Republic* 19:4 (1999): 691–712; Joanne Pope Melish, "The 'Condition' Debate and Racial Discourse in the Antebellum North," *Journal of the Early Republic* 19:4 (1999): 651–72; Patrick Rael, *Black Identity and Black Protest in the Antebellum North* (Chapel Hill: University of North Carolina Press, 2002), chapters 4 and 5; Elizabeth Bethel, *The Roots of African-American Identity: Memory and History in Free Antebellum Communities* (New York: St. Martin's Press, 1997), chapter 5; Frederick Cooper, "Elevating the Race: The Social Thought of Black Leaders, 1827–50," *American Quarterly* 24 (December 1972): 604–25; Robert S. Levine, *Martin Delany, Frederick Douglass, and the Politics of Representative Identity* (Chapel Hill, NC: University of North Carolina Press, 1997), 22–32; R. J. Young, *Antebellum Black Activists: Race, Gender, Self* (New York: Garland Publishing, 1996), 110–11; and Julie Winch, *Philadelphia's Black Elite: Activism, Accommodation, and the Struggle for Autonomy, 1787–1848* (Philadelphia: Temple University Press, 1988). For a discussion of the concept of racial synecdoche, see Rael, *Black Identity,* 179.

3. Rael, *Black Identity,* 150–55; 6–7. Most of the scholarship on gender in antebellum black political culture focuses on a different question: how did African American women (and men) reconcile their feminist politics with their racial identity and abolitionist activism? See Rosalyn Terborg-Penn, "Black Male Perspectives on the Nineteenth Century Woman," in Sharon Harley and Rosalyn Terbor-Penn, eds., *The Afro-American Woman: Struggles and Images* (Baltimore: Black Classic Press, 1997), and *African American Women in the Struggle for the Vote, 1850–1920* (Bloomington: Indiana University Press, 1998); Philip S. Foner, ed., *Frederick Douglass on Women's Rights* (Westport, CT: Greenwood Press, 1976); Jean Fagan Yellin and John C. Van Horne, eds., *The Abolitionist Sisterhood: Women's Political Culture in Antebellum America* (Ithaca, NY: Cornell University Press, 1994); Linda Perkins, "Black Women and Racial 'Uplift' Prior to Emancipation," in Filomina Steady, ed., *The Black Woman Cross-Culturally* (Cambridge, MA: Sheckman Publishing, 1981); Gayle Tate, *Unknown Tongues: Black Women's Political Activism in the Antebellum Era, 1830–1860* (East Lansing: Michigan State University Press, 2003).

4. E. Anthony Rotundo, *American Manhood: Transformations in Masculinity from the Revolution to the Modern Era* (New York: Basic Books, 1993).

5. Deborah Gray White, *Too Heavy a Load: Black Women in Defense of Themselves, 1894–1994* (New York: W. W. Norton, 1999), chapters 1–3; Evelyn Brooks Higginbotham, *Righteous Discontent: The Women's Movement in the Black Baptist Church, 1880–1920* (Cambridge, MA: Harvard University Press, 1993); Glenda Elizabeth Gilmore, *Gender and Jim Crow: Women and the Politics of White Supremacy in North Carolina, 1896–1920* (Chapel Hill: University of North Carolina Press, 1996); Michelle Mitchell, *Righteous Propagation: African Americans and the Politics of Racial Destiny after Recon-*

struction (Chapel Hill: University of North Carolina Press, 2004); Kevin Gaines, *Uplifting the Race: Black Leadership, Politics, and Culture in the Twentieth Century* (Chapel Hill: University of North Carolina Press, 1996), 12.

6. Gail Bederman, *Manliness and Civilization: A Cultural History of Gender and Race in the United States, 1880–1917* (Chicago: University of Chicago Press, 1995), and Martin Summers, *Manliness and Its Discontents: The Black Middle Class and the Transformation of Masculinity, 1900–1930* (Chapel Hill: University of North Carolina Press, 2004) both analyze shifts from Victorian conceptions of manliness to more modern twentieth-century notions of masculinity.

7. Most analyses of ideals of African American manhood in early-nineteenth-century America limit the discussion to representations and celebrations of male self-assertion, aggression and violence, labor, and political power. See Ronald T. Takaki, *Violence in the Black Imagination, Essays and Documents,* expanded edition (New York: Oxford University Press, 1993), 17–36, 79–102; Stanley Harrold, *The Rise of Aggressive Abolitionism: Addresses to the Slaves* (Lexington: University Press of Kentucky, 2004), 29–36, 41, 120–23; James Oliver Horton and Lois E. Horton, *In Search of Liberty,* 166–67, and "Violence, Protest, and Identity: Black Manhood in Antebellum America," in *Free People of Color,* 80–96; James Horton, "Freedom's Yoke," 102–4; Maurice O. Wallace, "'Are We Men?': Prince Hall, Martin Delany, and the Masculine Ideal in Black Freemasonry, 1775–1865," *American Literary History* 9 (Autumn 1997): 396–424; R. J. Young, *Antebellum Black Activists,* 57–59, 69–83; David Levernz, *Manhood and the American Renaissance* (Ithaca, NY: Cornell University Press, 1989), 108–33; and Jim Cullen, "'I's a Man Now': Gender and African American Men," in Catherine Clinton and Nina Silber, eds., *Divided Houses: Gender and the Civil War* (New York: Oxford University Press, 1992), 76–91.

8. Jacqueline Bacon, *Freedom's Journal: The First African American Newspaper* (Lanham, MD: Lexington Books, 2007). Scholars have long considered the publication of the *Freedom's Journal* to be a benchmark in the growth of black political consciousness. In her early article on the subject, Bella Gross wrote that "the *Freedom's Journal* marked the beginning of a national movement among the colored masses, and ushered in the Negro Renaissance. It was the first attempt at national race-solidarity," in "*Freedom's Journal* and the *Rights of All,*" *Journal of Negro History* 17 (July 1932): 245. See also Frederick Cooper, "Elevating the Race: The Social Thought of Black Leaders, 1827–50," *American Quarterly* 24 (December 1972): 604–25; Elizabeth Rauh Bethel, *The Roots of African-American Identity: Memory and History in Free Antebellum Communities* (New York: St. Martin's Press, 1997); Martin E. Dann, *The Black Press, 1827–1890: The Quest for a National Identity* (New York: G. P. Putnam's Sons, 1971). Beginning with *Freedom's Journal* in 1827, the range of black-controlled newspapers became an important vehicle for the dissemination of ideas through an increasingly wider audience. Later black publications include the *Weekly Advocate,* the *Colored American,* and the *North Star,* all of which echoed the *Freedom's Journal*'s intent to act as a "channel of communication [. . .] through which a single voice may be heard, in defence of *five hundred thousand free people of colour*"—*Freedom's Journal* (16 March 1827).

9. "Letters to Country Girls," *North Star* (4 May 1849); "Elevation," *North Star* (4 May 1849).

10. *The Constitution of the American Society of Free Persons of Colour, For Improving*

Their condition in the United States; for Purchasing Lands; and for the Establishment of a Settlement in Upper Canada, also the Proceedings of the Convention, with their Address to the Free Persons of Colour in the United States (Philadelphia: J. W. Allen, 1831), 5; reprinted in Howard Bell, ed., *Minutes of the Proceedings of the National Negro Conventions, 1830– 1864* (New York: Arno Press, 1969).

11. *Colored American* (15 July 1837).

12. "Elevation," *North Star* (4 May 1849).

13. Leslie Harris noted a similar discrepancy during the Black National Convention of 1833, where the all-male delegates made no reference to the education of women when discussing education for the race. Leslie Harris, *In the Shadow of Slavery: African Americans in New York City, 1626–1863* (Chicago: University of Chicago Press, 2003), 178.

14. *Colored American* (23 November 1839).

15. Bruce Dorsey, *Reforming Men and Women: Gender in the Antebellum City* (Ithaca, NY: Cornell University Press, 2002), 102. These ideas about the innate morality of women circulated as part of the ideology of the emerging middle class in the urban Northeast. See Mary Ryan, *Cradle of the Middle Class: The Family in Oneida County, New York, 1790–1865* (Cambridge: Cambridge University Press, 1981), and Nancy Cott, *The Bonds of Womanhood: "Woman's Sphere" in New England, 1780–1835,* 2nd ed. (New Haven, CT: Yale University Press, 1997).

16. *Freedom's Journal* (9 November 1827).

17. "Means of Elevation," *Colored American* (22 June 1839).

18. Maria Stewart, "An Address Delivered at the Boston Masonic Hall" (27 February 1833), in Richardson, ed., *Maria Stewart,* 60.

19. *Colored American* (16 February 1839).

20. Dorsey, *Reforming Men and Women,* 19. Sean Wilentz explores the masculine culture of early-nineteenth-century life in *Chants Democratic: New York City and the Rise of the American Working Class, 1788–1850* (New York: Oxford University Press, 1984).

21. *Colored American* (16 June 1838).

22. Maria Stewart, "An Address Delivered at the Boston Masonic Hall" (27 February 1833), in Richardson, ed., *Maria Stewart,* 60.

23. *Colored American* (22 June 1839).

24. Bruce Dorsey notes, "Reformers [. . .] cast the problem of excessive drinking as dependence." Dorsey, *Reforming Men and Women,* 8–9; Rotundo, *American Manhood,* 179.

25. "To Young Men," *Weekly Advocate* (11 February 1837).

26. *Colored American* (25 April 1840).

27. "To Young Men," *Weekly Advocate* (11 February 1837).

28. Nancy F. Cott, "Marriage and Women's Citizenship in the United States, 1830– 1934," *American Historical Review* 103:5 (December 1998): 1451, 1452.

29. David R. Roediger, *The Wages of Whiteness: Race and the Making of the Amerian Working Class* (New York: Verso, 1991), 43–64; Joyce Appleby, *Inheriting the Revolution: The First Generation of Americans* (Cambridge, MA: Harvard University Press, 2000), 142.

30. See Frederickson, *The Black Image in the White Mind,* especially chapters 1–3; Mia Bay, *The White Image in the Black Mind: African American Ideas about White People,*

1830–1925 (New York: Oxford University Press, 2000), 38–50; Dorsey, *Reforming Men and Women,* 8–9; Paul Gilmore, *The Genuine Article: Race, Mass Culture, and American Literary Manhood* (Durham, NC: Duke University Press, 2001), 56–59; and Kristin Hoganson, "Garrisonian Abolitionists and the Rhetoric of Gender, 1850–1860," *American Quarterly* 45 (1993): 579.

31. Harris, *In the Shadow of Slavery,* 133.

32. Litwack, *North of Slavery,* 175.

33. *Colored American* (9 February 1839).

34. Austin Steward, *Twenty-Two Years a Slave, and Forty Years a Free Man; Embracing a Correspondence of Several Years, While President of Wilberforce Colony* (1856; repr. New York: Negro Universities Press, 1968), 167.

35. Ibid.

36. *Colored American* (16 June 1838).

37. The emphasis on property ownership also reflected the extent to which the Northern black leadership placed the popular ideal of the "self-made man" in the service of the elevation project. See Rotundo, *American Manhood,* 3–4; and Rael, *Black Identity and Protest,* 131–32.

38. Harris, *In the Shadow of Slavery,* 178.

39. *Colored American* (15 April 1837).

40. For a discussion of the eighteenth-century ideology of republicanism, see Daniel T. Rodgers, "Republicanism: The Career of a Concept," *Journal of American History* 79:1 (June 1992): 11–38; Steven J. Ross, "The Transformation of Republican Ideology," *Journal of the Early Republic* 10:3 (Autumn 1990): 323–30. Strains of republicanism continued to be deployed in the early-nineteenth-century North. See Eric Foner, *Free Soil, Free Labor, Free Men: The Ideology of the Republican Party before the Civil War,* 2nd ed. (New York: Oxford University Press, 1995), 14–15, 27.

41. *Liberator* (7 February 1835).

42. *Colored American* (15 April 1837).

43. 1843 National Colored Convention, 16.

44. A distinction should be made here between higher education and early education. As Linda Perkins notes, Northern blacks did create schools for girls as well as coeducational institutions where the children of their communities could learn basic skills. Linda Perkins, "The Impact of the 'Cult of True Womanhood' on the Education of Black Women," *Journal of Social Issues* 39:3 (1983): 22–24. The Free African School of New York City was one such school, as was the school run by Sarah Mapps Douglass in Philadelphia. The black press's discussion of "ideal" male and female education principally applied the more advanced training necessary for young men and women to fulfill their appropriate gender-specific adult roles.

45. *Freedom's Journal* (10 August 1827). Herbert Aptheker describes the letter as the first black "expression of a 'women's rights' viewpoint"—*Documentary History of the Negro People* (New York: Citadel Press, 1951), 89. Dorothy Sterling describes the letter as "close to being a feminist statement" in *We Are Your Sisters: Black Women in the Nineteenth Century* (New York: W. W. Norton, 1984), 98.

46. *Colored American* (30 September 1837).

47. *Colored American* (23 November 1839).

48. *Colored American* (16 June 1838).

49. *Minutes of the National Convention of Colored Citizens* (Buffalo, NY, 1843), 27.

50. *Liberator* (7 February 1835).

51. *Colored American* (11 May 1839).

52. "To Young Men," *Colored American* (7 July 1838).

53. *Weekly Advocate* (18 February 1837).

54. For more examples of differences as well as relationships between African American men's and women's literary societies, see Elizabeth McHenry, *Forgotten Readers: Recovering the Lost History of African American Literary Societies* (Durham, NC: Duke University Press, 2002), 50–79. For examples in later decades, see Emma Jones Lapsansky, "'Discipline to the Mind': Philadelphia's Banneker Institute, 1854–1872," in Hine and Jenkins, eds., *A Question of Manhood*, 399–414.

55. In *Sketches of the Higher Classes of Colored Society,* published in 1841, Joseph Willson makes a special point of noting that in Philadelphia, men's societies, including the Philadelphia Library Company of Colored Persons, the Rush Library Company and Debating Society, and the Demosthenian Institute, all sponsored debates and other public activities. The women's literary societies he highlights do not. See Julie Winch, ed., *The Elite of Our People: Joseph Willson's Sketches of Black Upper-Class Life in Antebellum Philadelphia* (University Park: Pennsylvania State University Press, 2000), 111–17.

56. Rotundo, *American Manhood,* 68.

57. *Liberator* (7 February 1835).

58. Willson, *Sketches* (1841), 111–17.

59. *Colored American* (2 February 1839).

60. Schor, *Henry Highland Garnet,* 11, cites the *Liberator* (19 April 1834).

61. Ibid.

62. The connection between manhood rights, citizenship, and property ownership would inform the African American perspective on emigration in the 1850s as well. See Bruce Dorsey, "A Gendered History of African Colonization in the Antebellum United States," *Journal of Social History* 34:1 (2000): 77–103.

4

Masculinizing the Pulpit

The Black Preacher in the Nineteenth-Century AME Church

JULIUS H. BAILEY

On March 13, 1869, in the latest installment of a series on "Pioneers of the AME Church" in the *Christian Recorder,* the official denominational newspaper, Henry Highland Garnet highlighted the achievements of the Rev. William Paul Quinn, Third Bishop. Garnet described one religious meeting on the Western frontier threatened to be disrupted by "ruffians" until Quinn grabbed "an ample green stick" and sprung into action:

> Thus armed, he walked out among the rioters, who received him with a storm of jeers and derisive shouts. But the tables were speedily turned. Right and left the undaunted Quinn swept his ponderous weapon, and right and left ruffians fell like, wheat before the reaper's scythe. Piercing cries for mercy began to be heard, instead of oaths and obscene epithets. On and on brother Quinn went through the band of villains, just precisely as though he was threshing corn. Some cried to the Holy Virgin, and others called on the twelve Apostles, and some in bad English called in earnest on the name of the second person in the Trinity, and others invoked the assistance of the blessed martyrs, and very many more saints than were generally known to be recorded in the sacred calendar

of the Roman Church. Astonished at the boldness of a single man, and intensely pained by his blows, the ranks of the enemy were broken, and they fled like chaff before a tempest . . . Rev. gentleman did not speak a single word, and when the work was finished, he calmly took his seat on the stand, and since that time Methodist camp meetings have never been disturbed in Allegheny county.[1]

While narratives of manly exploits in the West are hardly unique for this time period, what is distinctive is the particular manifestations of the anxiety over achieving "true manhood" expressed by many male African Methodist Episcopal Church leaders. The founder of the denomination, Richard Allen, and others had established a tradition of robust leadership after refusing to be mistreated in the white St. George's Methodist Episcopal Church in Philadelphia at the end of the eighteenth century, and early itinerants proved their manhood on the western national boundary—but post-emancipation AME leaders had few comparable outlets to put to rest any doubts about their own masculinity. While younger men had new frontiers to conquer by performing missionary work among the newly freed slaves or traveling abroad to evangelize their African brethren, elder statesmen and leaders in the church had neither the physical ability nor the desire to engage in such activities. Instead, the pulpit, which had historically been a space where both men and women expressed and lived out their divine calling to share the Gospel message, became increasingly masculinized and the vocation of minister synonymous with manhood.

Anxieties over Female Preaching

Gender roles were fairly malleable in the early-nineteenth-century African Methodist Episcopal Church, but by the late 1830s, male AME Church leaders gradually separated positions by gender. Richard Allen heralded Jarena Lee, a female preacher from New Jersey, as one of the most powerful orators in the church and gave her carte blanche to speak at his Bethel AME Church in Philadelphia. However, in 1839, in Philadelphia, she was prohibited from ascending to the pulpit. She remembered, "I remained in the city about three months and received appointments in our churches on Thursday nights, although in years past I always had them at any time, Sunday afternoons not excepted." Jarena Lee was not alone. A few years earlier, Rebecca Cox Jackson sought to preach in the AME denomination but was prohibited from doing so based on the church discipline. She eventually left the black church in favor of the Shaker tradition.[2]

The denials of Lee and Cox from speaking in the pulpit were a result of the dramatic change in requirements for AME preachers in the 1830s. Because from its inception the AME Church made only subtle distinctions between the positions of exhorter and preacher, women regularly spoke from the denomination's pulpits. The 1836 General Conference of the AME Church separated the callings of preacher and exhorter in its legislation: "It is not expected that an exhorter will attempt to preach formally, to read a text, announce a theme, and divide his subject; but he will sing, pray and then read a passage of Scripture, and make such remarks as he may feel disposed."[3] However, the imprecise phrasing that granted exhorters the opportunity to "make remarks" allowed for quite a bit of leeway in the interpretation of the line between exhorter and preacher and consequently, the enforcement of the passage varied from church to church in the tradition.[4] By the late 1830s, male AME Church leaders had sharpened the distinction between preachers and exhorters. Practically, this meant that female exhorters were increasingly denied access to the pulpit. Though in the early nineteenth century women had spoken at revivals, church meetings, and conferences of the AME Church, male leaders began to limit their opportunities.

However, the increasingly gendered space of the pulpit would not exist without a fight. Female members aspiring to the ministry and the Daughters of Zion petitioned the AME General Conference, calling for the denominational leadership to officially sanction female preachers in 1844, 1848, and 1852. In each case the request was refused by a large margin.[5] Further pleas received little notice and by 1864 the General Conference did not even call for a vote on the issue.[6] Although unsuccessful in their motions, by petitioning the General Conference, these female members called for the right to lead and made the question of gender politics part of the public language and literature of the AME Church.

The prospect of women preaching illumined the fragility of the black male psyche at mid-century. From 1840 to the late 1860s, the discourse in the public literature of the AME Church centered on the achievement of manhood. David Leverenz has suggested that a new understanding of manhood emerged in the mid-nineteenth century, which defined manhood based on "individual enterprise," "competitive success," and "power over others." Unlike earlier notions of manhood, such as wealth and education, these traits were understood to be attainable by all men. Because the ideology presumed a level playing field, if men failed to demonstrate their prowess in each of these areas, they had only themselves to blame. One's manhood had to be perpetually proven, inducing a pervasive insecurity among many men; Leverenz therefore defined the ideology of manhood during this period as a "compensatory response to fears of humiliation."[7] Historian Gail Bederman asserts that in the second half of the nineteenth century, middle-class whites equated manhood with "bodily strength and social authority." Manliness was not bestowed upon birth but was a "standard to live up to, an ideal of male perfectibility to be achieved."[8] In the nineteenth century, facing both de jure and de facto racial discrimination in America, African Americans had access to few societal outlets and professions that would allow them to demonstrate their acumen in the public spheres and arenas of power presupposed in popular notions of masculinity. Because becoming a preacher was one of the few careers available for talented and educated African Americans, often the best and the brightest entered the ministry. This historical trend coupled with the ambiguity of nineteenth-century conceptions of manhood raised the stakes regarding access to the pulpit.

Reconstruction witnessed unprecedented political opportunities for African Americans. The year 1865 witnessed the passage of the Thirteenth, Fourteenth, and Fifteenth Amendments, which banned slavery and granted African Americans full citizenship and enfranchisement, and the Union presence in the South allowed blacks to organize and register voters in record numbers. African American men ascended to positions that would have been unimaginable just a few years previously, and during Reconstruction fourteen African American men were elected to the House of Representatives and two to the Senate. However, in 1877 the removal of federal troops from the South left African Americans to fend for themselves in the face of violent white "redeemers" such as the Ku Klux Klan, who felt blacks had stepped out of their rightful subservient place. Post-Reconstruction saw these gains taken away as African Americans were thrown out of office and poll taxes, literary tests, and property requirements were reinstated. The post-Reconstruction "nadir" in African American history only elevated the material and symbolic importance of the black male preacher. By the 1880s, in their collective participations and revisions of manhood, many AME authors did not look to the educated and refined ministers of the contemporary church. Instead, they turned to the past for men who engaged in the strenuous life of the itinerant ministry, demonstrating bodily strength and "manly" courage. Historians in the AME Church looked back to a golden age of masculinity that they hoped could be recaptured in the present generation, and they constructed images of the vocation of minister and life on the road that held up the itinerant preacher as the exemplar of true manhood.

Historicizing Manhood

AME historians emphasized the ability of early male itinerants to eschew luxury and brave the harsh conditions of the mission field. In 1885, H. T. Kealing, in his *History of African Methodism in Texas,* closely linked manhood with his description of the first AME missionaries in Texas. He wrote, "We are not content, even, that the Missionary should remain on a level with the great men of earth. We claim for him the highest type of admirable manhood, in that he leaves the cushioned pew, and sure salary for the doubtful allurements of hardships, deprivation, and misrepresentation." Kealing depicted the early missionaries in that region as pioneers who were uneducated men and therefore did not owe any of their success to "showy attainment, or glamour, but entirely to natural force of character, and superior cast of mind." He underscored that many itinerant preachers traveled long distances and preached in log cabins, and other ministers suffered through hunger, wore worn-out clothes, and slept outside on the ground with only a rock as a pillow. In these accounts, the strongest men confronted whites face to face without fear.[9] Kealing's narratives of missionaries focused on particular incidents in Texas that exemplified their leadership qualities, self-assertion in the face of adversity, and fearless independence, even when opposed by white Americans.

Likewise, in his 1867 work *An Apology for African Methodism,* Benjamin T. Tanner described the early missionaries as men who did not need many material possessions to complete their mission. Tanner defined the necessary spiritual qualifications for an AME preacher as a strong heart and voice, and an uncompromising faith in God; armed with those traits, the preacher needed only "a horse, a saddle-bag, a Bible, a hymn-book, and a glorious field for work." Tanner, like other AME historians, invoked the size and strength of the church's preachers who "are the very men to do it, of strong muscles, a strength not to be resisted, with a will that recognizes no impossibilities, they are just the men to work at the oar, and work they do!" Tanner compared the AME itinerants to another male leader, Moses, because they too were sent miles away with little or no money in their pockets: "Trusting God, they took up the march, and like Israel, as they advanced, obstacles gave way; many a stubborn river stood up in heaps, when their feet touched the waters."[10]

Not surprisingly, William Paul Quinn figured prominently in the narratives. Tanner held up Quinn, who had led the church's expansion westward in the first half of the century, as the standard bearer for all ministers who would follow. Quinn, Tanner averred, embodied the physical and mental makeup required to be successful on the rugged frontier: "God in his providence, having eminently endowed him with the necessary qualifications for the arduous and often dangerous task of planting the 'standard of the Cross' in those then Western wilds."[11] Garnet gushed over Quinn's stature, declaring, "No one, who then knew him, will accuse me of exaggeration when I state, that probably there was rarely to be found a man of finer personal appearance, even in that populous city. Standing more than six feet in height, full and roundly built, with every limb and feature well shaped, and proportioned, and of a beautiful olive complexion-fine forehead, and a bright and kindly beaming eye, and withal moving with elastic step, and possessing polished, and courtly manners, William Paul Quinn was a ruler, and a prince." Although women such as Jarena Lee had preached across the country, AME Church historians focused on the autonomy, rugged endurance, and powerful physical appearance in celebrating the achievements of the early male itinerants in their denominational histories in order to construct models of manhood for the contemporary church. Into the late nineteenth century, the published literature of the AME Church continued to wrestle with notions of manhood. In 1891, in the preface to his, *History of the* AME *Church,* Daniel A. Payne wrote that the formation of the AME Church allowed African Americans to "feel and recognize our individuality and our heaven-created manhood."[12]

Domesticity and the Masculinization of the Pulpit

Daniel Payne was one of the first to respond publicly to the petitions of the Daughters of Zion for preaching licenses. In his letter to the *Christian Recorder,* Payne contrasted the life of a preacher with the duty of a woman to her family. He argued that such preaching infringed upon the "sacred relationships which women bear to their husbands and children, by sending them forth as itinerant preachers, wandering from place to

place, to the utter neglect of their household duties and obligations."
Although Payne had preached for years regarding the necessity of an
educated ministry, he dismissed the idea of female preachers by invoking
the cult of true womanhood, describing the harm that would result by
women leaving the domestic realm. Payne concluded that the idea was
"antiscriptural, anti-domestic, and revolutionary."[13] While education was
important to Payne, his ultimate qualification for the ministry was masculinity.

Payne's celebration of the "sacred relationships" of women to their
husbands and children was no accident, for he believed that the Daughters of Zion had overstepped their bounds in the church and forgotten
their central duty to the home. However, his concern for domestic religious life, genuine as it might have been, was not his only motivation
for his oratorical challenge. To the contrary, Payne wrote his response to
vindicate himself and his fellow ministers in the church who, because of
their own insecurities about their manhood, felt threatened by the prospect of female preachers. A spokesman for the African American race
and an established figure in the AME Church, Payne wanted to coun-
ter the sense of degradation that came from viewing images of African
Americans in the white press that depicted them as less than men. He
did so by demonstrating a central perceived component of manhood,
control over women in the church. For Payne, squelching the rebellion
of women in the church was an act on the behalf of the family and the
preservation of the divinely ordained gender roles of the AME Church.

When Payne reflected upon the efforts of the Daughters of Zion to
create their own conference to empower female preachers, he took their
failure as a sign of God's disapproval. Payne recalled that "certain women
members of the A.M.E. Church, who believed themselves divinely commissioned to preach by formal licenses, subsequently organized themselves into an association with the avowed intention of laying out a field
after the manner of our Annual Conferences." He proclaimed, "They
held together for a brief period and then fell to pieces like a rope of
sand."[14] While Payne may have been concerned that the authority of the
General Conference was being undermined, he seemed pleased about
the demise of the women's efforts. For Payne, the failure of the movement validated his belief that female preaching violated the universal laws
of nature.

Payne was not alone in his assessment, for early African American
female preachers also recognized a tension between motherhood and the
ministry. In her autobiography, Jarena Lee remembers leaving her sick son

to preach for a week at a church that was thirty miles away. She recalled that "during the whole time, not a thought of my little son came into my mind; it was hid from me, lest I should have been diverted from the work I had to [do], to look after my son." Since her friends and family had taken good care of the child, she wrote, "I now began to think seriously of breaking up housekeeping, and forsaking all to preach the everlasting Gospel." Throughout her autobiography, she recalls leaving her children, believing divine intervention lessened her maternal attachments. Another female preacher, Zilpha Elaw, could not comfort her daughter who converted during a revival. "Many a mother strongly felt with me on that occasion," she wrote, "though my position would not allow me to leave the pulpit."[15] While it would be unwise to interpret Lee's and Elaw's experiences as entirely typical for female preachers, they do illustrate the tensions they felt between their commitments to the ministry and their obligation to their children. Throughout the second half of the nineteenth century, particularly in times of heightened insecurity about their own manhood, male AME Church leaders would invoke women's "natural" duty to the home to squelch the aspirations of women. Within antebellum racial discourse, women's place, many men argued, remained in the home.

Although Payne invoked domesticity to oppose the movement to license female preachers, his concern for the spiritual life of the home was not disingenuous. Joining the AME Church in 1841, Payne perhaps more than any other member of the AME Church, wrote passionately about the importance of the domestic religious life of a family. In 1850, Payne wrote a book of poetry entitled *The Pleasures and other Miscellaneous Poems,* which appeared shortly after the deaths of his wife, Julia Ann Payne, on November 6, 1847, and his nine-month-old daughter on July 12, 1848.[16] Having lost his own father at the age of four and his mother at the age of nine, Payne perhaps had his own personal losses as a reason to perpetuate a distinct vision of the importance of family in the life of the church. In his autobiography, Payne focused on his father's role in his early religious and educational instruction. He remembered regularly being awakened by his father's morning prayers and hymns, fondly recalling his father's instruction in the alphabet, and receiving punishment for "neglecting his lessons." His father named him after the Prophet Daniel, baptized him as an infant, returned home, and, Payne writes, "on bended knees, my pious father holding me in his arms, again dedicated me to the service of the Lord." After his father's death, his mother "took him by the hand" and led him to the church and sat by his side. Having never experienced a traditional family life for any extended period, Payne sought not only to be, as he viewed his father, a "faithful observer of family worship," but to perpetuate that practice in the AME Church.[17]

Payne's vision of domestic life was intimately linked with a masculine ministry. At the time of Payne's membership in 1841, the question of licensing and ordaining female congregants divided the AME Church. As women challenged the traditional roles of men and women in the church and the home, discussions of the appropriate domestic religious life moved from the prescriptive columns to the front page and editorial sections of the *Christian Recorder*. Notions of domesticity informed the discourse about the appropriate role of women in the AME Church. Many male AME Church leaders staked their claim to the leadership positions in the church based on domestic ideology, relegating women to the role of "helper."

In addition to gender concerns, Payne sought to increase the educational standards to enter the ministry. During his first assignment as an itinerant minister in Washington, DC, Payne began a movement to create an educated AME Church ministry, which had a lasting impact on women and unschooled men aspiring to the pulpit. Payne envisioned a well-educated male ministry in the AME Church, and he pressed the AME leadership to comply. At the 1844 General Conference, Payne proposed that the AME Church construct a "course of studies for the education of the ministry." To Payne's surprise, the conference defeated his resolution. After the vote, some members of the conference threatened that if no form of the proposal was adopted, they would form their own "ecclesiastical establishment." The following day, the General Conference passed the resolution. Bishop Brown assigned Daniel Payne, H. C. Turner, David Ware, Richard Robinson, Abram D. Lewis, W. R. Revels, and George Weir to "select a proper course of studies" for young ministers.[18]

For a brief period, the interests of uneducated men matched with those of female preachers, and many male ministers continued to argue that a converted heart and a gift for preaching were more important than a formal education. Uneducated AME Church leaders faced the real possibility that additional requirements for preachers might cost them their ministerial positions. Similarly, in their autobiographies, female preachers in the early AME Church downplayed the importance of an educated ministry. Zilpha Elaw felt the "wise and learned" often did not embrace "the heavenly discipline of God's Holy Spirit." Similarly, Jarena Lee believed that in many cases the uneducated had a unique sensitivity to the "operations of the Holy Spirit."[19] While early female preachers made similar arguments minimizing the necessity of education, most male AME Church leaders saw gaps in education as an easier divide to cross than the difference in gender and viewed them as the competition for ministerial positions rather than as potential allies.

As his influence grew in the AME Church, Payne increasingly linked education and manhood to the role of preacher. In 1845 in a series of essays on the "Education of the Ministry," Payne argued that a well-educated ministry would preach more effectively, tying masculinity to the pulpit. He wrote, "Knowledge will become just what the Creator designed it to be, an element of your manhood, in which you may live and move and have your being." According to Payne, women, rather than fully participating in this "glorious reformation, should support men in their efforts to achieve education. Payne later proclaimed, "Venerable mothers of Israel! We call upon you to aid us in this glorious reformation. Give us your influence; give us your money; give us your prayers."[20] While Payne pushed for an educated clergy and more sharply defined positions in the church, access to those positions increasingly fell along gender lines. In their public literature, male AME Church leaders regularly defined ministerial positions and education as endeavors exclusive to men.

Although there was an element of self-interest involved in Payne's opposition to female preaching, Payne never wavered from his perceived duty to protect the family. Having experienced personal trials in his own familial life, Payne was committed to preserving the sanctity of the home. In 1847, Payne married his first wife, Julia A. Farris. Within the first year of marriage, Julia died while giving birth to their daughter. Payne's daughter lived only nine months before also passing away. Perhaps because of the dramatic loss of his parents at such a young age, coupled with the deaths in his own family, Payne viewed himself as a defender of the home. Despite emphasizing the "natural nurturing" ability of mothers in the home, the central AME church text on domesticity was written by him, and his *Treatise on Domestic Education* (1885) appeared at an opportune historical moment. Published only one year after the licensing of female preachers, Payne's work was readily received by an eclectic audience that included those critical of mothers who "abandoned" their families for the pulpit as well as others who observed devaluing of the contributions of women in the church and the home. In the midst of the turmoil surrounding the licensing of female preachers, Payne offered his notion of mothers as "domestic educators" as a means of uniting the divided constituency of the AME Church. Payne was one in a long line of ministers who viewed the licensing of female preachers as a threat not only to the family but to his sense of male authority as well. The ambiguity of the duties of fatherhood only increased the importance of the pulpit as a site to demonstrate true manhood.

Elusive Fatherhood

Early in his term as editor of the *Christian Recorder* from 1868 to 1884, Tanner, like Payne, assumed a masculine ministry in his writings and viewed preaching from the pulpit as an important demonstration of one's manhood.[21] However, while many authors wedded the attainment of manhood with activities performed outside of the home, Tanner was one of the few leaders in the AME Church who regularly connected manhood not only to the public sphere but to fatherhood and the religious leadership of the home. While masculinity could be clearly delineated in narratives of the rugged mission field, Tanner exerted enormous effort to construct an image of fatherhood that was not "feminized" by association with the domestic realm.

While Tanner was unique in his emphasis on fatherhood in the domestic space, he, like many of his ministerial brethren, believed that manhood was more easily demonstrated in the public sphere. For Tanner and other contributors, manhood could be demonstrated by standing up against racism and achieving success in business. In addition, Tanner viewed a man's role as a husband as intimately linked with the public realm. In one article he wrote that a husband should go "out into the world in a conqueror's spirit." Although manhood could be attained without becoming a father, once an individual embraced marriage and had a family, Tanner made it clear that fatherhood entailed caring for children. Rather than confronting men in the church about their parental duties, Tanner often communicated points of morality through stories and narratives; in the case of manhood, Tanner included sketches of men that modeled correct manly behavior in the home and society.[22]

Because much of the discourse of manhood in the *Christian Recorder* focused on a man's success in business and society; where notions of true womanhood were central to the domestic realm, a father's role in the home, while important, was difficult to reconcile with the public nature of "true manhood." This struggle to merge the public and the private realms of manhood and womanhood is exemplified by the advice given to young men. In one article, the Reverend A. E. Dickinson encouraged fathers to teach their sons self-reliance and the ability to perform essential physical activities such as splitting wood but also to be versed in the "uses and proprieties of kitchen, dining-room and parlor."[23] Articles in the newspaper that addressed the roles of men in the home struggled to balance the importance of a deep spirituality in the father without "feminizing" his role in the home. The compromise that emerged ascribed the formal leadership of the family's religious service to the father but granted mothers the responsibility for the day-to-day maintenance of the home and the keeping of the children. With this model in mind, it was the father's duty to put his "faith" in the mother's ability to nurture the children and the family.[24] Fathers modeled the correct religious behavior through a private piety that entailed retiring to their closets to pray for their wife and children.[25]

While articles encouraged all children in the church to strive to improve the condition of the race,[26] the father was charged with instilling manhood in boys. Tanner wrote, "If a young man deserves praise, be sure to give it to him else you not only run a chance of driving him from the right road by want of encouragement, but deprive yourself of the happiest privilege you will ever have of rewarding his labor."[27] In a similar vein, James C. Waters wrote, "It is conceded that young men are the pillars of any government . . . young men occupy, or should occupy a position in the Church, which at once constitutes them columns in the edifice; and this is particularly true with respect to the young men of the A.M.E. Church."[28] Articles encouraged young men to rise further in the ranks of society than their fathers and challenged them to take advantage of the opportunities made available to them through the sacrifices of those who came before them. Augustus W. Watson wrote, "Bishop Richard Allen, Morris Brown, Edward Waters and William Paul Quinn, suffered and labored in an age which dates back a few years, before I was born; but every word of their eloquent suffering was for me; they fought for truth and conscience, and I have as deep an interest in truth and conscience as they had."[29] Writers encouraged young men to begin their days early and "do something that will benefit their church and their race" and "not to get in their own way."[30] While contributors expressed concern about the spiritual development of children, many felt that as boys grew into men, they would face special challenges that would lead them away from the Sunday school system.[31]

Rather than a precise definition of fatherhood, constructions of manhood by AME church authors were often synonymous with living the life of a good Christian. The traits of manhood included such broad practices as being pious and meeting one's duty to God through obedience, engaging in labor and participating in industry, temperance, patriotism, and good character.[32] Advice dispensed to boys and men alike encouraged them to seek spiritual strength from the Lord, maintain good character, and choose the spiritual gifts over physical desires. Reverend T. H. Jackson wrote, "Young men there is a higher a better, a nobler life than the merely sensual."[33] However, character itself was not the sole purview of any race. In one editorial, Tanner wrote, "What has character, and the love of it, to do with color or the want of it?"[34] Reverend William D. Johnson constructed notions of manhood from his reflections on the life of his father, recalling his devotion to his mother and his marriage as well as an enduring abiding belief and faith in Jesus.[35] These AME leaders' recollections of the proper division of responsibility between men and women in the home saw their corollary in postbellum church legislation.

Women as "Assistants": Power Differentials of Gender and Race

The 1868 AME Church General Conference struck a compromise that created the position of stewardess and female superintendent. The General Conference decided that a pastor of a congregation could nominate a Board of Stewardesses, instituting the first official position for women in the church. The position did not require ordination, fell under the authority of the male leadership, and viewed women as "assistants" in the church. According to AME Church polity, stewardesses were a "collection of sisters, numbering not less than three nor more than nine, who assist the stewards, class leaders and pastor [. . .] but cannot always be recognized as a board, as they have no legislative or judicial discretion, but are merely assistants."[36] The General Conference stipulated that if the necessary "three to nine most influential women" could not be found in a congregation, men could hold the position. However, women could not occupy the position of steward. Male stewards as well as the pastor had the final say over potential candidates and the length of their tenure in the position. In contrast, AME Church legislation granted no power to allow stewardesses to remove stewards.[37] The General Conference also defined the duties of the female superintendent in relation to the male superintendent. While both were required to arrive at the schoolroom on time, the female superintendent was also required to "assist" the male superintendent in "preserving order in the school, especially among the females." In addition, the female superintendent oversaw female teachers and their classes.[38] Reticent to relinquish power, male AME Church leaders established positions for women with prestigious titles, but little real power.

In practice, AME Church leaders who appointed women to the position of stewardess met resistance. In 1873, Bishop Henry McNeal Turner appointed nine women to the role. Turner recalled that fellow preachers became "ashy over the matter" when they learned of his appointments and were "disposed to be troublesome." Turner handled the matter by telling the ministers that if they could not work with the stewardesses, "they had better vacate their positions at once; or I would vacate them without their assistance, and put other men in their places."[39] While the General Conference had instituted the position of stewardess, it had not defined specific duties for the position. This oversight meant that the duties of the position varied from church to church. Turner created a list of duties for the stewardesses under his charge in Savannah, Georgia. They included attending to the sick and poor and "search[ing] out" children for the Sabbath school. However, he also made special accommodations for the women. For example, rather than meeting with the official board, he met with the stewardesses biweekly at four o'clock on Friday afternoons, because it was not "proper to have ladies strolling around after night." For the most part, Turner limited their activities to working with women, but when they did work with men, he felt they were "abundantly successful." In general, Turner spoke very positively of the stewardesses. He wrote, "I have found my stewardesses worth more than all the male officers put together. They are more industrious, more regular to time, more concerned about the religious progress of the church, and they find out more that is going wrong."[40] Although many ministers supported the passage of legislation that expanded women's roles in the church on paper, few expected to enact the positions so swiftly.

Turner had a kindred spirit in a younger minister named Theophilus Gould Steward. Born April 17, 1843, two years after Payne joined the AME Church, Steward often clashed with the conservative stances taken by the many of the elder statesmen in the church. In April 1862, the AME Church licensed Steward to exhort and on September 26, 1863, he earned his preaching license. Although he had received little formal education, Steward proved to be an effective preacher and was appointed to the Macedonia AME Church in South Camden, New Jersey. Steward served as pastor there until early in 1865, when Daniel Payne assigned him to be a missionary in South Carolina.[41] T. G. Steward made the case that one could not define manhood in the same way for African Americans as one would for white Americans because of the racism that existed in American society. Manhood could be defined for whites based on their occupation and training; however, many African Americans, even after attaining education, had to work as farm workers, on steamboats, and as mechanics. He declared, "We cannot judge colored men by their occupation; and the fact that they are not ashamed of such occupation, but are contented in them argues nothing."[42]

Steward understood the barriers that faced many Africans Americans as well as the burden that came with the "curse of color." "Prejudice excluded colored people no matter how learned or talented from positions of honor or profit among whites, and colored people have not these positions to bestow."[43] Steward viewed such limits on an individual's profession as linked to the project of racial uplift, because the field in which a young African American male chose to work was important because it affected whether African Americans were to be viewed as dependent servants or independent agents. He wrote, "It should be the aim of every colored youth to take advantage of every privilege by which he may better his own condition and reflect honor upon his race." He continued, "There are too many young men growing up in this age who think they have no higher calling than to play the part of servants. While we do not wish to cast any reproach upon those who have chosen these occupations when no other doors were open to them, yet we think that the colored youth of this day should have a higher ambition."[44] Unlike the mission field, where a more rugged individual type was in place, the precise scope of manhood in the domestic realm remained elusive for most contributors to AME literature.

Steward, no stranger to dissent during his time as a member of the AME Church, became one of the most outspoken advocates for the expansion of women's roles in the church. In his effort to sway public opinion in AME Church newspapers, Steward challenged the patriarchal structure that had become entrenched in the denomination. He questioned why the public roles of the church—preaching from the pulpit, receiving ordination, and voting at Quarterly and General Conferences—were understood as exclusively male pursuits, while women were expected to support the church only at the local level by raising funds and supporting its programs. Although his stance was very unpopular among other male leaders, Steward made a case for the expansion of women's roles in the denomination.

Steward encouraged women to draw upon the power they already possessed in local congregations across the country. While men held the highest leadership positions in the church, women constituted the majority of the AME Church membership. According to the AME Church *Discipline,* any person seeking to be a licensed preacher or an exhorter had to be nominated by members of his congregation.[45] An individual aspiring to rise in the ranks of the church needed the recommendation of his local congregation. Because of this approval process, T. G. Steward made the case that women should be able to vote in all church meetings, including the election of the trustees. If female members voted throughout the career of a minister, he argued, "does not consistency alone, demand that it shall not be restricted in other instances."[46]

Skeptical about the ability of his fellow ministers to deviate from the status quo, Steward urged women to act on their own behalf. "It is well known that our brethren are seldom induced to inaugurate any improvement in our property until the complaints and calls of the sisters become as they fancy the greater evil." According to Steward, it was the "more progressive wives and daughters, sisters and mothers acting like fire upon the back of a stubborn turtle" that would "compel" the church to "strike out." If women could vote at church meetings, he argued, the "delays running through perhaps a decade, a score of years [would] be prevented by forcing a decision on the side of progress."[47] While Steward argued passionately for his position, there were a number of structural barriers in the church hierarchy to preempt the power of female congregants. For example, a local preacher received his license from the Quarterly Conference, which could deny a preacher a license or refuse to renew it "without any impeachment of his moral character, or finding any decrease of piety, talent or usefulness."[48]

Steward challenged the assumption of many male AME Church leaders that the role of leadership inherently belonged to men, which he felt presupposed a false male superiority: "This doctrine is based upon the barbarous idea of female inferiority and where men cling to it, clearly shows more love and tender regard for the gold of the temple, than for what is termed the spiritual interests." The assumption that female congregants were the "weaker vessels," Steward asserted, was used to justify the exclusion of women from positions of power. However, the AME Church still expected women to raise funds and to "shoulder about two-thirds, and in some extreme cases, nine hundred and ninety-nine one thousandths of the burden." Steward pronounced "the whole thing wrong—the practice and the grounds upon which it is based." Theologically, Steward supported his position with the biblical passage in Galatians 3:28: "There is neither Jew nor Greek, there is neither bond nor free, there is neither *male nor female;* for ye are all one in Christ Jesus."[49]

In 1874, through the *Christian Recorder,* Tanner called for "representative" women of the race to join the missionary efforts of the church. In response to Tanner's editorial, a group of bishop's wives sent an open letter to the sisters and wives of pastors in the church to join them in their efforts to form a women's missionary organization. The bishop's wives called upon all women in the church and especially "those of us who have consecrated our all, jointly with our dear husbands, for the universal spread of the gospel." They called for the pastor's wives to organize "Mite Missionary Societies" in their husband's churches. The women hoped that by gathering small "mites" from members of the church, the collective effort would result in a substantial amount of money to put towards missionary work. The founders of the organization were seven bishop's wives: Mary Quinn, Eliza Payne, Harriet A. E. Wayman, Mary A. Campbell, Maria Shorter, Mary L. Brown, and Mrs. Bishop Ward.[50] Officially, the WMMS fell under the authority of the missionary department and therefore served as a "helper" to the AME Church.

Although the WMMS was headed by women, male leaders asserted their authority over the organization, playing a large official role in the proceedings of the meetings. On May 8, 1874, at the inaugural meeting of the Bethel AME Church Women's Mite Missionary Society, although Mary A. Campbell presided over the meeting, Bishop Shorter opened the ceremony and Reverend Theodore Gould, Bishop Campbell, Tanner, and W. H. Hunter all spoke before the women began the organizational process and elected officers. Although the opening meeting was "unceremonious" and not very well advertised, fifty people attended the opening meeting, and Mrs. Bishop Campbell was elected the first president of the organization. Over the weeks following the first WMMS Convention on August 11, 1874, in Philadelphia, Tanner printed the minutes of the meeting along with the bylaws and the constitution of the new organization.[51]

The presumption that women were the assistants to the male leaders impeded the early efforts of the WMMS, particularly their attempts to form separate branches of organization. In response to Tanner's letter, Harriet Wayman expressed interest in forming a women's missionary society but needed the support of the elders, trustees, and stewards of the church. Only with their support, Wayman wrote, did they "have the power to work." The AME Church leadership, at times, posed a real power barrier to the involvement of women in the missionary efforts of the church. Wayman asked, without the encouragement of the pastor, "what can we do?" While the women were ready to organize and "help work for the cause of Christ," they needed the men to "loan the use of our Churches," and "call the people together and make known the objects of meeting."[52] Despite the desire of the male leaders to have a hand in the organization, the female leaders made the WMMS their own. From 1874 to 1878, Mary A. Campbell, the first president of the organization, raised money for local societies and missionary work in Haiti, Santo Domingo, and West Africa. In America, they focused their efforts in the North. While many male AME Church leaders referred to Africa as the "fatherland" that they would "conquer" with the Gospel,[53] many women in the WMMS viewed Africa as the "motherland" that needed support in the nurture of her children. The WMMS raised most of the money for the late-nineteenth-century missionary efforts of the church. However, the male leaders still defined the boundaries of the group and maintained final authority on the group's decisions. Consistent with its historical legacy, the AME Church male leadership limited female participation to the role of "helper" in missionary work as well.[54]

AT THE 1884 General Conference, in his opening address, Bishop William F. Dickerson challenged the AME Church to reach a final decision on the licensing of female preachers. He argued that if women were licensed to preach, a "proper adjustment of the pronouns" in the AME Church *Discipline* "may serve to give notice to all that we have risen to that height where sex is no barrier to the enjoyment of some of the privileges of the Gospel Ministry."[55] Although the motion passed, there was furious debate over the legislation. Among the faction of ministers who opposed licensing female preachers, the Reverend James A. Johnson was the most outspoken. In his rebuttal to the 1884 legislation, Johnson placed the pulpit at odds with the home. Johnson defined women as the "weaker vessel" and argued that women were physically incapable of dealing with the hardships encountered in the itinerant lifestyle. According to Johnson, women were intellectually and physically designed for the "particular sphere" of the home where they could be protected by a male, either a father or husband. Sanctioning female preachers, he asserted, would substitute man's will for God's will and do nothing more than "damage the church."[56] He concluded, "There is no advantage to be gained from it. God has circumscribed her sphere, and whenever she goes out of it, injury is done to society. The Bible said she should keep silence in the church."[57]

Johnson's transposition of the home and the pulpit was no accident, for the legislation represented a clear threat to the male dominance of the ministry by placing men in direct competition with women for congregations. By 1884, the home had become so closely tied to true womanhood that its mere invocation was meant to undo the aspirations of women in the church. By seeking a license to preach, the dissenters argued, women not only impeded the work of the church but disrupted home life and the nurture of children. The 1884 resolution of the General Conference to license female preachers challenged the male dominance of the ministry. The legislation implied that men would be in direct competition for congregations with women. On May 22, W. D. Cook proposed that licensed female preachers function only as traveling evangelists, rather than lead their own churches. Ministers opposed to the legislation employed the language of domesticity in their attacks. The Reverend G. W. Bryant spoke out "in favor of their staying home and taking care of the babies." Cook's resolution limiting women's roles passed 65 to 11.[58] The denomination would not elect its first female bishop, Vashti Murphy McKenzie, until the year 2000.

As we have seen, positions were fairly malleable in the growing AME Church in the early nineteenth century, exemplified by women such as Jarena Lee delivering sermons at Mother Bethel Church in Philadelphia. However, as the AME movement transformed into an institution, male leaders formalized rules, raised educational requirements to head congregations, and more rigidly mapped the boundaries of gender roles in the church, which increasingly limited the opportunities of women to assume leadership. There were numerous reasons for male ministers to seek to maintain control of one of the few public spaces and leadership roles available to African Americans, but this essay has concentrated on their concern of falling short of the standards of manhood. Romanticizing the manhood embodied by the strong early itinerant ministers and recanting the lore of their exploits on the frontier as they expanded the church westward in the first half of the century only accentuated the scarce outlets available to assert their own manhood. It is within this atmosphere that many AME leaders sought to masculinize the pulpit and engage the perpetual process of demonstrating their "true manhood."

Notes

1. Henry Highland Garnet, "Pioneers of the AME Church—No. III," *Christian Recorder,* 13 March 1869, 1.

2. David W. Wills, "Womanhood and Domesticity in the A.M.E. Tradition: The Influence of Daniel Alexander Payne," in David W. Wills and Richard Newman, eds., *Black Apostles at Home and Abroad: Afro-Americans and the Christian Mission from the Revolution to Reconstruction* (Boston: G. K. Hall, 1982), 138. Julius H. Bailey, *Around the Family Altar: Domesticity in the African Methodist Episcopal Church, 1865–1900* (Gainesville: University Press of Florida, 2005), 37–38.

3. Alexander W. Wayman, *Manual, or Guide Book for the Administration of the Discipline of the African M. E. Church* (Philadelphia: AME Book Rooms, 1886), 16.

4. Daniel A. Payne, *History of the African Methodist Episcopal Church* (Nashville, TN: Publishing House of the AME Sunday School Union, 1891), 121.

5. Bailey, *Around the Family Altar,* 38.

6. James A. Handy, *Scraps of African Methodist Episcopal History* (Philadelphia: AME Book Concern, 1902), 189–90; C. S. Smith, ed. *History of the African Methodist Episcopal Church* (New York: Johnson Reprint Corp., 1968), 476–96; Daniel A. Payne, *Recollections of Seventy Years* (Nashville, TN: Publishing House of the AME Sunday School Union, 1888), 109–10.

7. David Leverenz, *Manhood and the American Renaissance* (Ithaca, NY: Cornell University Press, 1989), 4.

8. Gail Bederman, *Manliness & Civilization: A Cultural History of Gender and Race in the United States, 1880–1917* (Chicago: University of Chicago Press, 1995), 8–27.

9. H. T. Kealing, *History of African Methodism in Texas* (Waco, TX: C. F. Blanks Printer and Stationer, 1885), 3–4, 33, 150, 165, 170.

10. Benjamin T. Tanner, *An Apology for African Methodism* (Baltimore, 1867), 135, 130, 138.

11. Ibid., 312–13.

12. Payne, *History of the African Methodist Episcopal Church,* 12.

13. Clarence E. Walker, *A Rock in a Weary Land: The African Methodist Episcopal Church during the Civil War and Reconstruction* (Baton Rouge: Louisiana State University Press, 1982), 26.

14. Payne, *History of the African Methodist Episcopal Church,* 237.

15. William L. Andrews, *Sisters of the Spirit: Three Black Women's Autobiographies of the Nineteenth Century* (Bloomington: Indiana University Press, 1986), 45–46, 103.

16. Payne, *The Pleasures and Other Miscellaneous Poems* (Baltimore: Sherwood & Co., 1850), 32–36.

17. Payne, *Recollections of Seventy Years,* 11–13, 16.

18. Payne, *History of the African Methodist Episcopal Church,* 169.

19. James T. Campbell, *Songs of Zion: The African Methodist Episcopal Church in the United States and South Africa* (New York: Oxford University Press, 1995), 45–48.

20. Payne, *History of the African Methodist Episcopal Church,* 194–95.

21. Tanner, "Preaching," *Christian Recorder,* 8 August 1868, 1; Tanner, "The Pulpit—Its Weakness and Its Strength," *Christian Recorder,* 15 August 1868, 1; Tanner, "Plain Preaching," *Christian Recorder,* 15 August 1868, 1; Tanner, "Pulpit Eloquence," *Christian*

Recorder, 31 October 1868, 2; Tanner, "Success in the Ministry," *Christian Recorder,* 22 May 1869, 2.

22. The Reverend Henry C. Potter, "The Black Man Is Not at Home Here," *Christian Recorder,* 6 April 1872, 4; Tanner, "Train the Boys for Business," *Christian Recorder,* 5 June 1884, 2; Tanner, "The Best Good at Home," *Christian Recorder,* 17 February 1876, 3; Tanner, "Boy's Courage," *Christian Recorder,* 17 February 1876, 3; Payne, "The Work of Life," *Christian Recorder,* 24 December 1874, 1; Tanner, "Sketches of Young Men," *Christian Recorder,* 15 August 1868, 4.

23. A. E. Dickinson, "What to Teach Our Sons," *Christian Recorder,* 12 August 1875, 3.

24. "A Family Experience," *Christian Recorder,* 18 May 1876, 2.

25. Tanner, "Child-Prayer," *Christian Recorder,* 1 July 1875, 6. "The Closet," *Christian Recorder,* 18 May 1876, 2.

26. P. Sheeder, "Religious Training of the Young," *Christian Recorder,* 16 January 1869, 1; Sheeder, "Religious Training of the Young," *Christian Recorder,* 30 January 1869, 1; C. B. M., "Advice to Youth," *Christian Recorder,* 17 September 1870, 3.

27. Tanner, "Encourage the Young," *Christian Recorder,* 30 January 1869, 4; Tanner, "Advice to Young Men," *Christian Recorder,* 1 October 1870, 2; "Bad Boys Make Bad Men," *Christian Recorder,* 31 August 1872, 6; "A Young Men's Hall," *Christian Recorder,* 8 January 1874, 7; George Cooper, "Give the Little Boys a Chance," *Christian Recorder,* 23 April 1874, 6.

28. James C. Waters, "The Young Men of the A.M.E. Church," *Christian Recorder,* 16 April 1870, 1.

29. Augustus M. Hodges, "Conversations with Young Men, By One of Their Number," *Christian Recorder,* 1 December 1881, 1; August W. Watson, "The Position and Responsibility of Our Young Men," *Christian Recorder,* 19 July 1883, 3.

30. Reverend J. F. Dyson, "A Talk to Young Men," *Christian Recorder,* 8 November 1883, 1; "Boys, Get Up," *Christian Recorder,* 29 June 1876, 2.

31. Reverend B. F. Watson, "What Shall We Do with Our Boys and Girls?" *Christian Recorder,* 22 November 1877, 1; Everett, "How Can We Keep Our Young Men in the Sabbath School?" *Christian Recorder,* 4 December 1884, 1.

32. Tanner, "The Temperance Question," *Christian Recorder,* 31 August 1882, 2; Tanner, "The Poor Drunkard," *Christian Recorder,* 13 January 1876, 6; John L. Davis, "What Are the Elements of True Manhood?" *Christian Recorder,* 11 May 1882, 2; "The Drunkard's Daughter," *Christian Recorder,* 6 July 1876, 6; "Maxims for a Young Man," *Christian Recorder,* 4 August 1876, 6.

33. "Maxims for a Young Man," *Christian Recorder,* 4 August 1876, 6; Reverend T. H. Jackson, "To the Young Men," *Christian Recorder,* 22 March 1877, 1.

34. Tanner, "Blydenism," *Christian Recorder,* 21 December 1882, 2.

35. Reverend William D. Johnson, "On the Death of My Father," *Christian Recorder,* 9 September 1880, 1.

36. Henry McNeal Turner, *The Genius and Theory of Methodist Polity* (Philadelphia: Publication Department of the AME Church, 1885), 165–66.

37. Bailey, *Around the Family Altar,* 49.

38. "The Sabbath School," *Christian Recorder,* 29 October 1870, 1.

39. Henry McNeal Turner, "How the Stewardess System Operates in the A.M.E. Church," *Christian Recorder*, 15 May 1873, 1.

40. Ibid.

41. William Seraile, *Theophilus Gould Steward (1843–1924) and Black America* (Brooklyn, NY: Carlson Publishing, 1991), 3–8.

42. T. G. Steward, "Colored Society—III," *Christian Recorder*, 23 November 1876, 1.

43. Steward, "Colored Society—VI," *Christian Recorder*, 28 December 1876, 1.

44. C. S. H., "Colored Youth and Education," *Christian Recorder*, 20 January 1876, 2.

45. Alexander W. Wayman, *Manual, or Guide Book for the Administration of Discipline of the African M.E. Church* (Philadelphia: AME Book Rooms, 1886), 26–27.

46. Steward, "Female Suffrage in Church," *Christian Recorder*, 30 July 1870, 2–3.

47. Steward, "Female Suffrage in Church," *Christian Recorder*, 20 August 1870, 2–3.

48. Wayman, *Manual, or Guide Book for the Administration of Discipline of the African M.E. Church,* 27.

49. Steward, "Female Suffrage in Church," *Christian Recorder*, 30 July 1870, 2–3.

50. Mary Quinn et al., "An Open Letter," *Christian Recorder*, 21 May 1874, 1; Campbell, *Songs of Zion,* 93.

51. Tanner, "The Organization of the Women's Mite Missionary Society," *Christian Recorder*, 23 July 1874, 2; Tanner, "The Women's Mite Missionary Society," *Christian Recorder*, 13 August 1874, 4; "The Convention on Organization," *Christian Recorder*, 20 August 1874, 2.

52. Harriet Wayman, "The Work of Women," *Christian Recorder*, 21 May 1874.

53. John W. Bowen, ed., "The American Negro and His Fatherland," *Africa and the American Negro* (Atlanta, GA: Gammon Theological Seminary, 1896). Wilson Jeremiah Moses, ed., *Classical Black Nationalism: From the American Revolution to Marcus Garvey* (New York: New York University Press, 1996), 221–27.

54. George A. Singleton, *The Romance of African Methodism: A Study of the African Methodist Episcopal Church* (New York: Exposition Press, 1952). See also Octavia W. Dandridge, *Eleven Decades of Historical Events* (Washington, DC: Women's Missionary Society A.M.E. Church, 1985); Dorothy Adams Peck, ed., *Women on the Way: African Methodist Episcopal Women Maximizing Their Human and Spiritual Potential* (Washington, DC: Women's Missionary Society A.M.E. Church, 1983); Campbell, *Songs of Zion,* 93–95.

55. *Minutes of the 1884 A.M.E. General Conference,* 133.

56. James H. A. Johnson, "Female Preachers," AME *Church Review* 1:2 (1884, 102–5.

57. Ibid.

58. Tanner, "The Late General Conference," *Christian Recorder*, 5 June 1884, 2; "The General Conference," *Christian Recorder*, 5 June 1884, 2.

5

"Shall I Trust These Men?"

Thomas Nast and Postbellum Black Manhood

FIONA DEANS HALLORAN

In a pair of illustrations printed August 5, 1865, Thomas Nast presented *Harper's Weekly* readers with two starkly contrasting models of masculinity: on the left, the "rebel chiefs" of the Confederacy knelt before "Columbia"; on the right, a black veteran stood proudly on his one remaining leg, his uniform in order and his gaze steady. "Shall I Trust These Men," Columbia asked, "And Not This Man?" In one stroke, Nast demanded national attention for black men.[1] Calling upon the undeniable relationship of military service to citizenship, Nast hammered away on behalf of black veterans, and symbols of citizenship reinforced the point. Black men appeared with the American flag, the ballot box, and other emblems of political identity, as Nast presented a version of black masculinity that offered the nation everything he considered ideal: patriarchy, self-control, and honorable self-sacrifice for patriotism. When Southern violence threatened the civil rights of the freedmen, Nast responded with a withering attack on former Confederates; in contrast to black men, these white Americans represented everything corrupt about white masculinity. If the North was to prevail in its quest to remake the South, it could not permit the Ku Klux Klan and other vigilante groups free rein. Black men demonstrated, with their wartime valor, the essential manliness on which the nation must rely in the postwar period.

However, Nast was an unreliable champion of racial equality. Though his drawings of black veterans include some of his most powerful images, the sympathy and outrage expressed in them resonating more than one hundred years later, his work simultaneously honored black men and accepted the tropes of minstrelsy. Just as he produced illustrations showing honorable black veterans, he drew illustrations in which black voters threatened the democratic process. In some cases, Nast even equated Irish immigrants and freemen, uniting them as "The Ignorant Vote," and by the time Reconstruction ended, Nast's outrage seemed grounded more in his hatred of Southern whites than his defense of Southern blacks. Nast thereby poses a challenge to understanding the role of black masculinity in postbellum American political culture. The nation's foremost political cartoonist, reaching an audience of more than one hundred thousand subscribers weekly, Nast occupied a commanding place in the public mind—and art can provide visceral expressions of the public will when words fail. Nast's representation of black men proves frustratingly mixed precisely because he reflects the racial ambiguities of his time and place. After the Civil War, Americans needed to know whether national conceptions of manliness included black men. Like Nast, many Americans took ambiguous positions on black citizenship, social status, and capacity for independent action, and as a result, artist and audience engaged the postwar crisis of masculinity in ways sometimes more confused than productive.[2]

Nast's Black Heroes

Thomas Nast's sympathy for black men probably originated in his childhood. Born in Bavaria in 1840, Nast immigrated to the United States in 1846, where he lived in a neighborhood bounded by Wall Street, Park Row, and Broadway. Most important for Nast's education in ethnicity and bias, the Five Points sat only six blocks away, and Nast often roamed the streets of Lower Manhattan, observing the riotous stew of life on its streets. Gangs, hot-corn girls, newsboys, German bakers, and Irish saloon owners all wandered in and out of this tableau. The small population of black Americans living in Five Points suffered periodic assaults from their immigrant and native-born neighbors, and years later Nast acknowledged the influence this violence had on his later work,

especially on his interest in the daily lives and activities of the underclass. Throughout his life, the artist sketched what he saw, whether it was
a rotund rider of the omnibus or a man on the street in Ecuador, and
for this ambitious, observant young man, the racial conflict among New
York's poor served as an introduction to American racism.[3]

More personal, and probably just as influential, was the social and
political atmosphere provided by Nast's wife, and through Sarah Edwards,
Nast entered a family that collected intelligent, politically active friends
for lively discussion. The circle included Jesse Haney, publisher of the
Comic Monthly; humorist Mortimer "Doesticks" Thompson; historian,
biographer, and antislavery advocate James Parton and his wife, the novelist Fannie Fern. Nast socialized with the Edwardses and their friends
beginning in 1859, and in 1861 he married Sarah. Just as national unity
began to disintegrate along sectional lines, Nast found himself in the
center of a group of literate, informed, and energetic observers of American politics. Several members of that group opposed slavery energetically
and in print, just as Nast would later do.

Nast's marriage coincided with his first real taste of steady employment. Though he began working as an illustrated journalist at fifteen,
none of his jobs provided sustained, consistent income until he began
regular work at *Harper's Weekly* in 1862. There, Nast joined a team of talented illustrators and engravers as part of the powerful Harper and Brothers publishing empire. Best of all, publisher Fletcher Harper acted as a
mentor for the young artist. Nast worked for the *Weekly* as an engraver,
but he also provided original illustrations, and Harper encouraged Nast
to spread his artistic wings, departing from the kind of work done by
field artists like William and Alfred Waud or Winslow Homer. Instead of
drawing what he saw, Nast drew what people on the home front felt, and
those drawings included scenes of homesick soldiers, lonely families, and
sentimental appeals to the South by Northern leaders.[4]

Thomas and Sarah Nast welcomed their daughter Julia into the world
on July 1, 1862. Julia's arrival likely reinforced for Nast the relationship between masculinity and fatherhood as he faced increasing family
and professional responsibilities. Six months later, Nast produced "The
Emancipation of the Negroes," a large illustration celebrating the Emancipation Proclamation that reflected both the antislavery views he had
come to hold and his new sensitivity to the burdens and pleasures of
patriarchy (see figure 1). Along the outer edges, Nast acknowledged the
ways that emancipation changed the status of black men: in chains before,
subject to the brutality of slave traders, whipped and branded, black men

Figure 1

Emancipation and the Black Family. Nast envisioned a transformed life for African Americans after emancipation, as they were welcomed into joining the community practices that were the birthright of all Americans.

would now enjoy wage labor and respect from their employers. With a respectfully tipped overseer's hat in the lower right of the drawing, Nast hoped for an entirely new relationship between black and white men. Emancipation meant dignity at work, with wages and decent conditions. It also meant security at home.[5]

In the center of the drawing, family took precedence. Watched by a benevolent Lincoln, the black family enjoyed a thoroughly middle-class life. "Here," *Harper's* explained, "domestic peace and comfort reign supreme, the reward of faithful labor." Respectably dressed, well-fed, and tidy, they gathered around the father, whose comfortable position in an easy chair signaled his authority and his paternal oversight, while behind his back, his daughter flirted gently with her beau, a patriarch in the making. What emancipation wrought for this father was the liberty to direct "all his honest earnings" to "the object he has most at heart—his children's advancement and education."[6] When he emphasized the primacy of fatherhood, Nast echoed abolitionist rhetoric, as activists like Frederick Douglass openly asserted the emasculating effects of slavery. Unable to defend themselves or protect as a father and husband should, enslaved men lost the masculine privileges and responsibilities inherent to patriarchy. They found themselves "beyond the range of human brotherhood," even as abolitionists insisted that enslaved men were both men and brothers. If so, patriarchal authority offered social power and gendered inclusion, and for Nast, the restoration of that authority formed the core of the Emancipation Proclamation. Freedom meant family life, safe from harm, sale, or helplessness. His illustration, subtitled "The Past and the Future," consumed two entire pages of *Harper's Weekly* and asserted in terms any reader would understand the value of black manhood for the nation.[7]

Nast's imagined black family contradicted a widespread literature devoted to former slaves, free black men, and black soldiers. In that literature, black masculinity posed at best a challenge and at worst a threat to American culture. According to some historians, writers and illustrators unable to deal easily with the implications of black manhood sometimes resorted to "narrative strategies" that "circumscribed or sharply limited the implications" of black freedom. Instead, popular literature and many illustrated magazines controlled the danger "through imagined white control of black actions, ridicule, or, most often, death." Nast rejected that dominant trend, and instead of the heroic but ultimately doomed black soldier, he offered readers black men who lived to establish stable families. Instead of objects of ridicule, Nast drew men worthy of respect and even honor. Even the presence of a benevolent Abraham Lincoln presiding over Nast's black family echoed the idea of white control, but in a fashion that acknowledged black patriotism and included African Americans in the national community. In short, Nast rejected some of the most common themes of his time and profession in favor of celebrating the black family and its patriarch.[8]

If black fatherhood formed the emotional core of emancipation, black patriotism formed its civic core. Nast was as profoundly optimistic after the war about the potential of black men to vote as he was impressed by their military service. His drawings portrayed black soldiers as brave fighters, implying that their service qualified them for full civil rights. Military service had been central to both masculinity and citizenship since ancient times, and Nast—a dedicated reader of history and mythology—knew exactly how powerful a symbol the Union uniform could be. In March 1863, Nast created a two-page illustration based on a description of an attack by the First Kansas Colored Volunteers. In the face of sword-wielding Confederates, Nast showed soldiers of the First Kansas attacking with vigor. Three men ran forward, while others fired their weapons or hoisted a tattered American flag, and a fallen soldier in the foreground highlighted the sacrifices that united black and white soldiers in battle. An accompanying article told the story of the unit's heroism and reinforced Nast's point: black soldiers offered the Union the potential to field "the steadiest rank and file in the world."[9]

The theme of heroic sacrifice emerged again in "Pardon" and "Franchise," which demonstrate the degree to which the potential of black veterans as citizens and Republican voters excited Nast's imagination (see figure 2). He frequently portrayed them with symbols of political participation. In these paired illustrations, the black veteran stands by Columbia, but also stands next to a ballot box and an American flag, potent symbols of citizenship underlining the symbolic power of rights previously denied and now the cause of war. Though the black veteran's leg is gone below the thigh, he nevertheless stands erect, his gaze steady and dignified. Columbia's hand rests on his shoulder, invoking the prohibition on physical contact between black men and white women. Barely visible behind her, the tattered edges of the flag remind the reader of two of the greatest and most notorious moments in the history of the U.S. Colored Troops: Fort Pillow and Fort Wagner. At Fort Pillow, readers would recall, black soldiers found no quarter despite their surrender. At Fort Wagner, after staggering losses, their bodies were dumped into a common grave along with their white commander by derisive Confederates.[10]

PARDON.
COLUMBIA.—"SHALL I TRUST THESE MEN,

Figure 2 **"Pardon" and "Franchise."** In these facing pages, Nast's pair of illustrations dramatizes the ethical dilemma of granting white men of the Confederacy the vote while withholding it from black men, here exemplified by the wounded veteran.

FRANCHISE.
AND NOT THIS MAN?"

Nast deftly played on his readers' sympathies, knowledge, and expectations. He blessed black voting with the white, feminine hand of the nation. Though grievously maimed, his veteran upheld the finest traditions of Union mythology, unbowed despite his wounds. Fort Pillow reminded readers that black soldiers had been denied the rights promised by the rules of war. Readers also recognized Nast's hint that the nation could repudiate the actions of men like Nathan Bedford Forrest by accepting black Americans into the body politic. Fort Wagner linked black veterans to the commitment made by many Northerners to racial progress and the end of slavery. In visual terms, Nast asserted that voting rights were the final step in the long march of antislavery activism.

Not all of Nast's work appeared in the widely read but ephemeral pages of illustrated newspapers, as he produced oil paintings as well. As a boy, Nast enjoyed a short period of academic training in art, and years later, during the Civil War, he called upon that training to produce a series of paintings devoted to war themes. These included *Entrance of the 55th Massachusetts (Colored) Regiment into Charlestown, S.C February 21, 1865*. Based on an engraving from March that year, the painting celebrated the connection between black military service and the end of slavery. The image carefully organized two groups so that they touched in the center, a triangular form Nast often used. On the right, the marching soldiers, their caps held atop their bayonets, happily waved to the crowd. On the left, meeting them, was a large group of ecstatic civilians, including women and children. In the center, the organizational and official weight of the image, rode the unit's white colonel. According to its caption, the soldiers sang "John Brown's March" as they entered the city. In one stroke, Nast connected military service to liberation, abolition, and white leadership. As *Harper's Weekly* presented it, the war had been "a revolution of citizens against their government," but had produced "a revolution quite as profound" between slave and master. By supporting black franchise rights, white Northerners, especially white men, could act in the same heroic vein as the colonel of the 55th. They could partake in the libratory aspect of the war and join the celebration.[11]

Three years later, Nast was less optimistic. In "This Is a White Man's Government," he dramatized the consequences of a victory for Democrats: violence, ignorance, and black disenfranchisement (see figure 3). The presidential election that year offered voters a choice between Horatio Seymour of New York and General Ulysses S. Grant, the Republican nominee. For Nast, both men triggered a personal response. Grant was Nast's hero. The savior of the Union, a man whom Nast believed to be

Figure 3 **"This Is a White Man's Government."** Nast's illustration argues that Democrats established an alliance of the Irish and the South backing Democratic candidate Seymour based on the suppression of the black vote.

committed to the rights of freedmen, and a rough soldier whose personal manners offered a simple masculinity rather than eastern refinement, Grant embodied Nast's idea of the perfect American leader. Seymour would have suffered by comparison in any event, but Seymour was a particular enemy of Nast's for reasons directly related to the latter's valorization of black masculinity. It was Seymour who in 1863 tried to reason with the New York draft rioters by calling them "my friends." Nast witnessed the Draft Riots, and they left an indelible impression on him; echoes of the riots appeared in his work for nearly a decade. In particular, Nast never forgot the sight of a black man hanging from a New York streetlight or the flames of the Colored Orphan Asylum after it had been sacked and set alight. Sympathy for black New Yorkers, based in part on outrage at their treatment during the riots, fueled Nast's support for them in his work and his contempt for Seymour.[12]

Given Seymour's link to the riots, Nast's opposition to the New York governor was bound to be vicious. Nast portrayed the nominee as Lady Macbeth, trying to wash the blood of the riots off his hands. Seymour's candidacy offered a compromise among three competing and often antagonistic groups: wealthy Northern Democrats, angry former Confederates, and voters from within the large Irish immigrant community all jostled for control of the party. Seymour hoped to appeal to many of those voters, especially the Irish and Southern factions, by emphasizing white supremacy. Nast used Seymour's campaign slogans against him. When Seymour argued that the nation must be operated by white men in the interest of the white race, Nast turned that idea on its head. To choose white men over black men, he argued in "This Is a White Man's Government," was to ignore the masculine virtue of the black man and embrace the worst examples of white manhood. His three figures represented three versions of that corruption.[13]

The Irish immigrant embodied the dangers of alien manhood—shiftless, drunken (he carried a bottle in his pocket), violent, and impossible to control. Behind him the Colored Orphan Asylum burned, and a lynched man dangled in Nast's vivid evocation of the Draft Riots. In the center Nast placed the ultimate boogeyman of Nathan Bedford Forrest as the representative of the unreconstructed South. Bearing the initials NBF on his hatband and carrying "The Lost Cause" as a dagger, Forrest symbolized not just slavery in his overseer's whip in his back pocket, but the impossibility of maintaining a healthy republic with treason lurking still. Unlike the simple, animal violence of the Irishman, the Southerner stood for a more complex, more problematic danger. He rebelled, broke the Union, cost hundreds of thousands of lives—yet, Nast complained, he voted still. Finally, on the right stands August Belmont, a major figure in Democratic politics and a New Yorker like Nast. Clutching a wallet full of "Capital for Votes," Belmont joins hands with his compatriots to buy the election if it could not be won by violence. His was the corruption of greed, and though less threatening than the others, his figure never-theless represented an aspect of manhood that Nast, and many Americans like him, held in contempt.[14]

What the republic needed, what would restore its democratic govern-ment under the leadership of an honest man, was the vote of the fourth man in the image. Prone, two boots and a fancy shoe pressed into his back, it was this man who embraced the symbols of the United States. The flag and ballot box, in combination with his Union uniform, left no possibility for misunderstanding. To vote Democratic was to disen-franchise this man. To accept his citizenship was to refute the idea of a "White Man's Government." Nast chose his title with care. The idea that the government ought to be restricted to white men appeared in a vari-ety of places in 1868. Debates in the Senate in February explored the "basis of representation" in some detail and with great passion. Senator Daniel Clark of New Hampshire embraced black political participation. Clark asked Americans whether they would reward the sacrifices of black soldiers during the war with rejection. When the nation asked for their help in wartime, "did you point to the sign over the door, 'Black men wanted to defend the white man's Government'?" Like Nast, he played on the Union soldier's uniform, asking "did you say, 'Don't disgrace it; this is the white man's Government?'" Masculinity played a central role here, as Clark acknowledged. "This right [of voting] is necessary to develop his manhood," and in so doing to "elevate" all black Americans.[15] In contrast, governors in South Carolina, Alabama, and North Carolina echoed the sentiment Nast and Clark decried. Governor Benjamin F. Perry of South Carolina publicly argued that "this is a white man's gov-ernment, and intended for white men only."[16] Seymour, running against U. S. Grant's reconciliatory message "Let Us Have Peace," warned against allowing black men to join the polity. As *Putnam's* wrote, the Democrats believed "that political rights shall be enjoyed by white men only, or, as they express it, under 'a white man's government.'"[17]

But Nast plumbed even deeper conflicts than the title suggested. His campaign illustrations in 1868 commented not just on the contest between Grant and Seymour but also on an ongoing effort to resolve the question of black suffrage in the nation as a whole. Although Radical Republicans in Congress sought to impose suffrage laws on Southern states, they could not manage the same trick in the North. The power to confer voting rights had long belonged to the states. Relying on that power, Northern states refused to permit black citizens to vote. So while Grant's platform advocated black suffrage, his party knew that the votes in question could come only from the South. Indeed, the votes of black men there helped to secure the White House for General Grant. His election, and the dominance of the Congress by Radical Republicans, finally gave black men a serious chance at nationwide voting rights. By supporting Grant, denigrating Democratic voters, and advocating on behalf of black men, Nast contributed to that fight. He could claim, without too much hubris, some small share in the success of the Fifteenth Amendment.[18]

In "Pardon" and "Franchise," as he had done in his emancipation drawing, Nast relied on simplicity. Freedom's promise lay in the role of father, husband, and citizen; as benefits accrued to black men, so would they help the nation. The best example of their potential lay in their military service, and brave, reliable, and worthy of the nation's respect, black soldiers fulfilled the promise of their freedom. Nast's drawings of black family men and black soldiers explored in detail the ramifications of black manhood for American society. "This Is a White Man's Government" approached the question differently. Far more complex in its political foundation, the illustration and others like it played on public statements, campaign slogans, the histories of not only the candidates but also various voting blocs. By 1868, Nast's optimism about black manhood had been tempered by the obvious opposition of many white Americans, but he remained committed to the idea of black citizenship. He assumed in "This Is a White Man's Government" that his readers agreed, as the drawing was less an argument for the valor and value of black men than a blow *against* the opposing qualities in white men. One figure from "This Is a White Man's Government" went on to become a central theme in Nast's later work.

No white men better served Nast's taste for contrast than the former Confederates. Nast despised them. During the same period of his career when he developed a stereotypical representation of the Irish thug, Nast produced an instantly recognizable Southern thug: based in part on Nathan Bedford Forrest, he wore a rough uniform and heavy boots and carried the whip of the overseer. This was the man in the center of "This Is a White Man's Government," and he would appear again and again.[19] Like his Northern counterpart, the Southern thug posed a danger to the nation, and he allowed Nast to compare the optimism of emancipation with the gritty resentment and terrible violence of the unreconstructed South. In drawing after drawing, he appeared as the agent of repression. However, Nast used Southern violence against freedmen not just to attack the South but also to honor the patriotism, families, and service of black men. As Southern vigilantes worked to reclaim their state governments—a process described without irony as Redemption—Nast objected ever more strenuously, though his early optimism about the potential to remake the South and integrate black men into American culture began to disintegrate in the face of constant violence.

"Patience on a Monument" offers one example (see figure 4). Though Nast used the sides of the drawing and quotes on the monument to attack Southern violence, the emotional center of the drawing rests on the shoulders of its hero. Perched atop the monument, a black veteran mourns his lost family, whose bodies lie at the base of the plinth. The howling Irish mob to the left finds its match in the gun-toting KKK mob on the right. Both have attacked children—the Colored Orphan Asylum and a Freedman's School—and both represent Nast's opposition to the combined powers of Irish immigrants, former Confederates, and the party to which both belonged: the Democrats. However, the black veteran plays no passive role here. His face shows his anger, and he sits surrounded by symbols of success: his broken chains, the discarded whip of the overseer, his rifle, and the note "Emancipated by A. Lincoln." Nast's frustration with national policy toward Southern violence found an outlet both in vilifying Southerners and in applauding the accomplishments and virtues of black men. At the base of the monument, Nast has quoted a Mississippi newspaper. The freedmen should be made to understand, it reads, that "we are the men we were when we held them in abject bondage." The point, as Nast saw it, was that the freedmen were no longer the men they had been then, and Southerners must be made to accept the change.

As he so often did, Nast here mixed symbolic elements from other artists' work. For example, the pose of his black veteran recalls "Freedman," a sculpture created by John Quincy Adams Ward in 1863. Like that small bronze, Nast posed his subject with chains but not in them, sitting but not kneeling, and poised between bondage and true liberty. Unlike "Freedman," Nast inserted unequivocal symbols of manhood and resistance: the uniform and the gun. Similarly, Nast invoked a wide range of sculptures, prints, and paintings by including Lincoln's name, but he chose not to pose Lincoln as standing emancipator, with a freedman as

Patience on a Monument.

Figure 4 **"Patience on a Monument."** Nast depicts the sacrifice at the root of all arguments for black men's enfranchisement.

the kneeling slave.[20] Nast's use of the uniform deserves a second look. In his examination of "Freedman," historian Kirk Savage emphasizes the interaction of male nudity and masculinity. He quotes a reviewer's comment on the "lusty negro" and points out that nudity in an image of a black man carries with it all the baggage of the erotic gaze. Later images, created during the later years of the Civil War and reflecting the successes of the Union, offered black men more dignity and more clothing. Still, they tended to portray black men partially nude, shaking off the bonds of slavery. Thus, for Nast to carefully dress his veteran in a soldier's garb, as he had also done in the second panel in figure 2, "Franchise," was to assert a dignity and honor for black veterans linked directly to their masculinity. Manhood lay, he insisted, not in the naked black body but in its symbolic value as a representative of the nation: a soldier.[21]

In case that point failed to convince, in other illustrations Nast used black nudity to his own advantage. In "The Modern Samson," nudity evoked not sexual danger but the power of enfranchisement. The white female figure of "Southern Democracy" cut off Samson's hair because it held his power, "Suffrage." This time, the violent rioters included Seymour, his running mate Union General Francis P. Blair, Nathan Bedford Forrest, and Robert E. Lee. Forrest, adding a last touch of atmosphere, held a torch to emblems of civilization, including the Bible. The link between nudity and vulnerability remained, but that vulnerability connected black men through Samson not just to slavery but to citizenship, strength, and virtue.[22]

Black manhood existed within the contested landscape of Reconstruction. Nast dramatized this with one of his favorite artistic devices, the triangle. In "Patience on a Monument" (figure 4), for example, his hero sat at the tip of the triangle, while on the right and left stood alternative versions of masculinity. The Irish rioter represented the dangerous element of white manhood against which Nast railed throughout his career. On the left the KKK demonstrated the danger posed to the republic by uncontrolled Southern violence. Nast loved juxtaposition and here used it perfectly, forcing readers to confront the superiority of his black veteran against the backdrop of white citizenship. Though the title emphasized his patience, the placement asked again the question from 1865, "Shall I Trust These Men? And Not This One?"[23]

As he demonstrated in *Entrance of the 55th Massachusetts (Colored) Regiment into Charlestown, S.C February 21, 1865,* Nast sometimes used his academic training in the service of his political beliefs. As a teenager in the 1850s, the young Nast worked with Theodore Kaufman and spent days minding the door (and copying the art) at a small private gallery in New York. The combination of his fine art background and his interest in allegorical and historical painting shows in some of the illustrations that employ the triangle. Sometimes, he used triangular forms to indicate emphasis. "Patience on a Monument" serves as one example, but "This Is a White Man's Government" relies on the same device, as the three sides of a pyramid rest on the base of the black voter.

The triangular form helped Nast to lead the audience's eye where he wanted it to go, but it also allowed for juxtaposition and balance. He returned to the form repeatedly, never with more power than in an illustration published by *Harper's Weekly* in September 1876.[24] In it, Nast dramatized the terror and death freedmen experienced in the Redemption South. As Southern Democrats moved to recapture state governments, they systematically disenfranchised black men, often targeting Union veterans for special terror. Because those men carried with them the dignity of military service and in many cases were armed, they became the particular targets of white rage. Horrified by the reports coming from Louisiana, South Carolina, and Alabama, Nast released all the venom and sympathy of his pencil. The central figure provided the triangular form, and his attitude both drew the reader's eyes down to the pile of bodies on the ground and up to the heavens. Like a spotlight, the triangle pointed straight to God, asking for justice.[25] As usual, Nast chose his caption well. "Is This a Republican Form of Government?" asked his subject. His question echoed Article 2, Section 4 of the Constitution, which Nast quoted in a letter the previous year: "The United States shall guarantee to every state in the [*sic*] union a republican form of government." The phrase must have seemed apt when he observed the fury of Southern whites and the confused attempts to find an appropriate reaction among Northern Republicans.[26]

Nast's Uncertainty and Ambivalence

Nast believed in the possibility that President Grant could ease the transition of freedmen into Southern (and national) society, but Grant's power and commitment proved unequal to the task. By the end of Grant's second term, bitterness crept into Nast's illustrations. Frustrated with the slow pace of change, outraged by the violence of the Redemption movement in the South, and bewildered at what he saw as the abdication of their responsibilities by Northern Republicans, Nast became more

pointed. Replying to the "Solid South" created by intimidation and murder, Nast again employed the image of a semi-nude black man (see figure
5). This time, the physical threat of his body was undisguised. This figure
offered an unequivocally dangerous message: he stood, his face angry,
muscles on full display and a rifle in his hands, the caption reading "He
Wants Change Too."

Both parties had by this time come to call references to the war "waving the bloody shirt," but in this case the bloody shirt lay on the ground.
His boot firmly planted on it, Nast's black Republican asked for nothing.
Though the image respected the power of black men, it also relied on
white fear of black masculinity.[27] In these and other images, Nast under-
lined the humanity and manhood of former slaves and Union soldiers.
As he had done during the war, he defended the idea that black men
had a valuable role to play in American society and politics. However,
the years after the war, particularly from 1868 onward, constantly tested
Nast's resolve, as Southern resistance to black civil rights seemed never
to ease. When national leaders struggled to determine the limits of their
commitment to change, Nast faltered.

He was never entirely consistent. Nast struck some hard blows for
black men. He invoked classic masculine virtues on their behalf, but he
was no reliable friend. At times he openly criticized black voters and
black politicians; more often, he relied on racist physical symbols evocative of the minstrel show. In both cases, Nast betrayed the sentiments he
so forcefully advocated in his pro-emancipation work. Even when he
offered a compliment, he sometimes added an insult. For example, in
"All the Difference in the World," the upper panel compared a filthy, lazy,
rum-drinking Irish farmer to an industrious freedman. The Democrats
courted the former while disdaining the latter, and Nast made obvious
his derision. But the lower panel of the same drawing ridiculed white
Democrats who reached out to black voters and employed three of the
commonplaces of minstrelsy: exaggerated lips, elaborate overdressing, and
a desire to socialize with white women. The point of the illustration was
to mock Democratic hypocrisy and to suggest plainly that the Republicans offered black voters dignity. Still, the use of racialized symbols
pointed to Nast's inconsistencies, and like so many of his contemporaries,
Nast's sincere support for freedmen had limits.[28]

In "The Ignorant Vote," Nast complained that black voters were to
the Republicans what Irish voters were to the Democrats, as in both
cases, in Nast's view, the parties sought the support of men unqualified
for the franchise (see figure 6). In his portrayal of the black voter, Nast

Figure 5 **"He Wants Change Too."** Nast's figure of the black male trades on tropes of black masculine physicality and threat of violence, albeit in an argument for their enfranchisement.

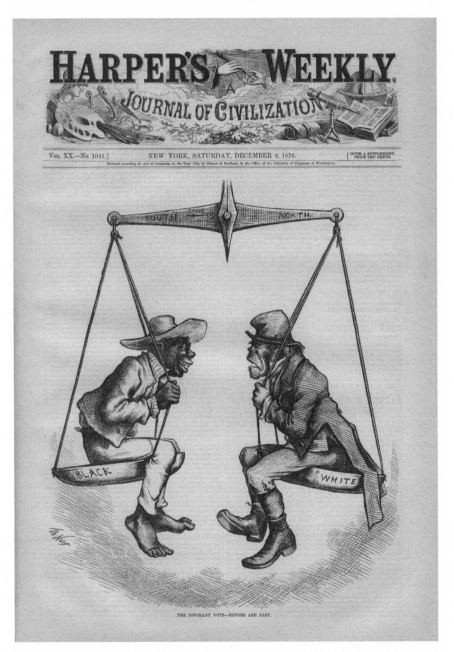

Figure 6 **"The Ignorant Vote—Honors Are Easy."** Equating the black Sambo and the bestial Irish, Nast feared that particular racial and ethnic groups correlated with a lack of ability to participate knowledgeably in the Republic.

relied explicitly on the commonplaces of minstrelsy: thick lips, bare feet, a vapid grin, and slumped posture. Gone were the upright spine, careful clothing, and intelligent gaze of other drawings. Worse, Nast compared the black voter to an Irish thug, who appeared wearing thick boots and a menacing expression. Portraying the black voter as less dangerous hardly constituted a compliment from the perspective of masculinity. What Nast did was to take away all the symbols of black manhood: veteran status, arms, paternalism, and dignity.[29] In their place he offered a harmless fool.

As historians have shown, the harmless black fool popularized by minstrelsy was never really harmless. Rather, he offered white Americans a way to diffuse the demands of black citizens and to ridicule their desire for full inclusion. For all his sympathy and righteous indignation, Nast adopted the symbols of minstrelsy in the same way. In "Colored Rule in a Reconstructed (?) State," he added his voice to a chorus of complaints about black legislators in South Carolina. Nast emphasized the waving fists and wide mouths of men who argued while Columbia fruitlessly demanded order. Chaos reigned. The drawing began with a report in the Charleston *News,* quoted by *Harper's Weekly.* Black legislators in South Carolina argued with one another and called one another "thieves, liars, and rascals." The result was "roars of laughter on the part of the House and an increased consumption of pea-nuts follow these outpourings of fish-fag rhetoric." *Harper's Weekly* earnestly urged South Carolinians to choose more worthy representatives from among the black citizens of the state. The article's sincerity, though, suffered a blow from its title, "Aping Bad Examples."[30] The contrast is stark between representations of black men in these later images and the men in "Pardon" and "Franchise" (figure 2), "Patience on a Monument" (figure 4), and "This Is a White Man's Country" (figure 3). Black men no longer bore the unmistakable stamp of greatness conferred by the Union uniform, and they no longer stood upright or appeared noble. Nast had been one of the greatest champions of black masculinity, insisting on its potential for that most important of nineteenth-century virtues, respectability. He had become, by the late 1870s, a much more ambivalent observer.

He could still strike a powerful blow. Fighting the presidential candidacy of Samuel J. Tilden in 1876, Nast showed the Democratic candidate standing approvingly over the bodies of black Republicans massacred at Hamburg, South Carolina. In the same issue, another illustration posed Justice with her scales. On one side, a single dead white man, on the other six black men. She angrily demanded "Equality." Two weeks later, Nast's masterful evocation of black suffering, "Is This a Republican Form of Government?" appeared. Clearly, atrocities like the Hamburg massacre still triggered Nast's protective instincts. But politics had become more complicated for him, and his views grew muddied. As the North moved away from the values of the Civil War era and toward the reform movements of the 1880s, Nast began to temper his position as well.[31] After the election of Rutherford B. Hayes in 1876, Nast's illustrations showed less and less of the fiery support for freedmen so common in the late 1860s and early 1870s. He still sympathized with black people, and in later years his illustrations on behalf of Chinese immigrants and Native Americans relied on references to black suffering and Reconstruction. However, Nast turned his attention to other issues in the 1880s. His deep involvement in party politics, his fight to retain editorial independence at *Harper's Weekly,* and his desperate financial situation after 1884 all sapped his commitment to racial equality.

ONE OF THE most difficult things about nineteenth-century politics is taxonomy. To place a senator, an editor, an activist, or an illustrator into any one category often proves impossible, and Nast offers a good example of the problem. Some of the work he produced resonated with very real sympathy, honoring the service of black veterans and predicting a stable, middle-class future for black families led by black patriarchs. Still, Nast embraced many of the commonplace racial ideas of his age. Despite his sympathy and optimism, he doubted the ability of black men to join society as the equals of white men. For Nast, black men fit into a social hierarchy somewhere near Irish immigrants: members of the political culture but not really to be relied upon. At times, such men even could be dangerous to democracy.

To insist on complexity in historians' view of nineteenth-century racial politics is nothing new, but Nast is a special case. For several reasons, Nast offers an opportunity to explore the way that race challenged nineteenth-century Americans to imagine a different world. As an illustrator he distilled politics to the satirical, the hypocritical, and the exemplary. In some ways, for all his sophistication, his greatest talent lay in his ability to be simple. Yet when it came to race he was anything but simple. He offered a personal, emotional, and specific vision of the potential for black men to become citizens; at the same time, he openly acknowledged the hesitation of equality so many Americans felt. Another reason he deserves attention is that his work is often used to demonstrate elements of nineteenth-century political culture. His anti-Irish illustrations, in particular, seem to appear in practically every treatment of resistance to immigration after the Civil War. In some ways, this approach makes sense, as political illustrations capture the emotions of the moment. Historians may declare that such works are ephemeral, but Nast's work denies that claim, as his drawings endure as examples in historical scholarship and in the classroom. Understanding Nast's position on race, and the difficulty of categorizing his views, matters.

Nast also connects art to the public sphere. Unlike many other artists of his time, Nast enjoyed an enormous readership. At times, *Harper's Weekly* reached a quarter of a million readers through issue sales alone, notwithstanding the likelihood of shared copies. Regularly, that number exceeded one hundred thousand. Since the paper often passed from hand to hand, and since bars often posted the paper and its illustrations for patrons' enjoyment, actual readership likely reached much higher. Moreover, *Harper's Weekly* traveled across the nation through the mail, so Nast's work—wildly popular throughout the late 1860s and 1870s—influenced Americans reading in Iowa as well as Poughkeepsie and Park Row. Finally, Nast's work reflected the multivariant nature of race and masculinity during his lifetime. An immigrant himself, Nast understood perhaps better than most that American identity could be defined in different ways. Delineating Americanness challenged Americans to embrace many kinds of change while trying to cling to some kind of common ground, and Nast chronicled that problem in his work. When he compared Irish and black men as citizens, when he elevated black veterans above Irish rioters, when he imagined a middle-class home with a benevolent black patriarch for freed slaves, Nast participated in a dialogue concerned not with black and white but with a multiplicity of ethnic, national, sectional, and religious identities. He knew then what it would take generations for scholars to recognize: race as a category never stood alone.

Notes

1. "Pardon" and "Franchise," *Harper's Weekly,* 5 August 1865, 488–89.

2. Scholarship on Nast is relatively thin, considering his influence. The best works are Albert Bigelow Paine, *Thomas Nast: His Period and His Pictures* (New York: Harper and Brothers, 1904); Morton Keller, *The Art and Politics of Thomas Nast* (New York: Oxford University Press, 1968); and Roger Fischer, *Them Damned Pictures* (North Haven, CT: Archon Books, 1996). Also useful to scholars are the volumes of the *Journal of the Thomas Nast Society,* Morristown, NJ.

3. Tyler Anbinder, *Five Points: The Nineteenth-Century New York City Neighborhood That Invented Tap Dance, Stole Elections, and Became the World's Most Notorious Slum* (New York: Plume Books, 2002). Sketches by Nast survive in the collection of the Houghton Library at Harvard University. In many, Nast drew images of the people he saw on his daily travels in New York City, for example, the pictures drawn on correspondence from his Boston publishers, Lee & Shepherd. See Houghton Library, Harvard University, Lee & Shepherd collection, two letters to Thomas Nast, July 29, 1868, and May 15, 1868. Numerous examples of Nast's doodling in Ecuador survive in the collection of the Rutherford B. Hayes Presidential Library in Fremont, OH. See, for example, RBH GA-33, TN Box 1, "Original Sketches—Misc."

4. Paine, *Thomas Nast,* 83.

5. Alice Caulkins, "Thomas Nast: A Chronology," *Journal of the Thomas Nast Society* 10:1 (1996): 120; "The Emancipation of the Negroes, January 1, 1863—the Past and the Future," *Harper's Weekly,* 24 January 1863, 56–57.

6. "Emancipation," *Harper's Weekly,* 24 January 1863, 55. The same emphasis on fatherhood appears in one of the illustrations following the New York Draft Riots in 1863. In "How to Escape the Draft," the artist has drawn a black father trying to protect his tiny daughter from the clubs of Irish rioters. While the drawing bears no signature, Nast provided other illustrations of the riots for *Harper's Weekly,* and there is every reason to think that this might be his work. In this case, the grooming, dress, and bearing of both father and daughter clearly are intended to suggest their class status, while the rougher clothes and flat caps of the rioters suggest poverty. "How to Escape the Draft," *Harper's Weekly,* 1 August 1863, 496.

7. Frederick Douglass, "Oration in Memory of Abraham Lincoln, delivered at the unveiling of the Freedmen's Monument in Memory of Abraham Lincoln, in Lincoln Park, Washington, D.C., April 14, 1876," *Inaugural Ceremonies of the Freedmen's Memorial Monument to Abraham Lincoln, Washington City, April 14, 1876* (St. Louis, 1876), 16–26; Frederick Douglass, "Why Should a Colored Man Enlist?" *Douglass' Monthly,* April 1863; James McPherson, *Marching toward Freedom: Blacks in the Civil War, 1861–1865* (New York: Facts on File, 1965), 5–13; Kirk Savage, *Standing Soldiers, Kneeling Slaves: Race, War, and Monument in Nineteenth-Century America* (Princeton, NJ: Princeton University Press, 1997), 117–18.

8. Alice Fahs, *The Imagined Civil War: Popular Literature of the North and South, 1861–1865* (Chapel Hill: University of North Carolina Press, 2001), 150–81.

9. "A Negro Regiment in Action," 168–69, and "Negroes as Soldiers," 174, both in *Harper's Weekly,* 14 March 1863. A Nast drawing depicting the attack by the Massachusetts 54th on Fort Wagner shows that terrible engagement with much of the same emotional content. See Russell Duncan, ed., *Blue-Eyed Child of Fortune: The Civil War Letters of Colonel Robert Gould Shaw* (Athens: University of Georgia Press, 1992).

10. On Fort Wagner, see Duncan; on Fort Pillow, see Albert Castel, "The Fort Pillow Massacre: An Examination of the Evidence," in Gregory J. W. Urwin, ed., *Black Flag over Dixie: Racial Atrocities and Reprisals in the Civil War* (Carbondale: Southern Illinois University Press, 2004), 89–103; and Derek W. Frisby, "'Remember Fort Pillow!': Politics, Atrocity Propaganda, and the Evolution of Hard War," in Urwin, ed., *Black Flag Over Dixie,* 104–31. As Frisby points out, the propaganda value of Fort Pillow outweighed the clarity of the evidence surrounding the incident. Even now,

historians disagree about what happened there, but Nast sought to trigger the Northern public's belief in Confederate violence against black soldiers, not to engage in detailed historical inquiry.

11. "'Marching on!' The Fifty-Fifth Massachusetts Colored Regiment Singing John Brown's March in the Streets of Charleston, February 21, 1865," *Harper's Weekly,* 18 March 1865, 165. *Harper's Weekly* identifies the officer as Colonel Bennett and provides the quote, 172; see also Harold Holzer, "'Spirited and Authentic': Thomas Nast, Civil War Artist," in Carol Bere, ed., *Thomas Nast & The Glorious Cause: An Exhibition by Macculloch Hall Historical Museum* (Morristown, NJ: Macculloch Hall Historical Museum, 1996), 18.

12. Nast's account appeared August 1, 1863, and shows many of the features he later recalled about the riots, particularly attacks on black New Yorkers and the desecration of the body of a police sergeant by women and children. Later *Harper's Weekly* illustrations that use symbols of the draft riots include "The Chicago Platform," 15 October 1864, 664–65; "This Is a White Man's Government," 5 September 1868, 568; "Lead Us Not into Temptation," 19 September 1868, 600; "All the Difference in the World," 26 September 1868, 616; "The Modern Samson," 3 October 1868, 632; "Patience on a Monument," 10 October 1868, 648; "Matched. (?)" 31 October 1868, 700; "The Chinese Question," 18 February 1871, 149; "Something That Will Not 'Blow Over' July 11 and July 12, 1871," 29 July 1871, 696–97; and "It Is Only a Truce to Regain Power ('Playing Possum')," 24 August 1872, 652.

13. "This Is a White Man's Government," *Harper's Weekly,* 5 September 1868, 568. Nast made the same point in other illustrations as well, for example, "Why the Nigger Is Not Fit to Vote," *Harper's Weekly,* 24 October 1868, 673.

14. Regarding the Irish in caricature, see L. Perry Curtis Jr., *Apes and Angels: The Irishman in Victorian Caricature* (Washington, DC: Smithsonian Institution Press, 1997). For Forrest, see Eddy W. Davison, Daniel Foxx, and Edwin C. Bearss, *Nathan Bedford Forrest, In Search of the Enigma* (New York: Pelican Publishing Company, 2007). For Belmont, see Irving Katz, *August Belmont: A Political Biography* (New York: Columbia University Press, 1968).

15. William Horatio Barnes, *History of the Thirty-Ninth Congress of the United States* (New York: Harper and Brothers, 1868), 389–92.

16. Eric L. McKitrick, *Andrew Johnson and Reconstruction* (New York: Oxford University Press, 1988), 167; Vincent Harding, *There Is a River: The Black Struggle for Freedom in America* (New York: Harcourt, 1981), 311.

17. *Putnam's Magazine of Literature, Science, Art, and National Interests* 2:11 (November 1868): 616–17.

18. Xi Wang. *The Trial of Democracy: Black Suffrage & Northern Republicans, 1860–1910* (Athens: University of Georgia Press, 1997), 39–48.

19. Nast's thug did not originate in a caricature of Forrest, but in some later images he appears as Forrest, as in "This Is a White Man's Government."

20. Savage, *Standing Soldiers, Kneeling Slaves,* 52–62.

21. Ibid., 61–62.

22. "The Modern Samson," *Harper's Weekly,* 3 October 1868, 632.

23. Savage asserts that Nast intended to demonstrate the black veteran's powerlessness in the face of white violence (175). While this is one accurate reading of the

drawing, read in combination with Nast's other comments on Irish immigrants and Southern vigilantes, the illustration clearly points to the comparative value of black citizenship and black masculinity to the nation.

24. Paine, *Thomas Nast,* 16–17. Nast minded the door and copied large paintings at The Bryan Gallery of Christian Art, at Broadway and Thirteenth Street—see "Important Old Master Paintings: The Property of The New-York Historical Society," Sotheby's Auction Catalogue (12 January 1995).

25. On the redemption movement, see Nicholas Lemann, *Redemption: The Last Battle of the Civil War* (New York; Farrar, Straus & Giroux, 2007); Stephen Budiansky, *The Bloody Shirt: Terror After Appomattox* (New York: Viking, 2008); and Eric Foner, *Politics and Ideology in the Age of the Civil War* (New York: Oxford University Press, 1981).

26. TN to Fletcher Harper, 10 February 1875. Princeton University Library, C0120, Box 1, Folder 15. Nast's quote misuses "the" when the Constitution actually reads "this."

27. "He Wants Change Too," *Harper's Weekly,* 28 October 1876, 872–73.

28. "All the Difference in the World," *Harper's Weekly,* 26 September 1868, 616. Other examples in which Nast used physical symbols taken from minstrelsy include "Another Step toward Civilization," *Harper's Weekly,* 31 May 1879, 421; and "The Civilization of Blaine," *Harper's Weekly,* 8 March 1879, 181.

29. "The Ignorant Vote—Honors Are Easy," *Harper's Weekly,* 9 December 1876, 985.

30. "Colored Rule in a Reconstructed (?) State," *Harper's Weekly,* 14 March 1874, 229. "Aping Bad Examples," *Harper's Weekly,* 14 March 1874, 242. On minstrelsy, see Eric Lott, *Love and Theft: Blackface Minstrelsy and the American Working Class* (New York: Oxford University Press, 1995); Sarah Meer, *Uncle Tom Mania: Slavery, Minstrelsy, and Transatlantic Culture in the 1850s* (Athens: University of Georgia Press, 2005); Annamarie Bean, James V. Hatch, and Brooks McNamara, eds., *Inside the Minstrel Mask: Readings in Nineteenth-Century Blackface Minstrelsy* (Middletown, CT: Wesleyan University Press, 1996); and William J. Mahar, *Behind the Burnt Cork Mask: Early Blackface Minstrelsy and Antebellum American Popular Culture* (Urbana: University of Illinois Press, 1998).

31. "The 'Bloody Shirt' Reformed," *Harper's Weekly,* 12 August 1876, 652; "Declaration of Equality," *Harper's Weekly,* 12 August 1876, 656. See also James McPherson, *The Abolitionist Legacy* (Princeton, NJ: Princeton University Press, 1976).

6

Charles W. Chesnutt, *Harper's Weekly*, and Racial Caricature in Postbellum, Pre-Harlem America

PETER CASTER

> All over the United States the Associated Press had flashed the report
> of another dastardly outrage by a burly black brute,—all black brutes
> it seems are burly,—and of the impending lynching with its prospective
> horrors. This news, being highly sensational in its character, had been
> displayed in large black type on the front pages of the daily papers.
>
> —Charles W. Chesnutt, *The Marrow of Tradition*[1]

The above epigraph, a provocative passage from Charles W. Chesnutt's
novel *The Marrow of Tradition* (1901), sardonically lances the popular
expectation of the "burly black brute" even as it demonstrates how racist visions appear in the "large black type" of print journalism, thus staging the complementary nature not only of history and fiction, but also
of visual image and printed text in producing black masculinity in the
national imagination. Chesnutt's 1901 novel joins the irony and use of
dialect from his tragicomic post-plantation tales of the previous fifteen
years with the sentimentality of his passing narrative *The House Behind
the Cedars* (1900) in a sensationalist plot, which culminates in a fictionalization of the 1898 Wilmington massacre as white rioters killed many
African American citizens and overthrew the elected Republican government in North Carolina's then-largest city. His anger at the event,

related to the novelist by many of his friends and family who had seen it firsthand, exacerbated his longstanding frustration with post-plantation fiction and led him to reconfigure in his fiction widely understood racial caricatures of black men.

In *The Marrow of Tradition,* he recasts the threatening "buck" figure and the submissive servant as, respectively, heroic and a white construction. These literary depictions contrast with the illustrations of *Harper's Weekly's* Thomas Nast and lesser-known artists such as Sol Eytinge Jr. and S. G. McCutcheon, wherein African American men often appeared as simple, submissive, even childlike, whether in that magazine or the others published during and after Reconstruction, some of them the very periodicals in which much of Chesnutt's short fiction initially appeared. This essay demonstrates how the illustrations of the nationally popular, middle-class *Harper's Weekly* helped naturalize and promulgate stereotypical images of black men in the decade following Reconstruction, the very caricatures Chesnutt contested through adapting and transforming them.

Catalogs and critiques of the stereotypes common to what Chesnutt called the "Post-Bellum–Pre-Harlem" era are not new. As Thomas L. Morgan points out, "In late-nineteenth- and early-twentieth-century fiction, the majority of African American images in popular fiction were confined to Southern-based pastoral depictions that restricted black identity to stereotypically limited and historically regressive ideas."[2] Most often, the masculine types fell into a number of discreet categories: the physically formidable and dangerous "brute" alluded to in the passage of *The Marrow of Tradition,* a figure reminiscent of Nat Turner, Gabriel Prosser, or more fictional but equally fearsome (to some white audiences) insurrectionary figures; the at some times "comic" and at others violent and "debased" but always obeisant Sambo; the sullen Jack, suspended between the polarized versions of rebel and servant; the character of minstrelsy, the singing and dancing entertainer Jim Crow; the elderly uncles Remus and Rastus, the post-plantation storyteller and the often dimwitted but harmless elderly black man, respectively, appearing in Joel Chandler Harris's fiction and elsewhere; and most famously, Uncle Tom, the self-sacrificing and loyal servant of Harriet Beecher Stowe's 1852 novel.[3]

The enduring power and historical overwriting enacted by racist stereotypes are perhaps best evidenced in Uncle Tom. Stowe's character became the caricature of the subservient older black man, yet the historical figure of Josiah Henson, widely believed to be the basis for Stowe's literary type, presents a model of heroic resistance, not acquiescence. The April 21, 1877, issue of *Harper's Weekly* lionizes Henson in terms more reminiscent of Frederick Douglass's courage than Stowe's sacrificial lamb, and paired engravings made from photographs of Henson and Douglass are joined by brief biographies. The biographical sketch of the former celebrates his leading his family to freedom and thereafter his "noble service of liberty and humanity" in aiding the escape of others. However, through the decade following Reconstruction, such distinguished illustrations appeared far less frequently in *Harper's Weekly* than the more negative images of black masculinity from the very same issue, including the cover, one of Nast's ambiguous portrayals of a grinning servant, and a cartoon in the final pages lampooning a clownish beggar.[4]

These illustrations of racial caricature dominated popular periodicals of the nineteenth century's closing decades, the period that paradoxically saw the emergence of American literary realism, a movement concomitant with but not definitive of Chesnutt's writing.[5] Of realism and caricature, Henry B. Wonham argues, "These two aesthetic programs, one committed to representation of the fully humanized individual, the other invested in broad ethnic abstractions, operate less as antithetical choices than as complementary impulses."[6] Caricatures became loci of cultural consensus regarding ethnic, racial, and gendered types that served as starting points for particular characterizations. Especially for African American writers, working within these expectations could prove extremely limiting, and Morgan points out, "Once these types of characters had been established in the public's mind, they became a part of the formulaic structure through which realism's mimetic efficacy was measured. Fiction that did not replicate acceptable literary types was dismissed for its lack of fidelity to the established codes of ethnic description."[7] What constituted realistic fiction thus meant descriptions of people, settings, and events that matched the expectations of the reading public, which generally meant the white literate middle class—who, especially after Reconstruction, became accustomed to stories of African Americans set in the antebellum South that often romanticized plantation life and race relations.[8] Chesnutt engaged this readership in his early sketches and short stories, which Wonham suggests employ "the thick brush of ethnic caricature" not to reify racist expectation "but to explore the psychological consequences of stigmatization upon human beings of every racial variety." According to Wonham, it was in *Puck,* the weekly magazine that published nine of Chesnutt's early short works from 1887 to 1891, in which the author learned "to challenge the dehumanizing force of ethnic caricature in his own writing by inhabiting, rather than resisting, the forms that threatened to limit his aspirations."[9] In Wonham's reading, Chesnutt dwelt within the outline of black caricature rather than trying to redraw its shape.

However, *Puck* was a little lower brow than the more widely distributed *Harper's Weekly,* and the Chesnutt of the 1880s certainly aspired, most famously, "to be an author," and to the wealth, prestige, and class advancement he hoped that would bring.[10] Wonham reads Chesnutt's sketches in *Puck* in relation to the caricatures of that magazine's pages, but while that magazine's subtitle—"What Fools These Mortals Be!"— may have appealed to the writer's sardonic edge, the tagline of *Harper's Weekly* declared it "A Journal of Civilization," and its illustrations celebrating Republican ideals, domestic prosperity, and "genteel" manners certainly depicted a world Chesnutt sought to join. Those illustrations played a significant role in the magazine's success, as it outstripped its closest competitor *Frank Leslie's Illustrated Newspaper* after the end of the Civil War. The editor of *Frank Leslie's* in 1875 acknowledged that in comparison with his publication's emphasis on current, transitory events, *Harper's Weekly*'s illustrations offered "pictures of sentiment" that "*last* in the mind of the purchaser."[11] Images depicting the inequities of class and racial difference may well have lasted in the mind of Chesnutt, who had access to such magazines and read thoroughly in the 1870s and 1880s and onward in his effort to improve himself and better his circumstances in becoming an author.

Born in 1858 in Cleveland to African American parents, Chesnutt's racial lineage was sufficiently mixed that he easily could have passed, a characteristic shared by several of the protagonists of his novels. However, unlike those characters, the writer consistently described himself as mixed race, both as he grew up in Fayetteville, North Carolina, and in his later return to Cleveland.[12] Chesnutt's literary career provides a valuable barometer of the possibilities and limits of life on the color line in the late nineteenth and early twentieth century; he grew up in the rural South and lived later in the urban North, spatial borderlands counterpart to the divisions of the period Chesnutt described as "post-bellum, pre-Harlem" also understood as the nadir of African American experience. As a light-skinned man designated as black both by the one drop rule and by his own choice, the writer negotiated widespread stereotypes of black masculinity as he sought to establish a public voice, even as he left a record of private frustration with both the Southern African American community and the Northern literary establishment. Racial essentialism trumping class advancement proved vexing for Chesnutt during much of his professional life and connected to his unease regarding his racial identity and his dissatisfaction with dialect stories.

Early on, Chesnutt demonstrated his profound ambivalence regarding his understanding of himself vis-à-vis the larger category of African Americans. In a journal entry from 1875, when he was seventeen, he expresses frustration with his African American students, condemning them as "good-sized liars, hypocrites, inquisitive little ~~nigger~~ wenches."[13] Dean McWilliams comments that "the imperfectly erased epithet enacts, in capsule form, the problem with which Chesnutt struggled throughout his early journals, and indeed, throughout his literary career."[14] Also in 1875, Chesnutt remarks of his African American neighbors, "Uneducated people, are the most bigoted, superstitious, hardest headed people in the world!"[15] In an 1879 letter sent to the *Christian Union,* though not printed there, he refers to "the colored people" and their "political rights": "In most parts of the state ~~they~~ we have a fair proportion of jurors."[16] Chesnutt felt divided in his willingness to throw his lot in with a social body he often felt more apart from than a part of, particularly in terms of the education and class mobility for which he worked much of his life. Nevertheless, as the third-person plural *they* is struck through and replaced by *we,* he acknowledged in this early stage of his development as a writer, however grudgingly, his membership in a racial community.

That shaped the topic of his writing early on, especially as he took note of the success of writers such as Albion Tourgée, author of the popular *A Fool's Errand, by One of the Fools* (1879), a white Northerner's account of the Reconstruction South. Chesnutt sought to follow such work and move beyond it, declaring in an 1880 journal entry, "I shall not record stale negro minstrel jokes, or worn out newspaper squibs on the 'man and brother.'"[17] To Chesnutt, the minstrelsy humor so common to the pages of *Harper's Weekly* cartoons would certainly be "stale," but they must not have seemed so to the magazine's editors and their anticipation of their readers' desires. In like fashion, the author found the well-known 1787 Quaker medallion depicted a kneeling manacled bondsman declaring, "Am I not a Man and a Brother" to be "worn out," but the slogan is referenced in two 1879 *Harper's Weekly* covers illustrated by Nast, one featuring a craven Sambo figure.[18] To readers of *Harper's Weekly* in the 1870s and 1880s, the very reading public Chesnutt sought to engage, antebellum tropes of blackness remained well-trod terrain.

Illustrations of Black Masculine Stereotypes in *Harper's Weekly*

We have no way to know if Chesnutt read *Harper's Weekly,* though it was the nation's most popular news and literary magazine, with an effective circulation of a half million people, so he would certainly have been aware of it, especially as he undertook a rigorous reading schedule in an ambitious plan of self-education. We know he was familiar with the weekly's sister publication, as in an 1880 journal entry, he described a local bookseller recounting "a paragraph in *Harper's* [*Monthly*] *Magazine,*" though the episode in question is not a paragraph from an article but part of the caption of a three-panel illustration—so easily do image and text confound.[19] The readers of *Harper's* were the very audience he sought to engage in his fiction, and Chesnutt recounts his plan of reading and describes his motives to head North for a literary career, writing, "I pine for civilization and 'equality.'"[20] *Harper's Weekly* promised the former, and while its articles made some effort to promote the latter, the frequent illustrations tell a different tale. The nation's most popular weekly provides an illustrative record of imaginations of black men broadly held by the white middle class, the very readership Chesnutt sought to cultivate. Even as that "journal of civilization" often declared in print its commitment to racial justice, its illustrations more generally capitulated to racist stereotypes of black men.

Two images appeared on facing pages in the August 23, 1879, issue of *Harper's Weekly* in a fashion that starkly dramatizes the polarized and competing versions of black masculinity (see figure 7). On the left-facing page, a detailed, stand-alone engraving featured a baby-faced black man with a watermelon under each arm and one balanced on his head, smiling and looking at the reader, followed by a young boy, perhaps his son, struggling with another melon. They are leaving a field, and a crescent moon indicates night, perhaps implying that their harvest is theft. The caption reads, "Water-Millions Is Ripe" and identifies the artist as Sol Eytinge, a frequent contributor to the weekly magazine and illustrator for editions of Elizabeth Barrett Browning, Charles Dickens, and Alfred Tennyson. The right-facing detailed engraving matched its opposite in size, occupying three-quarters of the page, and depicted "A Zulu Scout" peering from brush, his eyes wide and expression serious. He holds a carbine in hand, bears a shield and bandolier of cartridges, wears prominent earrings, and is shirtless. The accompanying article, "The Vanquished Zulus," like most in the magazine, was unattributed and begins beneath

"WATER-MILLIONS IS RIPE."—Drawn by Sol Eytinge, Jun.

Figure 7 **"Water-Millions Is Ripe"** and **"A Zulu Scout."** Two versions of black masculinity: these facing pages of the August 23, 1879, issue of *Harper's Weekly* indicate the polarized and competing Sambo and Nat stereotypes.

A ZULU SCOUT.

the unrelated illustration to finish on the next beneath the second image, chronicling "another one of England's long successions of little wars" in the defeat of the Zulu nation, leaving power with the English.[21] Literally underwritten by a justification of African colonization, the two images illustrate the opposite poles that dovetail precisely with the Sambo and Nat stereotypes prevalent since the antebellum era: one version is child-like, simple, nonthreatening, and happy in a rural setting of likely pov-erty; the other is adult, serious, armed, and potentially violent. While we cannot know what editorial process led to the commissioning of these two images and their adjacent publication, their side-by-side appearance invites at least one simple interpretation: African men could be warriors, but *Harper's Weekly* preferred its black men at home to present less potent forms of masculinity.

In the decade immediately following Reconstruction and the period of Chesnutt's decision to become an author, *Harper's Weekly* kept the eye of the nation turned southward. A lead article in 1877 on "The South-ern Question" began, "As slavery was the commanding question of our politics for a generation before the war, so the 'Southern question' which grows out of Reconstruction will long be the most important of all our political problems. The first step in its wise and peaceful solution is knowledge of the situation."[22] The magazine sought to increase the nation's understanding of race relations in the South, and 1880 alone saw *Harper's Weekly* publish one of Sherwood Bonner's dialect tales, over thirty illustrations of African Americans, and a four-part series of two-page articles focusing on black rural life in Georgia, South Carolina, and Alabama.[23] For three of those four Southern articles, one-third of the space of each first page was dedicated to illustrations—for the fourth, over half of the column inches were images (over half of each second page is advertisements). That relative proportion of text and image actu-ally underestimates the degree to which *Harper's Weekly* relied on increas-ingly inexpensive engraving reproduction in the 1870s and 1880s, as publishers found frequent illustrations a powerful selling point,[24] and between 1877 and 1887, eight to eleven of the typically twenty pages of each issue were entirely or predominantly images, while generally six pages included only text, with the remainder a balance of images, articles, and advertisements. In terms of column inches, the magazine offered more image than text. Visuals varied among minimal sketches, cartoon-ish caricatures, extremely detailed figures with exaggerated features, pho-torealistic engravings often copied from photographs or paintings, and reproductions of photographs.

The variations of black masculinity in these engravings of 1877 to 1887 balanced among clinging to antebellum stereotypes, offering mostly accurate but limited and limiting accounts of rural poverty and satirizing the efforts of African Americans to enter the middle and upper classes. While Nast sometimes portrayed black men in the South as a voting bloc in a tug-of-war between Republicans and Democrats, more common were depictions of black men as variously lazy, lying, happy and smiling, petty thieves, and nostalgic for "old massah." The last of these fostered romanticized versions of slavery and subordinated African American men to the paternalism of white mastery.[25] These pages depicted black men almost uniformly as rural and poor; occasional middle-class depictions, often in Sol Eytinge's Blackville series, generally lampooned aspirations of social mobility. Almost exclusively, African American speech was offered as dialect in phonetic spelling, as a rule for comic effect and with pronunciations that likely reflect linguistic minstrelsy rather than any authentic dialect, and, with the exception of Douglass, only black men in Africa were offered as warriors and leaders.[26] Such depictions tightly bound meanings of class and gender with race. That is, the professional occupations most available to black men in the mid- to late nineteenth century were the ministry and education. Preaching, teaching, and the educational preparation increasingly undergirding each in their professionalization made knowledge, proper dress, and speech the defining characteristics of middle- and upper-class manliness. Lampooning ignorance, nonstandard dialect, and foolishness not only generally denigrated blackness but specifically attacked black masculinity. Furthermore, given the associations of honor and truthfulness—a man's word being his bond—portrayals of black men as lying implied their lack of honor and thus lack of manhood.[27]

Criminality is among the most pernicious of the expectations fostered in the images. A drawing by C. M. Coolidge from the February, 9, 1878, issue offered a detailed caricature of a seemingly guileless young black man denying the apparently outrageous accusation from a white man that he has stolen chickens, only to be undone by the chicks peering out from his hat (see figure 8). The caption for this image reads, "Injured Innocence—[Drawn by C.M. Coolidge.] 'I hain't seen nuffin of yer Chickens! Do you took me for a Thief? Do you see any Chickens 'bout me? Go 'way dar, white man! Treat a boy 'spectable, if he am brack!'" His shirt and broad hat are in tatters and suggest a rural setting, and the dark skin, exaggerated lips, and dialect clearly mark his blackness. His eyes meet those of the *Harper's Weekly* readers, and his address

INJURED INNOCENCE — [Drawn by C. M. Coolidge.]

"I hain't seen nuffin of yer Chickens! Do you took me for a Thief? Do you see any Chickens 'bout me? Go 'way dar, white man! Treat a boy 'spectable, if he am brack!"

Figure 8 **Petty Thieves and Liars.** The caption for "Injured Innocence" reads, "I hain't seen nuffin of yer Chickens! Do you took me for a Thief? Do you see any Chickens 'bout me? Go 'way dar, white man! Treat a boy 'spectable, if he am brack!"

to the "white man" directly invokes the race, if not the gender, of many of those readers. The intended humor lies in the ironic distance between the evidence of the crime and the umbrage of his wounded pride at the accusation and demand to be treated "'spectable." Better concealed than the chicks in this scene was the potential violence an African American man could face in the South of 1878 for this mix of lie, theft, and perceived insolence.

A seemingly insatiable lust for chicken and watermelon harbored by black men appeared in numerous images of *Harper's Weekly* from 1877 to 1887. A May 4, 1878, cartoon featured a black man fleeing a farm at night, his arms full of stolen chickens, and the caption laments, "Oh, why does the white man follow my path?"[28] An August 4, 1883, detailed half-page caricature managed at once to depict black masculinity as lazy, impotent, and criminal, as a black man in the foreground holds a rifle but slouches in sleep, his foolish grin clueless as two black children steal watermelons behind him.[29] A full-page, detailed engraving and accompanying brief interpretive sketch from October 23, 1886, detailed the trial of "The Village Pest," a general class of youth likely to make town "lively" through petty thievery. Though the drawing in question depicted an African American boy, the short article that served as an extended caption seems to pitch its defense of the boy in a light-hearted, ironic register, as "the abstracted fowls have no connection with the accused boy," and his mother defends him. "There can be little doubt that the case will be dismissed."[30] While the text indicates such a pest "is oftener white than black," the image is part of a larger pattern for a different story.

Chesnutt addressed this appetite in both "A Virginia Chicken" (1887) and "A Victim of Heredity; or, Why the Darkey Loves Chicken" (1900). In the first, he overturns the stereotype by demonstrating how all hungry men appreciate roast chicken and in dire circumstances will steal to get it. In the second, the narrator and his wife are white upper-class sojourners in the South, and she declares, "There are thieves wherever there is portable property, and I don't imagine colored people like chickens any better than any one else." Chesnutt's longstanding storyteller Julius corrects her and offers a tale explaining that overworking starving slaves led to a back-and-forth of conjuring between white and black, finally resulting in an exceptional hunger for chickens in the race.[31] Though humorous in tone, "A Victim of Heredity" in particular maintains the underlying tragedy that lays bare the relationships among poverty, race, crime, and punishment, as the narrator's capture of a young

African American chicken thief encourages him to set an example, and "five years in the penitentiary would be about right"—a draconian sentence dodged when the narrator's wife has Julius set the captive free after hearing the latter's tale.[32]

Petty crime and its punishment provide the basis of an August 13, 1887, cartoon (see figure 9) appearing in *Harper's Weekly* the same year as the publication of "A Virginia Chicken." A magistrate addresses a shabbily dressed black man, telling the defendant, "It's ten dollars or thirty days, Uncle Rastus. You can take your choice." Rastus replies, "Well, yo' kin gimme de money, sah," a misunderstanding of the penalty of fine or incarceration, to which the bailiff responds with a look of shock.[33] It is a sophisticated cartoon, a static image that, although static, not only depicts in its caption a brief passage of time—*"after some contemplation"*—but, read left to right, charts the question, the answer, and the bailiff's response of surprise at the answer. This brief narrative time and space is itself bracketed by the presumed prior action of Rastus's unnamed crime and the subsequent punishment, undoubtedly the jail sentence, given his implied economic position. Another layer of interpretation remains available as well. The judge holds his hands together in a fashion similar to Rastus's gesture of contemplation: his right fingers under his chin, so that his hand mirrors that of the white judge. Moreover, Rastus's very dark skin contrasts with his white lips, evoking the characterization of blackface. Illustrated in all likelihood by a white engraver for a primarily white middle-class readership, this drawing of the stereotypically named Uncle Rastus operates as a trope of minstrelsy, the popular racist white imaginations of black life that reached their height in the antebellum period but remained in some vogue through the 1870s and 1880s.[34]

The Rastus figure of the perpetually smiling, older black man as the butt of one joke or another was one of the most frequent figures in the relatively small cartoons (generally one-sixth of a page) independent of any article that appeared regularly in the penultimate page of *Harper's Weekly*. The willingness to cast black people in general and men in particular as the object of humor reached such a height that 35 of the 157—almost one out of every four—issues of the magazine from 1885 to 1887 featured such depictions in those cartoons. These often crude caricatures characterized black men as careless, frightened, foolish, lazy, poor, and greedy, and what humor they intended often relies on the malapropisms and misunderstandings common to minstrelsy. In one panel, an Uncle Abra'm reads in a broadsheet that a black murderer has been executed and muses, "Why'd 'ey wait till de murderin's all dun 'fo' dey hang 'im?

HIS CHOICE.

MAGISTRATE. "It's ten dollars or thirty days, Uncle Rastus. You can take your choice.".
UNCLE RASTUS (*after some contemplation*). "Well, yo' kin gimme de money, sah."

Figure 9 **Truth and Consequences.** The caption for "His Choice" reads, "It's ten dollars or thirty days, Uncle Rastus. You can take your choice." "Well, yo' kin gimme de money, sah."

'Pears like 't 'ud be pow'ful sight better to hang de murd'rer b'fo' he kill sumbody."[35] The character's literacy and formal dress—he wears tails and a top hat, a common ironic counterpoint to minstrelsy's expectation of black inferiority—are undone by a fundamental lack of understanding regarding cause and effect. Also explicit in his brief speech is the recommendation to incarcerate black men before they commit crimes. Another cartoon also relied on fractured dialect and misunderstanding, an especially poignant episode suggestive of the legal inequities of the jim crow South. An Uncle Moses tells a younger man that he has been cleaning a lawyer's office for almost thirty years, and all the same books are still there. Though "*ignunt* people may think de law done change," he says, "dem whar knows, knows better."[36] The speaker's misunderstanding of case law and the irony of his aspersion of "*ignunt* people" operated as one layer of potential comedy—though not for Chesnutt, who passed the bar exam in 1887, the year this cartoon was published. The fundamental failure of Southern law to change meaningfully in the jim crow era presents an underlying tragedy and another layer of meaning.

Most of these caricatures simulated African American dialect for intended comic effect, and a September 25, 1886, cartoon titled "Funatic Spelling" shows a middle-class black man wearing glasses and reading the newspaper, sitting next to a rural laborer (see figure 10). One asks the other a question, and though it is not explicit which speech belongs to either speaker, the implication seems to be that the gentleman reading the paper poses the question to the other, asking his opinion of "de projected refo'm in spellin'." He explains, "in de place of spellin' hoss h-o-r-s-e, in dat roun'bout way, yo' jes cut it sho't an' spell it h-o-s, like it soun's." The other man responds in an almost bestial grunt, "Ugh—hugh—seems to me dat's sensable."[37] What pleasure white readers took in this exchange seems likely rooted in the speech common to these two men. One is clearly literate and, based on his fine clothing, of comfortable means and perhaps a professional or at least a well-heeled servant, while the other is likely a member of the uneducated, rural working class. Nevertheless, both speak in dialect because both are black.

Imitations of African American speech throughout *Harper's Weekly* illustrations from 1877 to 1887 demonstrated the popularity of the black dialect, an esteem that frustrated Chesnutt. In an 1889 letter to Tourgée, Chesnutt wrote, "I think I have about used up the old Negro who serves as a mouthpiece [. . .] and I shall drop him in future stories, as well as much of the dialect."[38] However, the dialect stories sold, as indicated in Chesnutt's many post-plantation stories published individually in various

FUN-ATIC SPELLING.

"Mistah Borey, what yo' tink of de projected refo'm in spellin' dat's bein' agitated?"

"Doan b'lieve I jis un'erstan' de nater on it."

"Waal, yo' see, for instance, in de place of spellin' hoss h-o-r-s-e, in dat roun'bout way, yo' jes cut it sho't an' spell it h-o-s, like it soun's, 'liminatin' all de silent soun's."

"Ugh—hugh—seems to me dat's sensable."

Figure 10 **Race, Class, and Dialect.** The caption for "Fun-atic Spelling" reads, "Mistah Borey, what yo' tink of de projected refo'm in spellin' dat's bein' agitated?" "Doan b'lieve I jis un'erstan' de nater on it." "Waal, yo' see, for instance, in de place of spellin' hoss h-o-r-s-e, in dat roun'bout way, yo' jes cut it sho't an' spell it h-o-s, like it soun's, 'liminatin' all de silent soun's." "Ugh—hugh—seems to me dat's sensable."

magazines and in two 1899 collections, *The Conjure Woman* and *The Wife of His Youth and Other Stories of the Color Line,* the latter of which includes four detailed illustrations.[39] In a letter to *Atlantic Monthly* editor Walter Hines Page in 1898, Chesnutt lamented his fiction's continued reliance on African American speech: "Speaking of dialect, it is almost a despairing task to write it. [. . .] The fact is, of course, that there is no such thing as a Negro dialect; that what we call by that name is the attempt to express, with such a degree of phonetic correctness as to suggest sound, English pronounced as an ignorant old Southern Negro would be supposed to speak it, and at the same time to preserve a sufficient approximation to the correct spelling to make it easy reading."[40]

Regardless of his dismissal, throughout the period of the publication of almost all of Chesnutt's short stories, white impersonations of black dialect with dubious authenticity remained popular in captions for illustrations, as well as short fiction and published in the nation's popular weekly. In 1883, *Harper's Weekly* promoted its book publishing division's release of a collection of its contributor Sherwood Bonner's *Dialect Tales,* and the cover of that issue featured an illustrated dialect tale by Sophie Shepard. The 1885 article "The Creole Patois" celebrated "the slave poetry improvised according to African methods," for which the white "imitations of the slave songs" are inferior in value.[41] The promotion of Bonner's book declared that literary portraiture of dialect "will vanish rapidly," but that claim was belied by the magazine's very effort to maintain such language and image, often through cartoons lampooning rural black men and women, particularly those of aspirant class.

These satires of efforts at class mobility would have been particularly painful for Chesnutt, given the degree to which he aspired to affluence and social rank. The "Blackville" series of typically full- but occasionally half-page detailed caricatures ran approximately thirty episodes in *Harper's Weekly* from 1877 to 1884. Eytinge (and occasionally another illustrator) portrayed leisure, courtship, and family life in "Blackville," parodying the efforts of African American families to imitate predominantly white middle- and upper-class cultural practices. These included conventional speech and spelling, and an African American debate society's prominent sign "NO CONTEMPTIBIL LANWIGE ALLOWD" in an 1879 illustration unravels their effort at linguistic propriety. Another engraving that same year offered a black teacher's criticism of his pupil: "Yer bin to dis Cadermy eighteen months, an' dunno how to spell 'pork?' Yer nebriate, ye!"[42] The fractured spelling and pronunciation of the debating society and teacher, like the formally dressed man of "Fun-atic Spelling," indicate that in white imaginations of blackness, even the professionals could not master the very basics of white communication and privilege. The presumption of white supremacy and black inferiority produced attempts at comedy that can appear quite horrifying. In an 1879 drawing attributed to Eytinge—though the engraving is signed "J. P. Davis Se[nior]"—a white toddler in a dress aims a toy pistol at a shabbily attired smiling black child who clutches his head, while well-dressed parents and three boys also armed with toy guns admire the scene. The caption reads, "Fourth of July Morning—The First Shot."[43] Celebrating Independence Day by playfully shooting a young black child offered a gloss of legitimacy to white-on-black violence that would increase during and after the 1880s, including the 1898 Wilmington massacre that provides the culminating episode in Chesnutt's *The Marrow of Tradition*.

Perhaps some illustrators based their images on personal experience with African American communities, and their intent as well as the sensibility of the magazine publishing their work may have been lighthearted with no directed ill will. However, it seems more likely that, like the white portrayals of black behavior defining minstrelsy, the Blackville illustrations are products of racist white imagination unattached from observations of lived practice. After all, according to an 1883 profile in *Harper's Weekly*, Eytinge, "whose Blackville sketches are among his most popular contributions to this journal," lived in a "charming cottage adorned with profuse roses and climbing vines, affording from the piazza a superb view of New York."[44] Lacking a view of the rural South, where did the artist find inspiration for his work? We can glean an indication in the November 1878 issues of the magazine. The caption for an 1878 Eytinge Blackville drawing reads, "Decorative art has at last reached Blackville— 'Dat small Japan mug cum from de ruins of Pompy.'" The scene's realistic caricature demonstrates efforts of a black family to adopt the decorative arts and manners of white elites. Four weeks prior to Eytinge's illustration, *Harper's Weekly* featured an article with accompanying realistic illustrations depicting a decorative art exhibition in New York. Three weeks prior to the Blackville drawing, the magazine included the illustrated article "The Eruption of Vesuvius," chronicling the burial of Pompeii and recent tourist visits to the site.[45] A similar pattern occurred for other Blackville cartoons, and Eytinge's "Great Blackville Regatta" and its dilapidated rowboats on the river appeared four weeks after an illustration and article on a Delaware yacht race.[46] Given the recent publication of text and graphics on the decorative arts and the ruins of Pompeii, as well as the boating contest, the artist's lampooning of African American life and (failed) efforts at class mobility seem to employ as racial parody recent *Harper's Weekly* material chronicling upper-class leisure activities rather than any experience with rural African American life.

Harper's Weekly artists such as McCutcheon crafted realistic drawings relying less on the exaggerated traits and parodic settings, but that work—like Eytinge's—dramatized the poverty of African Americans who puzzled over how to participate in American society. The same month as Eytinge fused articles on decorative arts and Pompeii into a parody of black life, McCutcheon offered a detailed realistic image with the caption "Old and Weary," in which a well-dressed, elderly black man with white hair sits in the grass on the side of a wooded trail. Two young white girls eye him with curiosity or wariness as they walk past, and the poem indicated in the drawing's caption appears two pages later, reading, "Weary thou art; the world seems sad and strange, / Thou aged wanderer in our alien land; / The problem lies beyond thy widest range; / Its simplest rule thou canst not understand."[47] The poem, likely an adaptation of Hebrews 11.8–9 account of Abraham from the King James Version of the Bible, casts the African American man as moving aimlessly in a land not his own, one with rules he "canst not understand." Those rules, and another juxtaposition of black and white difference, were suggested in two illustrations from the 1881 New Year's issue, which offered a pair of otherwise unrelated depictions of Christmas dinner. In one, several generations of a caricatured black family crowd around a dinner of possum in a small image dwarfed by an extremely dark-toned sketch of a nighttime swamp hunt. The illustration includes this dialect in scrawl, "POSSUM FAT and SIMMON BEER KRISMUS COME but UNCE A-YEAR." A few pages later appeared the photo-realistic illustration of a well-dressed white family of four preparing for a dinner of roast pig.[48] Economic security, linguistic mastery, class privilege, and lifelike representation were the domain of white, not black, Americans.

The images of African American families in *Harper's Weekly* illustrations from 1877 to 1887 regularly depicted African American men (and less often, women) negatively: childlike, petty criminals and loafers, living in rural poverty, their speech an impoverished version of English, poorly imitating middle- and upper-class behavior, all for the intended amusement of white readers. Of course, the African American population of the United States immediately after Reconstruction was generally rural, often poor, and literacy varied. However, much of the magazine's readership likely saw in the illustrations of well-to-do white men and women dining, traveling, or otherwise engaging in leisure less an accurate reflection of their present circumstances than a wishful mirror, a portrayal of themselves as rich, cultured, literate, and who they aspired to be. Black families were depicted as poor, coarse, and foolish—emphasizing what a racist white imagination believed them to be. The contrast is under-scored by generally more realistic portrayals of white subjects in illustra-tions (aside from strictly political or comic works) and the more frequent caricatures of black subjects. Analysis of these illustrations does not dic-tate that *Harper's Weekly* or its illustrators were entirely racist, that men and women of African descent did not imitate the cultural practices of (largely white) middle and upper classes in hopes of social mobility, or that such effort may have at times fallen short. However, it seems much more likely that white illustrators drew their imaginations of blackness in a fashion both capitulating to the expectations of their predominantly white audience and to foster Southern white readership. For a reader and writer like Chesnutt, such caricatures may have spurred him to envision alternative representations.

Chesnutt's Reconfiguration of Racial Caricatures

Rather than the "stale" humor of minstrelsy or "worn out" appeals to antebellum tropes, the Chesnutt of 1880 dedicated himself to "come down to hard facts" in recording the "peculiar" and "interesting" aspects of black life in description and dialogue—but he faced a challenge in the popularity of plantation tales such as those by Harris and Bonner and the widespread practice of illustrations caricaturing black men as lazy, foolish, criminal liars incapable of proper speech or right action. Chesnutt's pub-lished literary work of the 1880s and 1890s challenged those stereotypes with the romantic trickster and tragic figures of his dialect tales published in *Puck,* the *Atlantic Monthly,* and many other magazines and newspapers, many of which were included in two 1899 collections.

Chesnutt's post-plantation fiction already distanced itself from his predecessors and contemporaries, in part through characterizing the ste-reotypes of black masculinity as racist imaginations even more clearly than the appetite for chicken overturned in two of his stories. His only use of the term "Sambo" in the short stories is applied to a man who is actually white, but undertakes an unwilling minstrelsy. In "Mars Jeems's Nightmare" from *The Conjure Woman,* the slave owner is conjured to appear as a black man, and overseer Mars Johnson asks "dat noo nigger," "W'at 's yo' name, Sambo?" to which the new man replies, "My name ain' Sambo."[49] The insolence in refusing to identify with a stereotype spurs the overseer to whip him, to which he responds by attempting to attack the offender, though he is wrestled to the ground (and likely saved from being burned to death) by the other slaves. When that conjuring abates, the again white Mars Jeems resolves to treat his slaves better, though not to free them. In the story "The Passing of Grandison," first published in the *Atlantic Monthly* in 1887 and reprinted in *The Wife of His Youth,* the titular character's passing does not refer to the attempt to appear white, but both his masquerade as a willing, subservient slave and his passages south and then north. A Kentucky plantation scion forcibly frees the seemingly meek slave Grandison to impress a woman, only to see the prodigal return from Canada by foot, an affirmation of fictive slave loyalty undone when Grandison escapes for good with his wife and kin.[50] The apparent unwillingness to escape and the return were thus acts of black minstrelsy, a mask of servility given to him by the white patriarch and worn as a tool to accomplish the freedom of his family.

Chesnutt's relative success with post-plantation fiction led him to suspend his stenography business and dedicate himself as a fulltime novelist, an experiment that lasted only briefly. Perhaps his strongest encouragement to do so came from a May 1900 review, an endorsement by critic and author William Dean Howells, arguably the nation's foremost man of letters, who volunteered an essay to the *Atlantic Monthly* in which he described Chesnutt's stories to date: "They are new and fresh and strong as life always is and fable never is," and they feature "[c]haracter, the most precious thing in fiction," which Howells described "as faithfully portrayed." Howells contrasted Chesnutt's stories with more familiar representations of blackness, "the grotesque and comical negro and the terrible and tragic negro."[51] This former editor of the *Atlantic Monthly* and later columnist for *Harper's Weekly* suggested that Chesnutt's stories operate in the register of realism, his watchword for turn-of-the-twentieth-century literary merit. Their relationship would quickly sour with the 1901 publication of *The Marrow Tradition,* which Howells described as "bitter, bitter,"[52] likely in part because its depictions of character, "the most precious thing in fiction," departed from what the eminent critic felt were true to life. However, Howells held expectations of racial identity described by one critic as "minstrel realism,"[53] a sensibility matching many of the detailed illustrations of *Harper's Weekly,* and thus "faithfully portrayed" African American men and women may have meant to Howells portrayals faithful to antebellum stereotypes sustained during and after Reconstruction.

The two novels published at this zenith of Chesnutt's literary trajectory coincided with what is commonly referred to as the nadir of postbellum African American history, and of *The House behind the Cedars* and *The Marrow of Tradition,* the latter far more emphasizes and reconfigures the racial caricatures so prevalent in *Harper's Weekly* as Chesnutt began his literary career. Chesnutt's first published novel offers a sentimental narrative of passing that ends in the death of its heroine, Rena, one example of Howells's "tragic negro" (in this case, mulatto), who is spurned by her white lover when he learns of her background and pursued unto death by an unscrupulous black suitor. Between these two thwarted relationships is another, her friendship with the devoted Frank Fowler, a black man, who seeks throughout the novel to love and protect Rena. A number of critics dismiss Frank as a negative stereotype, "displaying a doglike fidelity to Rena that results in more than one scene of self-debasement, [who] reinforces the image of the docile, servile black."[54] We might ask, is Frank's loyalty to love really so terrible? Rena's devotion to George Tryon and her mother's fierce and lasting love for her children are presented as feminine virtues, so sentimental attachment as "servile" presents a flaw only for black men, making the claim to Frank's failure not one of race but masculinity.

If the dark-skinned and loyal Frank represents one type of black masculinity, Chesnutt increased the diversity of such representations in *The Marrow of Tradition,* even as he both exposed the degree to which caricature as a foundation of character is not restricted to African Americans and overturned the racial calculus of those types. The novel's complex plot charts the entwined genealogies of the Carteret and Miller families, united through a common patriarch's second and secret marriage to a black woman. Hidden wills, withheld inheritance, and denied legitimacy offer the backstory to the plot that begins with the birth of the new Carteret heir, a domestic scene paired with that of the unacknowledged black sister, her husband, Dr. Miller, and their young son. The elder Carteret schemes with Captain McBane and General Belmont to disenfranchise black citizens of the town and reassert white supremacy. Meanwhile, two young men, the decadent plantation son Tom Delamere and the reformist-minded Ellis, compete for the niece of the Carterets. On the other side of the color line, Dr. Miller encounters Josh Green, a black man who seeks vengeance on McBane for the death of his father and madness of his mother. Tom masquerades as a black Delamere servant, on whom he blames his robbery and murder of a widow, and Carteret, McBane, and Belmont precipitate a race riot, during which Josh kills McBane and is immediately slain. The massacre claims the Millers' son, and the distraught parents must then face the Carterets' impossible request in the final pages for Dr. Miller to apply his medical skills to save their child. The sentimentalism of the near-gothic racial and monetary patrimony runs parallel with the sensationalism of the plotting of the race riot and its conclusion, twin tracks that mirror those of the train that brings Dr. Miller back to the South again from Philadelphia to face a tragic conclusion.

The four central black male characters span a range of deliberate and recognizable types extending beyond the impoverished descriptions of *Harper's Weekly* illustrations. There is the obedient porter Jerry, who fawns over the white patriarchs at the *Morning Chronicle;* the faithful Sandy, accused of murder after he is impersonated by a cheat, thief, and murderer, the younger Delamere; Dr. Miller, the well-educated professional, husband, and father, a stand-in for Chesnutt himself; and Josh Green, the tough laborer who chooses brief, fierce liberty and death rather than subservience to the white mob. Jerry and Sandy are servants, Green is rural, and all three employ variations of dialect, but Dr. Miller's profession and speech differ sharply with broadly held expectations of black masculinity. All four initially appear as self-conscious types: the Southern aristocrat Carteret describes Jerry as "a black negro, of the pure type," while Sandy, according to the narrator, "would have presented, to one unfamiliar with the negro type, an amusingly impressive appearance." These types bear some resemblance to the brutal stigma of pointedly racist stereotypes such as Sambo, though as in its single ironic use in Chesnutt's post-plantation fiction, the only mention of Sambo in the 1901 novel occurs in the pages of the *Morning Chronicle,* the newspaper voice of white supremacist Southern Democrats.[55] The invocation of racial types suggests instead the impulse of caricature Wonham describes as coterminous with literary realism.

Introducing these men as types presents a starting point for their characterizations, but Chesnutt does not reserve the technique exclusively for black characters. In their own introductions, Dr. Miller and Dr. Burns, black and white, each "represented very different and yet very similar types of manhood," with Burns "representing a fine type of Anglo-Saxon"—which Chesnutt puns for comic effect when Jerry pronounces his alliance with the "Angry Saxon race." Also, "Sandy, no less than his master [the elder Delamere], was a survival of an interesting type."[56] As Wonham demonstrates of Chesnutt's early stories and those of his contemporaries, the shorthand caricature of types provided a starting point for representations; however, *The Marrow of Tradition* pushes far beyond his earlier literary work to demonstrate the inadequacy of those types and reverses Wonham's description of the magazine sketches, not inhabiting but resisting expectations.

Indeed, Howells's account of the book as "bitter, bitter" likely results from the inversion of white and black stereotypes, a reversal that occurs on the axis of gender. *Harper's Weekly* cartoons in the decade after Reconstruction regularly characterized black men as liars, thieves, and criminals, but it is white men (and to a lesser extent, women) in the novel who lie to themselves and others, steal, plot, and murder. Carteret, McBane, and Belmont, particularly with their claims to military rank, embody in their aggregate the caricature of Nathan Bedford Forrest that Nast excoriated regularly in *Harper's Weekly* as personifying Southern masculine racial hatred and violence, and it is they who incite the mob in the fictionalization of the 1898 Wilmington massacre.[57] Though differences of class seem to divide the three elder men, McBane's coarse arguments for racial genocide, as the more aristocratic Carteret admits, "in their last analysis, were much the same as his, though he would have expressed them less brutally."[58] Rapacious violence is a characteristic of white, not black, masculinity, and transcends class difference.

The logical heir to Carteret, McBane, and Belmont is the dissipated young Southern gentleman Tom Delamere, who similarly embodies the lying, stealing criminality popular white imagination attributed to black masculinity in *Harper's Weekly* and elsewhere. Tom's competing suitor Ellis describes him as "a type of the degenerate aristocrat," and as the narrator offers in Tom's introduction, "no discriminating observer would have characterized his beauty as manly. It conveyed no impression of strength, but did possess a certain element, feline rather than feminine, which subtly negatived the idea of manliness."[59] In denigrating Tom's lack of strength and other weaknesses, Chesnutt takes care not to equate his lack of masculinity with femininity but instead describes it as a bestial characteristic, itself a rhetorical reversal of the racist claims of African Americans as animals. The minstrelsy of Tom Delamere, whose "skill as a mimic and a negro impersonator was well known" even to his father, most fully demonstrates Chesnutt's inversion of raced expectations of masculinity. The character's impersonation of Sandy's dialect and his own dancing delight visiting Northerners at a cakewalk, and while the observer Ellis does not see through the disguise, he does recognize the performance as "somewhat overdone, even for the comical type of negro." Tom admonishes Sandy after the latter's reputation has suffered due to Tom's masquerade, "Brace up, Sandy, and be a man, or, if you can't be a man, be as near a man as you can!"[60] The cruelty in Tom calling to question the black man's masculinity is undermined by the speaker's own character, for the white man is a liar and murderous would-be trickster—in Chesnutt's portrayal, less than a man, a "degenerate," lacking strength, a "subtly negative" version of masculinity. The embodiment of violent criminality occurs in a white character whose blackface will falsely blame a black man, which implies instead that the "black brute" is a false construction of African American masculinity, a white invention.

Just as much a creation and inversion lies in the servitude of Jerry—whose last name, Letlow, a combination of *allowance* and *negative* perhaps provides an indication of how readers are to receive his character's subservience. He provides the titular figure of the chapter titled "A White Man's 'Nigger,'" wherein the quotes, like the strikethrough of "nigger" in Chesnutt's 1875 journal entry, set the final word apart, using the term while placing it at a distance. Where the earlier usage erases even as it writes the racist epithet, the 1901 chapter title ascribes to the "White Man" ownership not of the black man but, in the use of quotes, of the hateful language. Early in the novel Jerry declares that he "wush ter Gawd [he] wuz w'ite!" and in this chapter, he makes a point to read later a newspaper of the African American community, "an elegant specimen of journalism" Belmont scorns for, in addition to its critique of lynching and promotion of racial amalgamation, its advertisements for treatments to straighten hair and lighten black skin. Much later, Jerry will use the tonics and be ridiculed for it by Belmont, but his logic is simple: "he had realized that it was a distinct advantage to be white."[61]

The logic of white supremacy is predicated on the difference inscribed by the color line, but if Tom Delamere can cross it for his advantage, then Jerry will try as well. Of course, the narrator recognizes that like all the mortals of *Puck*'s tagline, "Jerry was a fool," but "not all kinds of fool."[62] His condition as a fool in some sense but not all gains clarity in comparison with an earlier passage describing Dr. Miller's journey southward on a segregated train car. Reconciling himself to this jim crow status requires that he recognize that "in order to live comfortably in the United States, he must be either a philosopher or a fool; and since he wished to be happy, and was not exactly a fool, he had cultivated a philosophy."[63] That philosophy, so bound in this instance to foolishness, seems to be the recognition of the false logic of racism coupled with an unwillingness to resist its strictures at personal cost. The subservience attributed to black masculinity thereby proves at once the product of white imagination and a consequence, not a cause, of racism.

If recognizing the inequity of white supremacy but not overtly resisting it makes one a philosopher, fool, or both, then Josh Green is neither. His bodily strength and capacity for violence make him, along with Jerry, part of what Andrew Silver identifies as the competing "[c]omic and savage typologies of blackness."[64] However, to reduce the two characters to opposite poles of humorous harmlessness and potential violence reads them exclusively in terms of the facing pages of the 1879 *Harper's Weekly* images of a comic smiling watermelon thief and a savage Zulu warrior. In Chesnutt's much richer pages, those types are starting points for the demonstration that the comedy, criminality, and servility expected of black men are consequences of racism, as in the cases of Tom Delamere, Sandy, and Jerry. For Josh Green, who resembles the "burly black brute" so sensationalized in the "large black type" of contemporary periodicals, his threat of violence results from historical awareness and sense of justice.

When Dr. Miller treats the "black giant" Green for a broken arm, the doctor recognizes "how inseparably the present is woven with the past, how certainly the future will be but the outcome of the present." Slavery and the rise of the Ku Klux Klan present "an old wound still bleeding," and Dr. Miller feels some hope that African American men will become capable of sacrificing their lives "to defend a right."[65] In the conclusion to the racial massacre, it is Green rather than his professional counterpart who will repudiate white supremacy at the cost of his life. Anticipating the conclusion of the resistance and refusing to join or lead Green's band, Dr. Miller feels at once "entirely convinced that he had acted wisely," and "conscious of a distinct feeling of shame and envy that he, too, did not feel impelled to throw away his life."[66] Dr. Miller's rational assessment and sentiment of shame complicate his character far beyond the existing caricatured types of black masculinity prevalent in the pages of *Harper's Weekly* and, presumably, the minds of its readers.

If Tom Delamere "negatived the idea of manliness"—wherein *negative* is both the reversal of manliness and the inversion of color—then Dr. Miller and Josh Green offer a counterpoint of positive manliness. These two characters indicated as opposite in their class difference, respective dialects, and opposite ends remain inexorably paired in the novel: their shared train journey southward, Miller's repair of Green's injury and reflection on the presentness of history, Green's assembly of resistance and Miller's refusal to join. Joseph R. McElrath Jr. joins other critics in declaring, "Unresolved as well is the question of exactly what Chesnutt was implying about different varieties of African Americans he pictures."[67] Part of what Chesnutt implies in the black men "he pictures" is that their diversity of character cannot be contained by the impoverished types prevalent in illustrations popular with many readers of the upscale weekly magazines—precisely the broad audience he longed for but failed to acquire and sustain in his time.

CHESNUTT'S ONLY appearance in *Harper's Weekly* occurred in 1905, after he had given up making a career as a full-time literary writer, and it was not one of his short stories or essays that appears, but a photograph of him at a table of eight, part of a gathering of nearly 150 people to celebrate the seventieth birthday of Mark Twain.[68] Twain's dialect story "A True Story, Repeated Word for Word as I Heard It" appeared in the *Atlantic Monthly* in 1874, twelve years prior to Chesnutt's first publication there. Thirty-one years later and just months before the honoring of Twain, Chesnutt saw the release of his last novel published in his lifetime, *The Colonel's Dream* (1905), which sold poorly and ended what hopes he still held for success as a novelist. The guests at the party included Twain, Howells, and Joseph Henry Harper of the Harper's publishing empire, as well as Andrew Carnegie, Willa Cather, and Nathaniel Hawthorne's son Julian. Chesnutt appeared in the photo somewhat in the background, seated at a table including seven other writers: May Isabel Fisk, a frequent contributor to *Harper's Monthly Magazine;* John Kendrick Bangs, then editor of *Puck* magazine, which had published nine of Chesnutt's early short works; naturalist Ernest Ingersoll, author of fourteen nonfiction books; Anna P. Paret of *Harper's Bazaar;* Roy L. McCardell, early film scenarist and prolific magazine writer; John Luther Long, author of the short story "Madame Butterfly" (1898), the basis of the play and opera; and poet Caroline Duer.[69] Here Chesnutt sat amidst the society he so aspired to join, and he likely felt a little of the ironic ambivalence so common to his narratives as he joined his esteemed company to honor a white Southern writer who earned his literary reputation and wealth in part through incorporating African American dialect and depicting black life.

Notes

1. Charles W. Chesnutt, *The Marrow of Tradition* (Ann Arbor: University of Michigan Press, 1990), 233.

2. Chesnutt's essay of this title appeared in *The Colophon* in February 1931 and is reprinted in *Charles W. Chesnutt: Essays and Speeches,* Joseph R. McElrath Jr., Robert C. Leitz III, and Jesse S. Crisler, eds. (Palo Alto, CA: Stanford University Press, 1999), 543–49. Editors Barbara McCaskill and Caroline Gebhard use the phrase as the title of their collection *Post-Bellum, Pre-Harlem: African American Literature and Culture* (New York: New York University Press, 2006). Thomas L. Morgan, "The City as Refuge: Constructing Urban Blackness in Paul Laurence Dunbar's 'The Sport of the Gods' and James Weldon Johnson's 'The Autobiography of an Ex-Colored Man,'" *African American Review* 38:2 (2004): 213.

3. The persistence of antebellum stereotypes during and after Reconstruction has been well documented. See George M. Frederickson, *The Black Image in the White Mind: The Debate on Afro-American Character and Destiny, 1817–1914* (New York: Harper & Row, 1971); John W. Blassingame, *The Slave Community: Plantation Life in the Antebellum South* (New York: Oxford University Press, 1972); Joseph Boskin, *Sambo: The Rise and Demise of an American Jester* (New York: Oxford University, 1986), 4; James F. Davis, *Who Is Black? One Nation's Definition* (University Park: Pennsylvania State University Press, 1991); Jan Nederveen Pieterse, *White on Black: Images of Africa and Blacks in Western Popular Culture* (New Haven, CT: Yale University Press, 1995); Eric Lott, *Love and Theft: Blackface Minstrelsy and the American Working Class* (New York: Oxford University Press, 1995); Sarah Meer, *Uncle Tom Mania: Slavery, Minstrelsy, and Transatlantic Culture in the 1850s* (Athens: University of Georgia Press, 2005). Boskin describes Sambo as generally "comic" (4), while Harriet Beecher Stowe's character of that name in *Uncle Tom's Cabin; Or, Life Among the Lowly, vol. II* (Boston: John P. Jewett & Co, 1855) is "debased" (271), but both are "servile" (136; 271). Harris's storyteller Uncle Remus served as a model for Chesnutt's own Uncle Julius, and Brer Rastus appears in "Uncle Remus's Church Experience," in *Uncle Remus: His Songs and His Sayings* (New York and London: D. Appleton and Company, 1880). For comparisons of Chesnutt's and Harris's plantation fiction, see Eric J. Sundquist, *To Wake the Nations: Race in the Making of American Literature* (Cambridge, MA: Belknap Press of Harvard University Press, 1993), 323–46; Tynes Cowan, "Charles Waddell Chesnutt and Joel Chandler Harris: An Anxiety of Influence," *Resources for American Literary Study* 25:2 (1999): 232–53.

4. While Douglass's physical and moral courage perhaps need no reminder, we might usefully recall his description of "that slave who has the courage to stand up for himself against the overseer," in *My Bondage and My Freedom* (New York and Auburn: Miller, Orton, & Co., 1857), 95. Douglass's portrait appeared on the cover of *Harper's Weekly* in 1883; *Harper's Weekly,* 24 November 1883, 773. One of Henson's own autobiographies offers his account of a physical battle with an overseer in *The Life of Josiah Henson, Formerly a Slave, Now an Inhabitant of Canada, as Narrated by Himself* (Boston, MA: Arthur D. Phelps, 1849), 15–17. The paired portraits and biographical sketches appear in *Harper's Weekly,* 21 April 1877, 305–6; the cover (301) follows Nast's consistent ambivalence regarding the citizenship and manliness of African American men

documented by Fiona Halloran (chapter 5). The cartoon (316) offers a "Seedy Applicant" dressed in patchwork rags, offering a presumable lie regarding his economic status.

5. Heather Tirado Gilligan emphasizes the competition between realism and sentimentalism with regard to race in Chesnutt's plantation fiction, in "Reading, Race, and Charles Chesnutt's 'Uncle Julius' Tales," *ELH* 74:1 (2007): 195–215. The ambivalences regarding Chesnutt's literary mode are demonstrated in the title and journal source of Joseph R. McElrath Jr., "Why Charles W. Chesnutt Is Not a Realist," *American Literary Realism* 32:2 (2000): 91–108. Drawing from an essay by Albion Tourgée, Henry Wonham titles a chapter "The 'Curious Realism' of Charles W. Chesnutt," in *Playing the Races: Ethnic Caricature and American Literary Realism* (New York: Oxford University Press, 2004).

6. Wonham, *Playing the Races,* 8.

7. Morgan, "The City as Refuge," 213–14. These understandings of American literary realism are indebted to Amy Kaplan's *The Social Construction of American Realism* (Chicago: University of Chicago Press, 1988).

8. C. Vann Woodward in *The Strange Career of Jim Crow* (New York: Oxford University Press, 1974) declares, "It was quite common in the 'eighties and 'nineties to find in the *Nation, Harper's Weekly,* the *North American Review,* or the *Atlantic Monthly* Northern liberals and former abolitionists mouthing the shibboleths of white supremacy regarding the Negro's innate inferiority" (70). See also *Myth and Southern History, vol. 1: The Old South* and *vol. 2: The New South,* both edited by Patrick Gerster and Nicholas Cords (Urbana: University of Illinois Press, 1989).

9. Wonham, *Playing the Races,* 159.

10. An issue of *The Nation* (31 August 1871) features an advertisement in which *Harper's Weekly* boasts that its "circulation is four times that of any similar publication" (152). In a journal entry dated March 26, 1881, Chesnutt writes, "It is the dream of my life—to be an author! [. . .] It is not altogether the money. It is a mixture of motives. I want fame; I want money; I want to raise my children in a different rank of life"; *The Journals of Charles W. Chesnutt,* Richard Brodhead, ed. (Durham, NC: Duke University Press, 1993), 154. For more on Chesnutt's own account of his development as an author, see *"To Be an Author": Letters of Charles W. Chesnutt 1889–1905,* Joseph R. McElrath Jr. and Robert C. Leitz, III, eds. (Princeton, NJ: Princeton University Press, 1997).

11. Joshua Brown in *Beyond the Lines: Pictorial Reporting, Everyday Life, and the Crisis of Gilded Age America* (Berkeley: University of California Press, 2002) describes *Harper's Weekly* as "stable and genteel" (4). He quotes *Frank Leslie's* editor James C. Goldsmith, 62.

12. For background on Chesnutt's early life, see Helen M. Chesnutt, *Charles Waddell Chesnutt, Pioneer of the Color Line* (Chapel Hill: University of North Carolina Press, 1952). Brodhead's edited journals and McElrath and Leitz's edited letters provide a valuable documentary record of his early literary development and professional life as a writer.

13. Chesnutt, *Journals,* 82.

14. Dean McWilliams, *Charles W. Chesnutt and the Fictions of Race* (Athens: University of Georgia Press, 2002), 24.

15. Chesnutt, *Journals,* 81.

16. Ibid, 107.

17. Ibid, 126.

18. *Harper's Weekly,* 8 March 1879, 181; *Harper's Weekly,* 31 May 1879, 421. The second of those offers Nast's hopeful vision of racial reconciliation in the South.

19. Chesnutt describes a dialogue with the vendor as follows: "Mr. Haigh read a paragraph in *Harper's Magazine,* where a lady requests her servant Bridget in a mild and deprecating tone, to perform some slight service, "if it was not inconvenient." He adopts a highly ironic tone concerning "the inconveniences that the rich have to suffer, that the poor are not troubled with" (126). Brodhead indicates that Haigh "was a man of conservative social and racial attitudes who gave Chesnutt a place to read and talk" (126n61). The three-part illustration titled "Mistress and Maid" charts the reversals of authority between mistress and servant in 1780, 1880, and 1980; *Harper's New Monthly Magazine,* April 1880, 800.

20. Chesnutt, *Journals,* 172.

21. *Harper's Weekly,* 23 August 1879, 672–73.

22. *Harper's Weekly,* 17 February 1877, 122.

23. Sherwood Bonner, "Dr. Jex's Predicament," *Harper's Weekly,* 18 December 1880, 816–17; "Inside Southern Cabins. Georgia.—No. 1," *Harper's Weekly,* 13 November 1880, 733–34; "Inside Southern Cabins. Georgia.—No. 2," *Harper's Weekly,* 20 November 1880, 749–50; "Inside Southern Cabins. III.—Charleston, South Carolina," *Harper's Weekly,* 27 November 1880), 765–66; "Inside Southern Cabins. IV.—Alabama," *Harper's Weekly,* 4 December 1880, 781–82.

24. Wonham, *Playing the Races,* 16–17; Brown, *Beyond the Lines,* chapters 5 and 6.

25. Holidays in particular seemed to inspire such nostalgia. A photorealistic illustration for Thanksgiving depicts a smiling young black man with a turkey saying, "Thirty-two pounds, massa!" *Harper's Weekly,* 19 November 1881, 777; a detailed illustration shows a black family presenting, according to the caption, "A Christmas Gift to Ole Marster and Missus" in *Harper's Weekly,* 22 December 1883, 820.

26. A series chronicling "Mr. H. M. Stanley's Anglo-American Expedition" in Africa appeared in March and April 1878 and included realistic illustrations of Africans, whether following Stanley, surrounding a burial, or in a tribal war. *Harper's Weekly,* 16 March 1878, 222; *Harper's Weekly,* 23 March 1878, 241; *Harper's Weekly,* 30 March 1878, 262–63; *Harper's Weekly,* 6 April 1878, 282–83. The magazine ran ads in July through September that year to promote their publication of Stanley's *Through the Dark Continent* (1878).

27. Scholarly attention to masculinity in general and black masculinity in particular has expanded tremendously in the past two decades. A representative but by no means complete list includes E. Anthony Rotundo, *American Manhood: Transformations in Masculinity from the Revolution to the Modern Era* (New York: Basic Books, 1993); Gail Bederman, *Manliness and Civilization: A Cultural History of Gender and Race in the United States, 1880–1917* (Chicago: University of Chicago Press, 1995); Kenneth S. Greenberg, *Honor & Slavery: Lies, Duels, Noses, Masks, Dressing as a Woman, Gifts, Strangers, Humanitarianism, Death, Slave Rebellions, the Proslavery Argument, Baseball, Hunting, and Gambling in the Old South* (Princeton, NJ: Princeton University Press, 1996); Darlene Clark Hine and Earnestine Jenkins, eds., *A Question of Manhood: A Reader in U.S.*

Black Men's History and Masculinity, vol. 1 (Bloomington: Indiana University Press, 1999) and *A Question of Manhood: A Reader in U.S. Black Men's History and Masculinity,* vol. 2 (Bloomington: Indiana University Press, 2001); Maurice O. Wallace, *Constructing the Black Masculine: Identity and Ideality in African American Men's Literature and Culture, 1775–1995* (Durham, NC: Duke University Press, 2002); Marlon B. Ross, *Manning the Race: Reforming Black Men in the Jim Crow Era* (New York: New York University Press, 2004).

28. *Harper's Weekly,* 4 May 1878, 360.

29. *Harper's Weekly,* 4 August 1883, 1389.

30. *Harper's Weekly,* 23 October 1886, 1557.

31. Chesnutt, "A Virginia Chicken," first published in *Household Realm* (August 1887). Reprinted in *The Short Fiction of Charles W. Chesnutt,* Sylvia Lyons Render, ed. (Washington, DC: Howard University Press, 1981). Chesnutt, "A Victim of Heredity; or, Why the Darkey Loves Chicken," first published in *Self-Culture-Magazine* 11 (July 1900). Reprinted in *The Short Fiction of Charles W. Chesnutt,* 125.

32. Chesnutt, *The Short Fiction of Charles W. Chesnutt,* 123, 131.

33. *Harper's Weekly,* 13 August 1887, 588.

34. Lott, *Love and Theft;* Annamarie Bean, James V. Hatch, and Brooks McNamara, eds., *Inside the Minstrel Mask: Readings in Nineteenth-Century Blackface Minstrelsy* (Middletown, CT: Wesleyan University Press, 1996); William J. Mahar, *Behind the Burnt Cork Mask: Early Blackface Minstrelsy and Antebellum American Popular Culture* (Urbana: University of Illinois Press, 1998).

35. *Harper's Weekly,* 19 February 1887, 139.

36. *Harper's Weekly,* 21 May 1887, 371.

37. *Harper's Weekly,* 18 September 1886, 628.

38. Chesnutt, *"To Be an Author,"* 44.

39. Chesnutt, *The Conjure Woman* (Ann Arbor: University of Michigan University Press, 1990); Chesnutt, *The Wife of His Youth and Other Stories of the Color Line* (Ridgewood, NJ: Gregg Press, 1967).

40. Chesnutt, *"To Be an Author,"* 105. Though Chesnutt challenges the legitimacy of the speech he used in his fiction, Lisa Cohen Minnick verifies the dialectical veracity of Chesnutt's conjure tales, tracing speech patterns to that of North Carolina former slaves; *Dialect and Dichotomy: Literary Representations of African American Speech* (Tuscaloosa: University of Alabama Press, 2004).

41. *Harper's Weekly,* 21 April 1883, 243, 241; *Harper's Weekly,* 17 January 1885, 43.

42. *Harper's Weekly,* 4 January 1879, 4; *Harper's Weekly,* 14 June 1879, 464.

43. *Harper's Weekly,* 12 July 1879, 548.

44. *Harper's Weekly,* 14 July 1883, 435.

45. *Harper's Weekly,* 23 November 1878, 928; *Harper's Weekly,* 2 November 1878, 872–74; *Harper's Weekly,* 9 November 1878, 897–98.

46. *Harper's Weekly,* 25 August 1877, 664; *Harper's Weekly,* 28 July 1877, 581, 590.

47. *Harper's Weekly,* 2 November 1878, 868, 870. Another McCutcheon illustration from later that year depicts an African American family puzzled by a jury summons; *Harper's Weekly,* 28 December 1878, 1023.

48. *Harper's Weekly,* 1 January 1881, 5, 12. In the first of the two images, the "N" of "SIMMON" is reversed.

49. Chesnutt, *The Conjure Woman*, 81.

50. Chesnutt, *The Wife of His Youth*, 168–202.

51. William Dean Howells, "Mr. Charles W. Chesnutt's Stories," *Atlantic Monthly*, May 1900, 700.

52. Howells, "A Psychological Counter-Current in Recent Fiction," *North American Review* 173 (1901): 882. McElrath documents the correspondence between Chesnutt and Howells in "W. D. Howells and Race: Charles W. Chesnutt's Disappointment of the Dean," *Nineteenth-Century Literature* 51:4 (1997): 474–99.

53. Gene Jarrett, "'Entirely Black Verse from Him Would Succeed': Minstrel Realism and William Dean Howells," *Nineteenth-Century Literature* 59:4 (2005): 498–99.

54. McElrath, *Critical Essays on Charles Chesnutt* (New York: G. K. Hall & Co., 1999), 18; Trudier Harris, "Chesnutt's Frank Fowler: A Failure of Purpose?" *CLA Journal* 22 (March 1979): 215–28; and SallyAnn H. Ferguson, "Rena Walden: Chesnutt's Failed 'Future American,'" *Southern Literary Journal* 15 (Fall 1982): 74–82. Sundquist is more favorable in his account, recognizing that "Frank, the novel's darkest-skinned character, is its most ethical, though he remains a minor figure" (*To Wake the Nations*, 400).

55. Chesnutt, *The Marrow of Tradition*, 24, 79, 246. In the actual town of Wilmington, a black man's appointment lent him the nickname "Sambo of the Custom House"; H. Leon Prather, *We Have Taken a City: The Wilmington Racial Massacre and Coup of 1898* (Rutherford, NJ: Fairleigh Dickinson University Press, 1984), 23.

56. Chesnutt, *The Marrow of Tradition*, 49, 90, 130.

57. Halloran, this book, chapter 5; also see Court Carney, "The Contested Image of Nathan Bedford Forrest," *Journal of Southern History* 67:3 (2001): 601–30. Bryan Wagner argues that the primary impulse of the riot is an attack on the black middle class, in "Charles Chesnutt and the Epistemology of Racial Violence," *American Literature* 73:2 (2001): 311–37.

58. Chesnutt, *The Marrow of Tradition*, 87.

59. Ibid., 16, 95.

60. Ibid., 118, 119, 122, 229. As Andrew Silver points out, given that the coat Tom has briefly stolen from Sandy was handed down to the servant from the elder Mr. Delamere, "when Delamere parodies Sandy, then, he also parodies his father"; *Minstrelsy and Murder: The Crisis of Southern Humor, 1835–1925* (Baton Rouge: Louisiana State University Press, 2006), 202n35.

61. Chesnutt, *The Marrow of Tradition*, 36, 84, 245.

62. Ibid., 243–45, 247.

63. Ibid., 60–61.

64. Silver, *Minstrelsy and Murder*, 167. However, Silver does not attend to the specifically gendered nature of those types in Chesnutt's fiction.

65. Chesnutt, *The Marrow of Tradition*, 109, 112.

66. Ibid., 285.

67. McElrath, *Critical Essays on Charles Chesnutt*, 19.

68. *Harper's Weekly*, 23 December 1905, 1884.

69. Ibid., 1914.

7

"So I Decided to Quit It and Try Something Else for a While"

Reading Agency in Nat Love

SIMONE DRAKE

When scholars discuss literary and cultural representations of black masculinity they often turn to the usual suspects. In regard to literature, the great triumvirate, Richard Wright, Ralph Ellison, and James Baldwin are called upon as representatives, with the occasional inclusion of Chester Himes. For cultural representations of black masculinity, Frederick Douglass, Booker T. Washington, and W. E. B. Du Bois are held up as narrative archetypes, while Malcolm X is a favorite, both visually and textually. Just as the literary and cultural representatives of black masculinity are predictable, popular culture representations are just as predictable, albeit generic. Popular film, music videos, and magazines are littered with images of the black male as thug, entertainer, athlete, and criminal. It is not surprising, then, that visual images of black masculinity in academic texts, particularly as cover art, also elect to present visceral images of black men and black bodies—nude and semi-nude images bearing sweat and brawn and generic close-ups of a black man's face. The exception to these images are found in texts dealing with Reconstruction, the Progressive Era, and the civil rights movement; these texts, instead, offer images in line with the middle-class decorum and respectability that framed racial uplift discourse—refined black men in suits or men in shirts and ties, protesting and marching. While there are, of course, exceptions to these literary and cultural representations of black masculinity, the aforementioned representations appear consistently enough to be considered commonplace. Considering the predictable and often stagnant narrative and visual attention to black masculinity, then, an important question arises: what can be gained by looking at unusual suspects?

Visual images of Nat Love, as well as his autobiographical narrative, *The Life and Adventures of Nat Love* (1907), offer contemporary readers and scholars a construction of black masculinity with a critical difference when compared to his contemporaries, Douglass, Washington, and Du Bois. Richard Majors and Janet Mancini Bilson coined the term "cool pose" as a way of describing how contemporary African American men utilize self-presentation as a survival mechanism, a means of retaining masculine self-control,[1] and that term can be projected usefully into the early twentieth century. Not only does Love offer an alternative model of racial uplift in the late nineteenth and early twentieth century, but the "self-making" in his narrative resonates with the "cool pose" of black masculinity that breaks from the modernist penchant for protest and lament for a masculinity that remains out of reach. Although the few scholars who have attended to Love's narrative cannot resist arguments that delve into racial authenticity, arguing that the West provided Love the space to transcend or erase blackness by embracing the myth of the racial frontier, or less frequently, to present Love as a mimicker of Booker T. Washington's accommodationist rhetoric, such analyses fail to consider critically Love's agency.[2] What scholars often fail to recognize is that Love made his choices of self-presentation based on his vision of himself and the black manhood that he sought to attain. From slavery and sharecropping in Tennessee to "the wild and wooly West" to the Pullman trains, Love was his own agent; he owned himself. Understanding Love as demonstrating a significant level of agency through his careers has the potential to offer scholars an alternative means of framing early-twentieth-century constructions of black masculinity.

An alternative reading of Love incorporates what Robert Reid-Pharr calls "the rhetoric of the freedom of choice"— in this case, the freedom to choose one's own race and act as one's own agent. Reid-Pharr asserts that "a much more expansive conception of freedom of choice" is needed when assessing African American cultural productions—a conception that recognizes, "One might not only choose one's room, one's books, one's music, and one's sexual partners, but also and importantly one might choose one's identity, indeed one's race."[3] Such an assertion informs this analysis of Love's rhetorical strategies in describing his "self-making" in a fashion that recognizes his agency and intellect without neutralizing or erasing his blackness.

We can interpret Love's "cool pose" of racial uplift in two important ways: visually and spatially. Only cursory attention has been given to the eight photographs that are included in the narrative, and examining the visual rhetoric of these photographs suggests important matters about Love's life outside of the autobiography, not the least of which is how his self-assertion offers an alternative account to the well-known progressive tradition of his contemporary Du Bois. Aside from his narrative, Love seems to have left no other remnants or artifacts attesting to his "life and adventures." However, U.S. Census records and state directories do confirm that he owned a home after the publication of his narrative. An analysis of the photographs and the significance of home ownership provide an opportunity to read Love as an important exemplar of how African American men negotiated life on the color line.

The House That Jim Crow Built

Nat Love was born into slavery in Davidson County, Tennessee, in 1854. He left his family home in 1869 for the Western plains, where, according to his autobiography, he became the roughest, toughest, and smartest cowboy on the frontier. *The Life and Adventures* is a multi-genre text that is divided into three distinct sections. The first section of five chapters describes Love's life as a slave, his family's hardships as sharecroppers, and his role as head of the house when his father died. The slave narrative section echoes the standard conventions of slave narratives, and more specifically parallels Washington's *Up from Slavery*. The second and longest section of twelve chapters records Love's life and experiences as a cowboy from 1869 to 1890. This section embodies the conventions of the dime novel, recounting superhuman feats—being shot fourteen times, for example—and encounters and friendships with famous cowboys and outlaws. The final section of five chapters chronicles Love's experiences as a Pullman porter and ends with nostalgia for life in the West.

The autobiography emphasizes Love's careers as strategies of economic improvement from life in slavery through individual heroics to middle-class success; nevertheless, a compelling symbol of Love's embodiment of the self-made man, home ownership, is not apparent in the narrative, because he did not purchase his home until after 1907.[4] His home ownership is significant, as it not only represents an act of "self-making" that many African Americans did not have access to during the Progressive Era, but also places Love's narrative within rather than outside of the African American literary tradition. The 1920 Census questionnaire for Los Angeles County records Nat and Alice Love owning a home at 1748 Twenty-Second Street in Santa Monica, California.[5] Not only does he own his home, but according to the questionnaire, his ownership is "free," meaning he does not have a mortgage. Only 22.3 percent or 542,654 of 2,430,828 American homeowners were African Americans in 1920. In California in 1920, African Americans owned 3,523 out of 376,173 homes, and the African American population in California was 38,763 or 1.9 percent.[6] The exact address of the Love's home in Santa Monica no longer exists, as I-10 runs through that neighborhood, and proximate addresses are industrial and office buildings. There is only one other black family listed on the schedule for Love's street and the two others on the list. The residents of the neighborhood are identified as "white," but almost all of them possess Spanish surnames, speak Spanish, and have parents who were born in Mexico. The racial demographics of these neighborhoods are, of course, complicated by the racial formations surrounding immigration during this time period.

Love's negotiation of the color line in the closing frontier perhaps precipitated his self-construction as a "bad man," and he also dueled with the expectations of jim crow on Pullman's trains. Perhaps only at the limit of the frontier, literally at the Pacific Ocean, could Love establish a home and by extension the self-ownership he lacked at birth. Because property has historically served as a racial signifier—slaves were property and thus blackness was a marker of property, and conversely, property ownership was itself a marker of race, of whiteness[7]—then Love's home ownership in the jim crow era becomes a symbol of racial transgression. Both the physical space and the domestic iconography of the home are critical determinants in achieving manhood within the confines of patriarchal assumptions of family stewardship. Thus, for a black man at the turn of the twentieth century, the acquisition of property functions as a designator of gender trumping race.

The Tales Photographs Tell

Prior to owning his home, Love constructed what we can recognize as a "cool pose" of racial uplift in his narrative through its sketches and photographs, which granted him opportunities of self-portrayal in terms of race and gender. In addition to the thirty-four pencil sketches, the auto-biography includes eight other pictures: one family photograph in the frontispiece, two cowboy photographs, four Pullman porter photographs, and one photograph of Love in his courier uniform. Representing him-self with the rugged individualism of a cowboy, as a polished professional porter, and as a successful family man, Love offers in these aggregate of images a compelling counter-argument to racist suppositions of black men as biologically inferior, undisciplined, and uncivilized—expectations that fueled white supremacy and lynching. The images strategically rein-force the conventional tenets of racial uplift at the same time that they disrupt those conventions by complicating assumptions of black middle-class decorum at the heart of such positivism.

The first page of the narrative is a frontispiece photograph of Love, his wife, Alice, who is identified only by name in the dedication, and, his daughter, who is never named. The caption under the photograph reads, "Nat Love, Better Known as Deadwood Dick, and His Family" (see fig-ure 11). This photograph is reminiscent of those Du Bois collected for his Georgia Negro album, because the photographs in that collection capture images of black people that the white media had no interest in representing: black people who were not domestics, sharecroppers, poor, or criminals. Like Du Bois's, Love's images of black middle-class advance-ment provide what Shawn Michelle Smith describes in another context as "a place from which a counter-history can be imagined and narrated," and they "underscore the ways in which both identity and history are founded, at least partially, through representation."[8] In addition to the family's clothing marking their class status, the very fact that they could afford to sit for a photograph was a significant marker as well, because photography at this time was an expensive art inaccessible to many. This photograph, then, seems designed to establish for the reader the Love family's middle-class status and respectability. As Kevin K. Gaines explains, in the wake of emancipation and on into the twentieth century, racial uplift was a pervasive ideology in black politics and culture that was compelling because it allowed African Americans to foreground the home and family, two images that bolstered "race building" by "making conformity to patriarchal family ideals the criterion of respectability."[9]

Love's conformity to uplift ideology merits scrutiny. In spite of the "image of the home and the patriarchal family" that stares back at the reader from the first page of the narrative, there remains something odd about this photograph, as census data on Love and his wife reveal informa-tion that calls into question the veracity of the family portrait, especially

Nat Love, Better Known as Deadwood Dick, and His Family

Figure 11 **"Nat Love, Better Known as Deadwood Dick, and His Family."** This studio portrait illustrates the transformation of the lone cowboy of the Wild West to the established paterfamilias. Used with Permission of Documenting the American South, The University of North Carolina at Chapel Hill Libraries.

the likelihood of the standing woman being his daughter. The photograph is not dated, so the only certainty is that it was taken prior to the publication of the text. The assumption can be made that the frontispiece and all but one of the Pullman photographs are taken at the same studio during the same time period.[10] The first photograph of Love in his Pullman uniform is a younger-looking man—no gray hair, a thinner face, and a sparser mustache—than the Love in the subsequent Pullman photographs and in the frontispiece. The first Pullman photograph also appears to have been taken in front of a different backdrop than the other Pullman photographs and the frontispiece. Considering these differences, the frontispiece photograph is perhaps the most likely to have been taken near the publication date. If, however, it was taken earlier in Love's Pullman career, then an even stronger case can be made that the younger woman in the photograph could not possibly be Love's daughter, who would have been only a toddler at the start of Love's Pullman career.

In the portrait, Love, who would have been about fifty-three in 1907, looks his age. According to census records, Love's wife, Alice, was also born in 1854 or 1855.[11] However, the two women in the photograph, presumably mother and daughter, appear to be closer in age, and neither of the two women appears to be in her early fifties. The seated woman's flat hat and attire mark her as a middle-class matron, and the standing woman's fashionable coordinated ensemble, with its cinched waist and elaborate hat, mark her as a younger woman. The argument could be made that the seated woman is Love's wife and has aged well, but this assertion does not address a variety of other discrepancies that this photograph, as well as the other photographs, present.

The 1900 Census schedule indicates that a Nat and Alice Love lived in Salt Lake City, Utah, and had been married for twelve years, and that Alice had given birth four times, with two children still living.[12] The peculiar aspect of this record is that there are no actual children listed as living in the Love household, as the only names recorded are Nat's and Alice's. Typically all of the children living in the home and their ages would be recorded below their parents' data. The older of the two living children should be approximately ten—so where are the living children? The 1910 Census schedule lists that Alice Love has given birth five times and there are no remaining children.[13] It is important to note the math here: Alice was thirty-four or thirty-five when she got married, which would make her in her mid-forties when the 1900 Census was recorded and in her mid-50s when the 1910 Census was recorded.

Not only would Alice have begun having children at a late age, according to the 1910 Census, but she would have continued having children well into her forties, and possibly her fifties. That is not to say this could not indeed be the case, but it is unusual and worth noting. Furthermore, Love never mentions having any children in his narrative. Based on this absence in his narrative and the census data that never identifies children living in Love's home, there remains the possibility that none of Love's children survived or remained with him at the time the photographs were taken. Lacking children would compromise his ability to fit the patriarchal model of racial uplift, so Love may have done for the photographs what he likely did throughout the autobiography—he fabricates, making a self that matches the expectations of the situation.

The frontispiece family photograph is not the only odd photograph in Love's collection. The next photograph is of a cowboy with a lariat, followed by one of a cowboy with a rifle. The caption below the first (see figure 12) reads, "The Roping Contest at Deadwood, S.D." Love presumably would have posed for most of the photographs on the same day in the same studio, changing from costume to costume so that there would be visual evidence of his various identities to support his narrative. Recognizing the highly staged aspect of these photographs is paramount to an alternative reading of Love's narrative, as such a recognition invites an expansion of Love's creative agency performing a black masculinity that frontier myths' racial erasure could not provide.[14]

The roping contest at Deadwood that Love references in the caption of the lariat photograph occurred, tellingly, on July 4, 1876. Love proclaims, "The name of Deadwood Dick was given to me by the people of Deadwood, South Dakota, July 4, 1876, after I had proven myself worthy of it, and after I had defeated all comers in riding, roping, and shooting, and I have always carried the name with honor since that time."[15] Scholars fail to acknowledge Love's intellect when analyzing his narrative, because he does not present his story as invested in self-assertions of intelligence crucial to narratives of racial uplift; instead, he seems to have written an entertaining autobiography in the dime novel tradition. However, Love is no fool. In lieu of either Du Bois's intellectualism advocacy or Washington's accommodation, Love opts for the African American signifying-trickster folk tradition. The full title of Love's narrative, with subtitle is *The Life and Adventures of Nat Love, Better Known in the Cattle Country as "Deadwood Dick," by Himself; a True History of Slavery Days, Life on the Great Cattle Ranges and on the Plains of the "Wild and Woolly" West, Based on Facts, and Personal Experiences of the Author.* Love

The Roping Contest at Deadwood, S. D.

Figure 12 **"The Roping Contest at Deadwood, S.D."** Used with Permission of Documenting the American South, The University of North Carolina at Chapel Hill Libraries.

uses the pseudonym "Deadwood Dick" on the front cover, the title page, and throughout the narrative. The persona of Deadwood Dick is not Love's creation, as the fictional outlaw dressed all in black appeared in many dime novels from 1877 to 1903. As Susan Scheckel observes, Love does not present his name as derivative of Wheeler's character; instead, he "encourages readers to see him as the original" because he earns his name in 1876, the year before Edward L. Wheeler's series began.[16]

Love does more than simply appropriate Wheeler's Deadwood Dick in an effort to establish the bona fides of his accomplishments. Love also signifies on this character's history and on his name. The first dime novel of the Deadwood Dick series "introduces the hero as an orphan victimized by politically powerful enemies; because the law will not protect him, he must become an outlaw to protect himself and his sister."[17] If Love's appropriation is considered in terms of race, nation, and masculinity, then his appropriation signifies on the instability of white masculinity. The frontier functioned as a critical space for warding off what Gail Bederman refers to as "racial decadence." Bederman points out how Theodore Roosevelt masked his "belligerent grab for a radically new type of nationalistic power" with racial decadence rhetoric that insisted, "A race which grew decadent, then, was a race which had lost the masculine strength necessary to prevail in this Darwinistic racial struggle."[18] When Love appropriates the name of Deadwood Dick, Love implies an awareness of the relationship between the denial of full citizenship to black people, meaning black men, and the nation's fear of black men gaining true freedom. Such recognition would have been informed by the controversy surrounding the Fourteenth Amendment that ultimately culminated in the "separate but equal" ruling of *Plessy v. Ferguson.* Love's appropriation, then, can be understood as a pun on the impotence of white masculinity—a dick that is like deadwood—a masculinity during the Progressive Era anxiously preoccupied with defining, performing, and defending a masculinity that was entirely "white" and "male."

Wheeler's character is an outlaw, because he was orphaned and unprotected from "politically powerful enemies." As a black man in the post-Reconstruction United States, Love is "victimized by politically powerful enemies," the nation and its fickle democratic ideals. Love has no protection, so he becomes a trickster in order to gain access to signifiers of whiteness: middle-class values, economic capital, and real estate. Love assumes the white Deadwood Dick's privilege and agency retroactively, on the centennial celebration of the nation, July 4, 1876. In other words, the liberated Love is born-again on the nation's birth date, a celebration that consistently fails to acknowledge that the Declaration of Independence does not grant freedom, rights, and protection to African Americans. In doing so, Love adopts a black masculinity disavowing both Washington's accommodation and Du Bois's lament of double-consciousness—instead, Love acts as his own agent, claiming the property of person he believes to be rightfully his.

Love's narrative and the accompanying photographs offer a counternarrative to the relationship between constructions of white masculinity and its relationship to the nation. Read this way, these photographs tell a provocative tale. The veracity of Love's narrative remains a place of contention; equally suspicious are the cowboy photographs, in which Love appears strikingly different from the other photographs included in the narrative. The incongruities in Love's narrative might lead the most suspicious reader to believe that he had not been a cowboy or lived in the West. An 1890 Denver directory confirms that Nat Love lived there then and that his occupation was a teamster, though there are no extant records of Love prior to that year. Another oddity lies in the picture of Nat with his gun, his hand is over its sight, a placement unlikely for a trained gun handler.

There are more significant oddities about the cowboy photographs. When the cowboy photographs are juxtaposed with the other images of Love, the only consistency is a black man in the photographs. Although there are some similarities in the eyes, the man in the cowboy photographs is slimmer than the man in all of the others, and he has higher cheekbones and a more angular jawline, suggestive of Native American features (see figure 13). None of the Pullman photographs exhibit these traits, and the facial and bodily differences cannot be attributed to time if all of the portraits were staged on the same day in the same studio. Census data confirms that Love resided in Denver in 1890, lived in Salt Lake City in 1900, and rented a home in the Los Angeles area in 1910.[19] It is unlikely that Love posed for his cowboy pictures in 1890 in Denver at the end of his career as was common for cowboys and then returned to Denver from Los Angeles later in his life to take the other photographs for the book. So, then, why wouldn't Love have posed in his own cowboy photograph? Analyzing the photograph could provide some insight on the presence of the "double" and insight about the freedom of choice Love exercises in the staging of the photographs, and more generally in his self-construction.

This cowboy photograph, "In My Fighting Clothes," is nearly identical to another one in which the figure holds a lariat rather than a rifle.

In My Fighting Clothes

Figure 13 **"In My Fighting Clothes."** Used with Permission of Documenting the American South, The University of North Carolina at Chapel Hill Libraries.

Like Edward Wheeler's Deadwood Dick, Love wears a shoulder-length wig with loose curls and bangs across his forehead, the only difference being that his wig is not blond. He is in full cowboy gear, with his saddle at his feet. This double with his black wig, high cheekbones, and angular jawline suggests a racial hybridity, a man who cannot be defined solely by blackness. He is brown, but his hair in particular creates a racial hybridity that disrupts the whiteness of Wheeler's character at the same time that it troubles how we define blackness. It is in the cowboy section of his autobiography that we learn not only that Love is engaged to a Mexican woman, but that he also speaks Spanish, further accentuating Love's interest in transcending rigid racial categorization in the West. Love ultimately embraced the "make your own self" ideologies that prevailed in the Dakota territories in 1876 when he claims to have won the roping contest, signified by the lariat lying on the floor in the photograph.

As with every element of his narrative, Love was strategic with his selection and costuming of what may have been his double. Twelve chapters of *The Life and Adventures* are dedicated to Love's life on the range, a life that suggests decreased circumscription from racism and jim crow law. Although Love never acknowledges that the frontier myth was indeed a myth, his inclusion of the cowboy photographs suggests that Love was all too aware of the failures of the frontier as a space of racial equality. Instead, he offers an idyllic image of the West: wherein blackness is not erased, the whiteness of Wheeler's Deadwood Dick disappears, and readers are confronted with the image of what may be a racially hybrid imposter who not only imposes on Love's narrative but inserts himself into the racial politics of the nation at the turn of the twentieth century.

The cowboy photographs deviate from the middle-class respectability illustrated in the frontispiece family photograph, the auspices of success the "race men" faithfully advanced. Love represents his life as a cowboy as wild, unruly, and lawless. He admits, "It was not an uncommon occurrence for us to have shooting trouble over our different brands. In such disputes the boys would kill each other if others did not interfere in time to prevent it, because in those days on the great cattle ranges there was no law but the law of might, and all disputes were settled with a forty-five Colt pistol." The cowboy chapters are circumscribed by similar "wild and wooly" exploits, laced with heavy hyperbole, including "the marks of fourteen bullet wounds on different parts of my body, most any one of which would be sufficient to kill an ordinary man, but I am not even crippled."[20]

These acts of participating in and surviving violent aggression do not necessarily present a contradiction to Love's middle-class image of the frontispiece. It makes sense that Love did not meet middle-class decorum while a cowboy. Life on the frontier provided Love the opportunity to be part of what Marlon B. Ross identifies as a New Negro promoter who wrote "highly personalized narratives [. . .] to reshape the collective identity of the race." The frontier, then, provided Love and others the space "to boast their individual hand-to-hand duels in overcoming the enemy known as Jim Crow."[21] The myth of the West, however, may have proven a myth in Love's case, and he surrendered the cowboy identity for the most respectable occupation available, that of the Pullman porter. Love concedes, "It was with genuine regret that I left the long horn Texas cattle and the wild mustangs of the range, but the life had in a great measure lost its attractions and so I decided to quit it and try something else for a while."[22] Love's decision exemplifies my argument about agency— "I decided to quit"—demonstrates a claim to ownership of his personhood and speaks to his freedom of choice. Love owns himself and he sees himself as an agent of change, adapting and moving on.

Pullman Porters: Mobility and Servility

Love traded the West, a geography of autonomous physical, "natural" masculinity, for viewing the national landscape through the windows of George M. Pullman's train cars. Despite Love's commitment, on the one hand, to the highest and most loyal servitude to his white passengers, he is unable to cover up the fact that the Pullman Company ultimately developed a new form of servitude with its low wages and the demeaning and patronizing nature of the porters' work. On the other hand, based on his autobiographical account, Love manipulated the system to the best of his ability in order to make it fill his needs.

His photographs as a Pullman porter and his final photograph as a courier grant him middle-class status and respectability and, apparently very importantly for Love, being a porter grants him a valuable freedom of mobility. Love recounts, "During my service with the Pullman company I have traveled from the Atlantic to the Pacific and from the Gulf of Mexico to the borders of Canada, over nearly all the many different lines of railroad." He continues, "I have visited all the principal cities and towns where the sound of the bell and the whistle is heard, and I have in a great measure satisfied my desire to see the country."[23] However problematically, the costume of porter provided Love with very real protection as he traveled through regions of a nation where lynching might vary in frequency, but always presented a threat. That Love declared that he felt at home and would ultimately make a home in the United States is noteworthy for a black man at the turn of the twentieth century.

While many readers and scholars read Love as a cowboy who wanted to escape race, or at best as a black man who embraced Washington's assimilationist and accommodationist rhetoric, a significant part of history would be lost in doing so. Love's approach to constructing a livable black masculinity has much to offer our understanding, particularly in his Pullman porter and courier photographs. Gaines asserts that it was the lot of Pullman porters "to pass their knowledge, ideals, and ambitions on to their children."[24] Based upon their absence in census records, Love's children may have been imaginative constructions, so he passes on his knowledge, ideals, and ambition to the reader, black or white, instead. The first Pullman photograph presents Love in his uniform, holding a pose reflecting a dignified pride with the caption, "My First Experience as a Pullman Porter" (see figure 14). In the next photograph, Love is once again exhibiting an air of pride, but this time with the added air of prestige and accomplishment. He is holding a fan in one hand and the coat sleeve of his opposite arm bears three stripes, marking his longevity as a porter, as well as his superb performance. The caption reinforces the image: "This is Where I Shine. Now I am Out for the Money" (see figure 15). The third Pullman photograph (see figure 16) has the caption "The Close of My Railroad Career." In this photograph we see Love in uniform with his hat tilted to the side, his arms crossed across his chest, and a look of satisfaction and refinement on his face. We see a similar aura in Love's pose in his courier uniform with the caption that simply reads, "With the General Securities Company." These poses can be interpreted through Gaines's more nominal definition of the goal and purpose of racial uplift ideology: "Generally, black elites claimed class distinctions, indeed, the very existence of a 'better class' of blacks, as evidence of what they called race progress. Believing that the improvement of African Americans' material and moral condition through self-help would diminish white racism, they sought to rehabilitate the race's image by embodying respectability, enacted through an ethos of service to the masses."[25] Love seemed to be convinced that his service to the white patrons on the train was indeed service to the racial collectivity. He uplifts the race by embodying respectability.

My First Experience as a Pullman Porter

Figure 14 **"My First Experience as a Pullman Porter."** Given the cost of staging photographs in the early twentieth century, Love likely would have had the studio photographs for the book, including this one, taken together. However, the men in the photos implied to be the same man do not resemble one another closely. Used with Permission of Documenting the American South, The University of North Carolina at Chapel Hill Libraries.

This is Where I Shine. Now I am Out for the Money

Figure 15 **"This is Where I Shine. Now I am Out for the Money."** Love trades the buckskin jacket of a cowboy for the buttoned coat of a porter. Used with Permission of Documenting the American South, The University of North Carolina at Chapel Hill Libraries.

The Close of My Railroad Career

Figure 16 **"The Close of My Railroad Career."** A self-satisfied, self-made man enjoys the fruits of his labors. Used with Permission of Documenting the American South. The University of North Carolina at Chapel Hill Libraries.

Love mirrors Booker T. Washington's racial uplift in the many ways that scholars have noted, but there are several pertinent ways in which he also reflects Du Bois's racial uplift strategies, particularly in his self-presentation. Shawn Michelle Smith's *Photography on the Color Line* and Hazel Carby's *Race Men* offer compelling analyses of Du Bois's visual rhetoric that can be applied productively to Love's rhetorical appeals to his white audience. Analyzing the Georgia Negro albums that Du Bois exhibited at the 1900 Paris Exposition, Smith argues that Du Bois compiles a photographic collection that "anchors his antiracist critique in a patriarchal model of an African American elite, envisioning a restrained and disciplined manhood figured in the discourses enabling lynching at the turn of the century."[26] One impetus for lynching and stripping black men of masculinity, and thus citizenship, was the nation's anxiety about a loss of national (white) manhood during the Progressive Era.[27] Racial uplift ideals were therefore directed at whites with just as much, if not more, fervor as they were directed at blacks. Instead of directing their appeals to sympathetic Northern whites comprising the slave narrators' audience, post-Reconstruction uplift rhetoric targeted unsympathetic whites.

By targeting this group, Gaines argues, "Elite blacks believed they were replacing the racist notion of fixed biological racial differences with an evolutionary view of cultural assimilation, measured primarily by the status of the family and civilization."[28] Love recognized the importance of these manly and refined poses, as well as the family photograph that meets the reader's eye on the first page of the narrative. Through his appropriation of the middle-class values reserved for white Americans, Love—like Du Bois—"reject[s] the whitewash of normative middle-class archives, claiming a space for African Americans within the middle classes."[29] Du Bois's albums and Love's photographs share the understanding of how the public gaze can be redirected, how the object of the gaze has some agency in determining how a person and perhaps a race are seen, as illustrated in figure 16.

Love's intended audience was not just white Americans, as he demonstrated a high investment in his black audience as well. For blacks, Love's photographs represent the possibility of a complex racial citizenship beyond the performance of career inherent in Love's occupations and photographs. This investment is evident in all of the photographs. Just as Hazel Carby argues that Du Bois "quite deliberately uses his own body as the site for an exposition of the qualities of black manhood,"[30] Love also asks his audience to recognize his body as evidence of defeating jim crow. The machismo of the cowboy photographs and the middle-class respectability of the family photograph, the Pullman photographs, and the courier photograph represent this effort.

Another photograph of Love's autobiography implies both machismo and middle-class respectability, combining two tropes of masculinity that are often incongruent. The penultimate photograph in the narrative is presumably of Love—it is hard to distinguish any detailed features— standing in front of a train with four white friends (see figure 17). The caption reads, "With Wm. Blood, My Old Cowboy Friend, and Other Friends at the Close of My Railroad Career." Arguably, this photograph conjures images of Washington's collusion with and efforts to appease whites, though not all interracial activity necessarily meant appeasement. More importantly, the image inserts Love's black body into a significant masculine space and history. In *Dixie Limited: Railroads, Culture, and the Southern Renaissance,* Joseph R. Millichamp points out that on the one hand, for white writers of William Faulkner's generation, "The newly important rail network represented the reconciliation, prosperity, and sophistication necessary for a Southern literary flowering." On the other hand, however, "African American writers from the days of the Underground Railroad through the great migration of the twentieth century saw the trains of the South as ambivalently situated symbols of both escape and entrapment."[31] The railroad tracks often were laid with the contract labor of largely black convicts, sometimes resulting in their deaths, and the trains were generally segregated, but trains also symbolized virility, entitlement, and progress. The five men standing in front of the train are dwarfed by its size. By appropriating the strength, technology, and mobility the railroad represents, Love establishes his own black masculinity, and it secures his citizenship by giving him wide access to the national landscape.

ALAS, THE TALES photographs tell are not always true. The pride of service that Love exhibits through his poses and narrative were surely at conflict with the demeaning nature of porters' work as servants to white clientele. In spite of presenting his experience otherwise, Love was not exempt from the inequities of Pullman's service. Many of the discharge records reveal that porters were employed for relatively short periods, and anywhere from less than one year to two or three years was the average, with occasional records showing six or seven years of service. Love was one of the earliest and longest serving porters, with fifteen years of

With Wm. Blood, My Old Cowboy Friend, and Other Friends at the Close of My Railroad Career

Figure 17 **Among Friends.** Nat Love stands before a train with friends and coworkers from his life in the West and his career as a porter. Used with Permission of Documenting the American South, The University of North Carolina at Chapel Hill Libraries.

service.[32] Love's discharge record reveals that he resigned October 17, 1906, with the notation that he "resigned not to be re-employed." The commentary under "cause" states, "The manner in which he absented himself from duty at Los Angeles on several occasions."[33] Absenteeism might be viewed as a reasonable cause to note that an employee ought not to be rehired; however, upon a review of the larger Porters' Discharge Records, as well as Employee Service Records for ("colored") porters and Chinese employees, a clear pattern emerges. African American and Chinese employees receive consistent negative notations in their records that are largely disproportionate to any negative notations in the records of their white coworkers. Similarly, his service record reveals that his salary was garnished several times and he was suspended for five- and ten-day periods on seven different occasions from September 15, 1902, to June 18, 1906, for "poor service," "not reporting for run," and a complaint in relationship to the buffet and lost property.

These infractions all occurred in the last four years of Love's service, and they easily could be attributed to Love losing interest in the job or his tiring of the demeaning servitude, but such an explanation would overlook the fact that a review of the Newberry Library's archive of Pullman Porters' Discharge Records reveal that porters' were routinely discharged for minor and arbitrary infractions. Love's long record of infractions and far longer record of service actually affirm his presentation of himself as a hardworking and conscientious employee, because he must have been to have worked for Pullman for fifteen years, more than twice as long as some of the longest employed porters. His citizenship and access to the national landscape, then, is indebted to Washington's urge that black men and women labor under the circumstances in which they found themselves. However, as Love's careers as cowboy and porter indicate, black men could determine the circumstances under which they chose to stop laboring. He could accommodate as long as necessary, and when that no longer works, he "*decided* to quit it and try something else for a while."[34]

Notes

1. Richard Majors and Janet Mancini Bilson, *Cool Pose: The Dilemmas of Black Manhood in America* (New York: Simon & Schuster, 1992).

2. For racial authenticity, see Blake Allmendinger, "Deadwood Dick: The Black Cowboy as Cultural Timber," *Journal of American Culture* 16:4 (1993): 79–89; Georgina Dodge, "Claiming Narrative, Disclaiming Race: Negotiating Black Masculinity in *The*

Life and Adventures of Nat Love," *a/b: Auto/Biography Studies* 16:1 (2001): 109–26; Kenneth Speirs, "Writing Self (Effacingly): E-Raced Presences in *The Life and Adventures of Nat Love,*" *Western Literature Association* 40:3 (2005): 301–20. For Booker T. Washington parallels, see Michael K. Johnson, *Black Masculinity and the Frontier Myth in American Literature* (Norman: University of Oklahoma Press, 2002); Susan Scheckel, "Home on the Train: Race and Mobility in *The Life and Adventures of Nat Love,*" *American Literature* 74:2 (2002): 219–50.

3. Robert Reid-Pharr, *Once You Go Black: Choice, Desire, and the Black American Intellectual* (New York: New York University Press, 2007), 7.

4. The 1910 Census lists Love as renting a home in Malibu, California.

5. Department of Commerce, Bureau of the Census. *Fourteenth Census of the United States: 1920—Population*. Census Place: Precinct 23, Santa Monica, CA. Although Love did not own a home at the time of publication, he did exhibit an investment in raising the funds to purchase the land for what he called "The Porters' Home," a "Home and Hospital, with adjoining farming land, for the benefit of old and disabled porters who were not able to perform their duties as Pullman car porters." According to Love, he actually proposed this idea to George Pullman in 1893, and Pullman signed a statement promising that if the porters succeeded at buying one thousand acres of land, he would erect the building on it. Presuming such a conversation took place, it seems likely that Pullman knew that the funds would never be raised for such a venture. The persistence with which Love pursued this endeavor, however, is significant, not only because it reflects the Washingtonian principle of property ownership, but also because it positions Love in the same field of activism as A. Philip Randolph, who would organize The Brotherhood of Sleeping Car Porters.

6. Zellmer Roswell Pettet and Charles Edward Hall, *Negroes in the United States, 1920–32* (Washington, DC: U.S. Government Printing Office, 1935).

7. Cheryl Harris, "Whiteness as Property," *Harvard Law Review* 106:8 (1993): 170–91.

8. Shawn Michelle Smith, *Photography on the Color Line: W. E. B. Du Bois, Race, and Visual Culture* (Durham, NC: Duke University Press, 2004), 10.

9. Kevin K. Gaines, *Uplifting the Race: Black Leadership, Politics, and Culture in the Twentieth Century* (Chapel Hill: University of North Carolina Press, 1996), 12.

10. Speirs also makes this assertion, but he does not make a distinction between the first Pullman photograph and the others, and he does not consider any of the photographs suspicious ("Writing Self (Effacingly))," 301–20).

11. *1870 United States Federal Census* (Provo, UT: The Generations Network, Inc., 2003) , accessed 20 November 2010, http://ancestry.com.

12. *Twelfth Census of the United States*. Year: 1900; Census Place: Salt Lake City, UT. Nat and Alice got married August 22, 1889, in Denver, Colorado, and they lived there until at least 1895, according to a Denver telephone directory.

13. Department of Commerce, Bureau of the Census. *Thirteenth Census of the United States: 1910—Population*. Census Place: Precinct 2, Malibu, CA.

14. Speirs offers an analysis of Love's staging of the photographs in which he argues that the pictorial images challenge readers to "move beyond assumptions that the story of his life is unraced" ("Writing Self (Effacingly))," 316). Speirs does not, however, offer a nuanced analysis of the photographs.

15. Nat Love, *The Life and Adventures of Nat Love* (Lincoln: University of Nebraska Press, 1995), 97.

16. Scheckel, "Home on the Train," 230.

17. Ibid.

18. Gail Bederman, *Manliness and Civilization: A Cultural History of Gender and Race in the United State, 1880–1917* (Chicago: University of Chicago Press, 1995), 185–86.

19. There is an eight-year gap in Love's narrative between the date of the last cowboy event in 1881 and when he leaves the range in 1890. The 1885 Kansas Census for Edwards County lists a Mahala Love, who may have been Love's mother, living with an N.A. Love, three other adults, and five children in Edwardsville County in 1885. "N.A." Love is the same age as Love.

20. Love, *The Life and Adventures of Nat Love,* 51.

21. Marlon B. Ross, *Manning the Race: Reforming Black Men in the Jim Crow Era* (New York: New York University Press, 2004), 90.

22. Love, *The Life and Adventures of Nat Love,* 130.

23. Ibid., 138.

24. Gaines, *Uplifting the Race,* 101.

25. Ibid., xiv.

26. Smith, *Photography on the Color Line,* 23.

27. Bederman, *Manliness and Civilization,* 185.

28. Gaines, *Uplifting the Race,* 4.

29. Smith, *Photography on the Color Line,* 4.

30. Hazel Carby, *Race Men: The W. E. B. Du Bois Lectures* (Cambridge, MA: Harvard University Press, 1998), 36.

31. Joseph R. Millichamp, *Dixie Limited: Railroads, Culture, and the Southern Renaissance* (Lexington: University Press of Kentucky, 2002), 12, 20.

32. In the Discharge Record volume that I examined, I did not come across anyone else employed for as long as Love was, though some of the entries are difficult to read.

33. The Newberry Library Pullman Company Archives, *Porters' Discharge Record,* vol. 1.

34. Love, *The Life and Adventures of Nat Love,* 130; emphasis added.

8

Cowboys, Porters, and the Mythic West

Satire and Frontier Masculinity in The Life and Adventures of
Nat Love

CHARITY FOX

The grand mythology of the American West drew and repelled the imagination and efforts of African Americans in the post-emancipation, pre–
Harlem Renaissance era. With its promises for land and home ownership,
making a "fresh start," and escaping strident and oppressive social conventions, the mythic American West seemed like a preferable alternative
to enduring the hierarchical tensions of the South or the moral risks of
the urban North. Prominent writers and race leaders like Ida B. Wells
and Booker T. Washington included westward expansion and small farming, respectively, as part of their projects for racial uplift, encouraging
African Americans to take advantage of relatively relaxed social rules,
less stringent segregation, and a popular sense of the West as a crucible
of opportunity. Easier transportation and the potential for large tracts
of land available through the Homestead Act blended with race leaders'
exhortations to trade the entrenched problems of the North and South
for a rugged, independent existence in the West. The promise of property ownership and pursuing equalizing opportunity left unfulfilled by
the failures of Reconstruction encouraged African Americans to consider moving west. However, opportunities at the frontier were mediated

by systematic institutional and economic barriers during what Rayford Logan termed the "nadir" of race relations in the United States, as the social and political gains blacks made during Reconstruction were rolled back.[1] Additionally, the fear of a "closing" frontier, as articulated in Frederick Jackson Turner's 1893 frontier thesis, encouraged those in control politically and socially to hold more tightly onto the suddenly scarce resources and opportunities of the West.

Though blacks are often left out of the romantic mythology of the frontier, many more African Americans moved west to work and homestead than popular representations and memories would indicate, and the most obvious blind spot occurs in the ethnic identities of the national icon of the cowboy. The figure of the cowboy was not an automatically beloved and heroic one in the 1800s, when a "cowboy" often presumed an uneducated and socially inept figure in middle- to high-brow literature.[2] However, this tide turned in the early 1900s, as the cowboy genre transformed into a nostalgic synecdoche for the country in heroic fictional portrayals in film, dime novels, and other popular culture—all of which proved distant from much of the actual work of the cowboy. Black cowboys have largely been absent from these popular representations of the American West; instead, the cowboy narrative of the Western genre usually represents white masculinity. Like many racial and ethnic groups disadvantaged at the turn of the twentieth century and ignored in much of the popular culture products of the time, African Americans could find greater social and economic mobility in the West for a time. Between the closing of the frontier and rise of increasing industrialization, possibilities existed for economic needs to trump racist values and foster at least some type of equality in the American West—as exemplified in the career of Nat Love.

In Nat Love's 1907 memoir *The Life and Adventures of Nat Love,* he claims to be the real-life inspiration for Deadwood Dick, a popular cowboy character in nearly one hundred dime novels published in the late nineteenth century. Love's autobiography details his path from slavery to the highest-regarded ranch hand and brand reader in the West. As the West "closed" in the early 1890s, Love took a position as a porter with the Pullman Company. In leaving his life as a cowboy to work as a Pullman porter, Love simultaneously gained a wife, a family, financial success, and quite a degree of middle-class respectability, as visually displayed through the photographs he includes in his memoir. Critical reception of Love's narrative varies greatly; some scholars of African American history include him in historical contexts as an "actual cowboy," while others have difficulty merging his dime-Western braggadocio into accepted canons of traditional African American writing. Whether one accepts Love's autobiography as factual (if exaggerated) or as complete fiction, his rocky transition from the ranch to becoming a Pullman porter often is ignored, an omission that causes readers to miss Love's larger purposes in writing. Reading Love's autobiography as satirical social commentary rather than parsing its veracity illuminates racial attitudes surrounding the American West, black masculinity, and economic opportunity in the late nineteenth and early twentieth centuries.

Closing the Frontier, Creating Western Mythology

In delivering his essay "The Significance of the Frontier in American History" at the 1893 American Historical Association, in conjunction with the 1893 Chicago World's Fair, Turner shaped a new and persistent way of thinking about America's history.[3] Though this thesis became synonymous with the idea of "the closing of the frontier," the majority of his argument focused on the role of expansion and mobility in shaping American history. For Turner, "The West" represented the continually shifting borderland between civilization and savagery. Turner envisioned the spread of "civilization" (or Western/European models of society) as occurring in waves, with each wave (pioneers, settlers, capitalists, etc.) building on the preceding groups' work to perfect the civilizing of the frontier. As civilization caught up with those fleeing it, the "frontier" moved west in another wave of conquest.[4] Turner's conceptualization of the frontier became an early argument for American exceptionalism. In situating the frontier as a wide-open, democratically available space, Turner suggests that discontented citizens who might otherwise become revolutionary have historically self-segregated by leaving and moving to the frontier rather than rebelling against constraining social order. Turner argues that surviving without the comforts—and implicitly, the constraints—of civilization created a distinctly different element in American society when compared to its European beginnings.

The difficult conditions of the frontier acted as a crucible that forged strong, self-reliant Americans out of overly civilized Europeans.[5] In the midst of claiming that a chapter was closing in American history, Turner uses the very language of the mythic West to lament its passing: "[I]n spite of environment, and in spite of custom, each frontier did indeed furnish a new field of opportunity, a gate of escape from the bondage of the past."[6]

His mythic rhetoric of escape and opportunity is similar to the rhetoric of abolition, emancipation, and early Reconstruction that contemporary race leaders like Ida B. Wells and Booker T. Washington incorporated into their writing encouraging African Americans to move west and pursue agricultural endeavors. However, Turner uses these phrases to claim that the frontier is full—there is no more room to continue this path of American expansion. Turner also revises the way that frontiersmen were seen. No longer scruffy miscreants unfit for civilized life, Turner makes the pioneers an all-important first step in conquest and expansion. He links Western pioneers to the revered white initial pilgrims, striking out to create new, specifically American ways of life. These rhetorical links imply that the pioneers were also white and also ideologically motivated to create a new Americanism in the course of taming the wild. By using the same rhetorical constructions of race leaders and arguing that this "period of American history" has closed, Turner's thesis can be read as implicitly simultaneously "closing" the promises of Reconstruction and the frontier as a space of opportunity for blacks. Where Wells and Washington were encouraging blacks to apply for Homestead Act grants to get their own "fields of opportunity," Turner was relegating those opportunities to the past as part of an increasingly mythic West that, in the eyes of his white audience at the World's Fair, no longer existed.

Economically Based Tolerance

Contrary to romantic attributions in American rhetoric of a social climate of Westerners' "natural" acceptance of other hardy and like-minded folks, C. Robert Haywood sees economic interdependence as a primary factor in creating the perception of the West as a land of opportunity. In his essay, "'No less a man': Blacks in Cow Town Dodge City, 1876–1886" (2001), C. Robert Haywood studies the newspaper records from notorious cow town Dodge City, Kansas, and concluded that the mythology of greater freedom, relaxed social rules, and less segregation in the West do in fact carry some historical weight.[7] However, Haywood attributes these social qualities to a tight job market and an even more tightly woven economic system, not to some social utopian cause for the level of acceptance and tolerance of racial differences. To keep the economic system profitable in areas with few potential workers, employers and employees alike literally could not afford to apply rules of segregation and racialized division of labor with the same stringency as in areas with a larger labor supply. The implication of Haywood's argument is that social and economic mixing among American racial groups in the West was acceptable when capitalist ventures were at stake; this economic tolerance was a by-product of the need to work together to achieve common economic goals, rather than a situation created by an ideology of the frontier.

Though later romanticized as the epitome of individual masculinity, the job that the cowboy performed was dictated primarily by the economic needs and to the advantage of cattle ranchers. Unlike government-registered homesteaders, whose grant of 160 acres would provide but a paltry start in the livestock industry, cattle ranchers required enormous plots of grazing land, sometimes utilizing unclaimed, publicly owned, or disputed land to feed their cattle. Until the close of the nineteenth century, when barbed wire technology finally became a cost-efficient fencing option, the cost of fencing in these large plots of land was astronomical.[8] Instead, ranchers relied on cowboys to act as a sort of human fence, keeping cattle in designated places, preventing herds from mixing, and protecting the cattle (and the rancher) from cattle rustlers and the massive economic losses they caused. This role as a mobile human fence shifted to one of a cowboy-enclosed mobile pasture when it came time to drive the cattle to railroad hubs. The thousands of head of cattle owned by large-scale ranchers required quite a number of cowboy fence posts; ranchers were economically dependent on hiring a large number of ranch hands, and hired blacks, whites, and Mexicans to perform these jobs. "Whites in the ranching business realized the importance of the contributions of all cowboys—black, white, or Mexican—and adjusted their prejudices accordingly."[9] As long as the economic fortunes of the ranchers and large landowners depended on retaining a large number of cowboy fence posts, discriminatory hiring practices were not an economically viable option.

However, invoking Turner, Haywood claims the spread of "civilization" and technology to Dodge City brought with it stricter rules for interracial interaction. The railroad's expansion lessened the need for long cattle drives to hubs hundreds of miles away, and the development of inexpensive fencing technology such as barbed wire decreased the need for a large number of ranch hands. As Haywood observes, "Once the economic impact of the trail herds was removed, these [racial and social] ambivalences were replaced by the standards and attitudes prevalent in the rest of the United States."[10] No longer economically dependent on black labor, the ranchers and the "townsfolk" of Dodge City traded their reputation for freer social interactions for more Victorian sensibilities.

Regardless of his actual duties and experiences as a human fence, the "cowboy" figure quickly became a stock character constantly romanticized in dime novels, early film, and other popular entertainment venues. Rather than focus on the mundane actions of working as a human fence, those who popularized the genre presented a solitary white cowboy as a combination of skilled gunman, brave unofficial soldier, and rugged masculine loner who avoids the stifling confines of over-civilization by women and their cult of domesticity. As the twentieth century progressed, the cowboy genre took on new importance as an iconic American figure in the ideologically charged climate of the Cold War, where the cowboy's character was often pictured as one of moral certainty in the face of terrible odds. Though the image of the cowboy has evolved somewhat, especially in the sense of a growing moral ambiguity in post-Vietnam Westerns, these qualities persist throughout the Western genre in its many incarnations.

Nat Love: From "Deadwood Dick" to "Daddy Joe"

On October 15, 1877, the publishing house Beadle and Adams published the first of what would become a long series of "Deadwood Dick" dime novels: Edward L. Wheeler's "Deadwood Dick, The Prince of the Road; or, The Black Rider of the Black Hills."[11] Wheeler's first description of his title character sets an ominous tone but still foreshadows Deadwood Dick's later displays of princely gallantry:

> His form was clothed in a tight-fitting habit of buck-skin, which was colored a jetty black, and presented a striking contrast to anything one sees as a garment in the wild far West. And this was not all, either. A broad black hat was slouched down over his eyes; he wore a thick black vail [sic] over the upper portion of his face, through the eye-holes of which there gleamed a pair of orbs of piercing intensity, and his hands, large and knotted, were hidden in a pair of kid gloves of a light color.
>
> The "Black Rider" he might have been justly termed, for his thoroughbred steed was as black as coal, but we have not seen fit to call him such—his name is Deadwood Dick, and let that suffice for the present.[12]

Though he never actually traveled to the American West, Wheeler wrote thirty-three Deadwood Dick novels until his death in 1885, and Beadle and Adams continued the franchise through ghostwriters until 1897, producing a total of ninety-seven Deadwood Dick dime novels.[13] Thirty years after the publication of the initial novel in the series, in 1907, Nat Love published his autobiography, whose full title and subtitle set the stage and style for the rest of the work: *The Life and Adventures of Nat Love, Better Known in the Cattle Country as "Deadwood Dick" by Himself; a True History of Slavery Days, Life on the Great Cattle Ranges and on the Plains of the "Wild and Woolly" West, Based on Facts, and Personal Experiences of the Author.*[14] In detailing his ascent from slave status to Western hero to Pullman savant, Love draws on multiple narrative styles, incorporating generic conventions of slave-to-greatness narratives, dime novels, captivity narratives, and travelogue.

According to the memoir, Love's father died soon after emancipation; although he was only fifteen and the youngest member of the family, Love took over as head of the family because he "was the most courageous, always leading in mischief, play and work."[15] He found odd jobs to support the family, one of which was "breaking" horses, or transforming them from wild to domesticated, at ten cents per horse. After ensuring financial security for his mother and nieces by selling a horse he won in a raffle, and securing an uncle to act as their male protector, Love decided to leave his family in February 1869 to see the world. As he becomes a prominent cowboy, Love's narrative style climbs to the heights of "unassuming" Western braggadocio. His first foray into this new Western life is in Dodge City, Kansas, where he applies for a job as a cowboy by successfully riding a bucking horse named "Old Good Eye" and impressing the camp boss and the men.[16] His new colleagues fit him out with a horse, saddle, and a gun rig, and bestow him with the name Red River Dick as a sign of his new beginning in the West. Love's dime-novel-style cowboy adventures begin immediately, as his group becomes embroiled in the first of many gunfights with hostile Indians as they journey back to the ranch.

> When I saw them coming after us and heard their blood curdling yell, I lost all courage and thought my time had come to die. I was too badly scared to run, some of the boys told me to use my gun and shoot for all I was worth. Now I had just got my outfit and had never shot off a gun in my life, but their words brought me back to earth and seeing they were all using their guns in a way that showed they were used to it, I unlimbered my artillery and after the first shot I lost all fear and fought like a veteran.[17]

After overcoming his initially paralyzing fear, Love becomes an immediate crack shot and quickly proves an indispensable member of the
ranching community, as he claims to have become one of the top brand
readers in the West. With the lack of fencing and clear land rights, cattle
were branded with the sign of their owner. Because of the uneven nature
of healing from the branding process, the ability to "read" the brands and
place each cow in the correct herd—and money thereby in the coffers of
the owner—was a more important job qualification for a cowboy than
conventional literacy, at least from the rancher's standpoint. Love's claim
of being a top brand reader indicates his awareness of the high value of
the skill and the senior ranking accorded to those who held it, and his
claims to excellence in that regard situate him as a key player in the economic interdependence of ranchers and cowboys.

Love claims to have earned the name "Deadwood Dick" as the result
of winning a roping and shooting contest in Deadwood, South Dakota,
on July 3, 1876, in which Love claims that he "roped, threw tied, bridled,
saddled and mounted my mustang in exactly nine minutes," a horse that
proved "wild and vicious." According to Love's account, "The time of the
next nearest competitor was twelve minutes and thirty seconds. This gave
me the record and championship of the West, which I held up to the
time I quit the business in 1890, and my record has never been beaten
[. . .] Right there the assembled crowd named me Deadwood Dick and
proclaimed me champion roper of the western cattle country."[18] Though
he regularly declares the name his own, Love makes no claims about
meeting Wheeler or any of the later dime novelists who wrote about
"Deadwood Dick"; he addresses the character's fame only obliquely, as
if his legend and renown apparently had surpassed the need for personal
acquaintance with mere writers.

By the end of his time as a cowboy, Love's fantastic adventures
included, among many others: numerous gunfights with Indians, but
never any trouble with other cowboys; capture and threatened marriage
to an Indian princess; daring escapes, one of which involved riding a
horse bareback 100 miles in twelve hours; almost freezing to death in
a snowstorm; and having at least fourteen horses shot from under him
in gunfights. By 1890, however, Love claims that the open range had
become "dotted with cities and towns" and the ranchers "had to give
way to the industry of the farm and the mill." He laments, "It was with
genuine regret that I left the long horn Texas cattle and the wild mustangs of the range, but the life had in a great measure lost its attractions

and so I decided to quit it and try something else for a while."[19] That "something else" included a move to Denver, Colorado, marrying his wife Alice, who is referenced in the dedication and approximately three sentences in the entire memoir, and a brief yet significant search for meaningful employment.

Love describes his job search as including a brief tenure of a single run as a porter for the Pullman Company, one of the few middle-class jobs available to black men at the time, but his first run left him "thoroughly disgusted." He wrote, "I wanted no more of it, so I turned in my keys, got my uniform and walked out."[20] Instead, he began selling produce and chickens from a wagon in Denver, a "profitable" enterprise that he worked for a year; however, claiming he was "yearn[ing] for more excitement and something a little faster" than the fruit cart, Love again secured a job as a Pullman porter.[21] From this point on, Love's memoir becomes a fawning showcase for the wonders of the Pullman sleeping cars, Pullman's system of ownership, and handy tips for the reader about pleasing a train car full of customers all at once. At times, this section of Love's travelogue-style narrative reads like early-twentieth-century advertising copy, especially when Love expounds on the way that sightseeing through the West by railroad will "[l]et your chest swell with pride that you are an American."[22]

Love's time with the Pullman service is full of nearly the same level of fantastic "insider" stories as his time as a cowboy. Much like his dime-novel style stories of meeting Billy the Kid and Frank and Jesse James, Love includes a section called "Tips and the people who give them," which includes encounters with the Rothschilds, the Knights Templar, and his personal interactions with George Pullman.[23] Like his claims to the popularized title of "Deadwood Dick," Love's unlikely claims of Pullman greatness and celebrity encounters continue his Western braggadocio. His experiences and stories echo the tall tales told about "Daddy Joe," the name given to the unknown first Pullman porter, whose legendary ability to please customers constantly grew among Pullman porters searching for information about their antecedents.[24]

Autobiography and Social Satire

Those critics who have approached *The Life and Adventures of Nat Love* generally accept Love's categorization of his book as an autobiography; consequently, his memoirs are generally examined either for their historical validity or for their literary worth to the canon of African American literature. In *The Negro Cowboys,* Philip Durham and Everett Jones argue that the Love's story is probably false, as he is one of many to lay claim to being the "real" Deadwood Dick. While Durham and Jones concede that Love's story is an entertaining piece of fiction, they have compared the names Love uses for his employers against records of Western ranchers and cattle brands and have been unable to match the names, thus demonstrating its fictionality.[25] In contrast, historian William Loren Katz, one of the more prolific documentarians of African American experiences in the West, includes Love and his exploits as fact in his chapter on black cowboys in *The Black West*.[26] Not only does Love's book provide evidence for Katz's numerous claims of African Americans' contributions to the building of the West, but Katz also uses Love and other black cowboys to argue that historical thinking about the American West cannot be complete without recognizing the roles that African Americans in paving the way for progress and civilization and the Western frontier.[27]

On the literary side, much of the criticism of Love focuses on how his Western-genre braggadocio prevents Love's work from being associated with more traditional "African American" writing and themes. This interference is accentuated by what Michael K. Johnson terms Love's "racial erasure."[28] In his first encounter with his ranching outfit in Dodge City, Love remarks, "There were several colored cow boys among them, and good ones too."[29] Johnson points out that, after this point in the narrative, Love virtually ceases referring explicitly to his own or others' black and white racial status or characteristics among the cowboys. In fact, Johnson argues that Love becomes "one of the boys" so quickly and thoroughly that the only references he makes to racial or ethnic difference are pointed denigrations of Native Americans.

In exploring this idea of racial erasure, Johnson also reads *The Life and Adventures of Nat Love* in connection to another black Westerner's semi-autobiography, Oscar Micheaux's *The Conquest*.[30] Through his many books and films, Micheaux tells and retells the story of his time as a homesteader in the American West. Johnson juxtaposes Love's complete lack of referencing his racial identity with Micheaux's tendency to downplay the hardships caused by his race. To make sense of this, Johnson asserts Richard Slotkin's theory of recuperative violence as the framework that makes Love's racial erasure possible.[31] Using ideas of recuperation through violence, Johnson theorizes that Love's concentration on the savagery and "othered" status of Native Americans allows him to picture himself as part of the dominant racial order. In this way, the interdependence of the cowboys when pitted against Native Americans allowed Love to ignore racial boundaries that would otherwise separate him from associating with whites. This racial interdependence is similar to Haywood's sense of the importance of economic interdependence. As long as the divide was between ranchers and Native Americans, the color of those fighting on the side of the ranchers was less important than banding together to win the battle.

While Johnson's arguments about Love's text are convincing, Love's "racial erasure" within the text may actually accentuate his feats for readers who consume the *visual* rhetoric of Love's memoir along with his *textual* rhetoric. In the absence of Love making specific textual references to his or others' race, there are constant visual reminders that Love is African American; the chapters are scattered with pencil drawings that illustrate the cowboy action in Love's stories (see figure 18). The central focus in these drawings is a character whose face is so shaded and blackened that his features are obscured almost completely. In addition to the line drawings depicting action scenes, there are also photographs of Love in various posed situations, including those taken with his family, in his cowboy outfit, and during his career as a Pullman porter (see chapter 7). Analyzing only the text will support Johnson's argument for racial erasure, but when the visual aspects of the book are included in the analysis, readers are given constant visual reminders of Love's race. Even while he visually enhances his role as an African American man, the absence of textual reference to his racial status could serve instead as an argument for the absurdity of using racial categories to measure a man's worth. Instead of reading *The Life and Adventures of Nat Love* as a bragging claim to greatness based on falsehood or an anomaly in the annals of African American literature, when the style of writing, visual aspects, and time period are considered equally, it is possible to see Love's work as a social satire.

Readers often expect "truth" from something claiming to be autobiography, but reading beyond the basic claims that Love writes and incorporating the visual aspects of the text and the historical context of the text provide a much deeper understanding of the cultural work that his memoir might be performing. If, as is commonly held, history is composed of the stories we tell about the past to make meaning of the present, then autobiography can be seen as the stories that one tells about oneself to make meaning of one's place in that larger story of history. Instead of questioning the historical validity or literary quality of Love's work, when read in this light, the questions become "Why would Love's stories about himself take this particular shape? What purpose could these

The Roping Contests at Deadwood, S. D.

The Big Wild Mustang Hunt—We Were Roping and Riding Them in
Fox Canyon

Figure 18 **"The Roping Contests at Deadwood, S.D."** Used with Permission of Documenting the American South, The University of North Carolina at Chapel Hill Libraries.

stories serve?" By satirizing conventions of slave-to-greatness, dime-novel Western, and railroad narratives, Love uses the genre of autobiography to comment on the social constraints regarding African American men in the postbellum, pre-Harlem era.

The first clue that *The Life and Adventures of Nat Love* might be a social satire rests in the way that the author's writing style, in its extreme exaggerations, seems to mock the very conventions on which his genres are based. His opening paragraph echoes stylistic choices made in prominent slave-to-greatness narratives. Love's story begins:

> In an old log cabin, on my Master's plantation in Davidson County in Tennessee in June, 1854, I first saw the light of day. The exact date of my birth I never knew, because in those days no count was kept of such trival [*sic*] matters as the birth of a slave baby. They were born and died and the account was balanced in the gains and losses of the Master's chattels, and one more or less did not matter much one way or another. My father and mother were owned by Robert Love, an extensive planter and the owner of many slaves. He was in his way and in comparison with many other slave owners of those days a kind and indulgent Master.[32]

In comparison, the opening paragraph of Booker T. Washington's memoir *Up from Slavery* reads:

> I WAS born a slave on a plantation in Franklin County, Virginia. I am not quite sure of the exact place or exact date of my birth, but at any rate I suspect I must have been born somewhere and at some time. As nearly as I have been able to learn, I was born near a cross-roads post-office called Hale's Ford, and the year was 1858 or 1859. I do not know the month or the day. The earliest impressions I can now recall are of the plantation and the slave quarters—the latter being the part of the plantation where the slaves had their cabins.
>
> My life had its beginning in the midst of the most miserable, desolate, and discouraging surroundings. This was so, however, not because my owners were especially cruel, for they were not, as compared with many others.[33]

Love's opening paragraphs clearly match the introductory paragraphs of Washington's autobiography, which in turn also mirrored the construction of Frederick Douglass's opening paragraphs in his autobiographies.[34] When Love shifts from his post-slavery narrative to his Western exploits, his deadpan delivery downplays the unusual nature of his adventures even while his dime-novel style exaggerates his personal importance and danger. The sheer number and generic similarity of Love's stories about the West and his days as a Pullman porter support interpreting his autobiography as a collection of tall tales.

Additionally, Love offers all of these life stories in written form, in spite of the fact that he claims within his text to be largely illiterate. Unlike Washington's detailed description of his quest for education, Love describes the extent of his "formal" education as happening between the end of the Civil War and his father's death: "Father could read a little, and he helped us all with our A B C's, but it is hard work learning to read and write without a teacher, and there was no school a black child could attend at that time. However, we managed to make some headway, then spring came and with it the routine of farm work."[35] At the end of his memoir, when describing his decision to leave the range for Pullman, Love states, "During my life so far I had no chance to secure an education, except the education of the plains and the cattle business"; in his stories of his work as a Pullman porter, Love's schedule leaves no time in his life to attain the education or advanced writing skills be necessary to produce his memoir.[36] This contradiction between his claims of illiteracy and his production of a written and published work is never explained, adding another cue for readers to approach the memoir as a social satire. Rather than take this as evidence that invalidates Love's claims of fact over fiction, this kind of contradiction in logic suggests the same sort of kernel of truth concealed within satire.

Love's transformation from a wild cowboy to a Pullman porter renowned for his abilities is another source of constant contradiction. Love's first experience with Pullman ended with his disgust in the passengers, in the job, and with the social position required of him as a porter. However, in his later effort at the occupation, the white Superintendent Smith gives him the key to success as a porter, declaring that "the whole secret of success was in pleasing all my passengers."[37] While the job, the social situation, and the passengers did not change since Love's first trip, his economic situation had in fact changed. After his profitable yet apparently boring turn as a produce salesman, Love states that finding a different job "was about as hard to find as the proverbial needle in the straw stack, at that particular time."[38] So, in the absence of any other options, Love promises Superintendent Smith he will "do better" than he did on his previous trip as a porter, and is rewarded with "increased responsibilities as well as increased profits and favors enjoyed."[39]

The implicit source of Love's improvement in his ability to please all of his passengers is the near-clairvoyant and omnipresent nature of Superintendent Smith. Love recounts how he would begin to report positive or negative incidents, and the superintendent would already have a full grasp of the situation, causing a confusing mystery for Love. Instead of "pleasing all of his passengers" out of some intrinsic part of his nature, then, Love was continually reminded that his actions and reactions potentially were under constant surveillance by his white boss. By extension, every white passenger could then be seen as a potential special agent, which accentuates the extreme constrictions on African American mobility and action even in this more middle-class employment.[40] Explicitly recognizing this sense of omniscient white surveillance alters the way that readers approach Love's stories; the sense that Love is constantly performing for a white audience surfaces and invites the question of whether all of his stories of slavery, cowboys, and porters are merely an exaggerated, performative way of addressing his readership.

Within his text, Love discusses these constrictions on African Americans and institutional levels of control in clear but subtle ways, usually through asides not related to what plot there is to his story. In his first aside, Love relays that his family's master, upon returning from the Civil War, refused to tell the slaves that they were free, so they continued working for him for "quite a while" until hearing the news for themselves.[41] This aside takes up a very short paragraph but acts as a very unpleasant personal reminder that the Emancipation Proclamation did not mean instant freedom and equality for African Americans. However, Love's clearest social-commentary asides are much more powerful. On at least two occasions, he shifts unexpectedly from his matter-of-fact braggadocio to a bitter and forceful tirade: one against the institution of slavery and the torture of blacks, and one against trusts and corporations.[42] In the first, Love details brutal whippings of men, women, and children because of the social status accorded them by the chance of their birth. Though ostensibly discussing the institutions of slavery, his description of lynching, whipping, destroyed families, and prohibiting education for blacks also can apply to the dangers facing blacks in the post-Reconstruction era. After this discussion, Love recommends that readers see the play *Uncle Tom's Cabin* to "see the black man's life as I saw when a child."[43]

BY EMPHASIZING need to "see" the play—rather than encouraging his readers to read the book—Love emphasizes the importance of visual as well as textual representation. If we read between the lines of his text, then, we should also read between the lines of his pictures. Love's photograph from his "cowboy days" stages a particular robust masculinity championed by no less than President Theodore Roosevelt at the turn of the twentieth century as a way of recapturing strong manhood at a time when the perceived weakness of urban work softened American men. However, while Love poses in stereotypical "Western" gear, he remains clearly in a photography studio (see figures 12 and 13 in chapter 7). The impressionistic painted background and props of saddle and rope serve to remove the ruggedness of an outdoor, Western context, while emphasizing the romantic nature of the life of a cowboy. Still, while middle-class white men's masculinity might be challenged by the lack of physicality in urbane work, its economic security presented an attractive aspiration for many black men. Success in such occupations did not necessarily erode black men's manhood but consolidated it in providing for a family guarded against want. Opposite the title page for *The Life and Adventures of Nat Love* is a picture of Love and his family, apparently consisting of his wife and daughter (see figure 11 in chapter 7). While working as a Pullman porter is considered by scholars and historians to have been a job providing entrance into a black middle class, in this photo Love and his family can be read as visually and physically representing themselves as upper-middle to upper class. The women's style of dress, especially the hats, gloves, and fur wrap, indicates their respectability and wealth. Additionally, Love's three-piece suit and tie also indicate more than middle-class status.

Taken together, these visual representations not only accentuate Love's racial identity in contrast to his textual erasure of race; they also accentuate the layers of performativity that visual representations can provide to textual representations, the degree to which images can confront viewers with contradictions and differences elided in text. Reading between the lines of Love's visual and textual rhetorics illuminates ways that his stories address social constrictions that assign ability, facticity, and class and physical mobility based on racial categories. With the inclusion of his visual texts as the main racial identifiers, Love implicitly argues through his claims to Deadwood Dick fame that a black man can perform all of the physical feats that a white man can—and can even perform them in a superior way. Even as he accommodates himself to the subordinate social position of Pullman porter in the written text, Love's visual representations of himself and his family argue for the economic abilities and representations of blacks, even within the strictures of socially assigned, race-based constrictions.

Love's satirized tall tales capture an essence of early-twentieth-century idealized masculinity; regardless of his race, his cowboy and porter tales create a man of mythic proportions. However, his reader, if reading astutely, is constantly reminded of the precarious positions that a black man often occupied in this time period. No matter how well liked he had been on the range or on the rails, Love had to continue to be of economic advantage to his employers in order to retain economic and social stability. On the range, lax and open racial rules were dependent on economic interdependence and banding together against the threat of battle with Native Americans. On the rails with Pullman, Love's acceptance and continued employment depended on pleasing all of his passengers all of the time, under constant and oppressive surveillance from his white supervisor. In *The Life and Adventures of Nat Love,* Love's primary message is that he constantly needed to prove his worth and indispensability within a multitude of complex economic and social systems, sacrificing his own principles and job preferences, in order to rise out of poverty, attain some form of personal freedom, and create and maintain a family that qualified as middle class.

Notes

1. Rayford Whittingham Logan, *The Betrayal of the Negro, from Rutherford B. Hayes to Woodrow Wilson* (New York: Da Capo Press, 1997).

2. Both sides of this "cowboy figure" can be seen in the main character Robert Clay, a "cowboy" who is actually a surprisingly well-educated civil engineer. Richard Harding Davis, *Soldiers of Fortune* (New York: Charles Scribner's Sons, 1897), accessed 21 November 2010, http://www.archive.org/details/soldiersfortune06davigoog.

3. Frederick Jackson Turner, "The Significance of the Frontier in American History," in *The Frontier in American History* (New York: Henry Holt, 1920), accessed 21 November 2010, http://www.archive.org/details/frontierinameric010200mbp.

4. Ibid., 19–22.

5. Ibid., 3–4.

6. Ibid., 38.

7. C. Robert Haywood, "'No less a man': Blacks in Cow Town Dodge City, 1876–1886," in *Racial Encounters in the Multi-Cultural West,* Gordon Morris Bakken and Brenda Farrington, eds. (New York: Garland, 2001), 235–57.

8. Earl W. Hayter, "Barbed Wire Fencing: A Prairie Invention: Its Rise and Influence in the Western States," *Agricultural History* 13:4 (October 1939): 189–207.

9. Haywood, "'No less a man,'" 235.

10. Ibid., 236.

11. Philip Durham and Everett L Jones, *The Negro Cowboys* (Lincoln: University of Nebraska Press, 1983), 189.

12. Edward L. Wheeler, "Deadwood Dick, The Prince of the Road; or, The Black Rider of the Black Hills," *Beadle's Half Dime Library* (1877), chapter 2, accessed 21 November 2010, http://www.gutenberg.org/ebooks/14902 .

13. Durham and Jones, *The Negro Cowboys,* 190.

14. Nat Love, *The Life and Adventures of Nat Love, Better Known in the Cattle Country as "Deadwood Dick"* (Los Angeles, CA: Wayside Press, 1907), accessed 21 November 2010, http://docsouth.unc.edu/neh/natlove/natlove.html.

15. Ibid., 21.

16. Ibid., 41.

17. Ibid., 42.

18. Ibid., 93.

19. Ibid., 130.

20. Ibid., 132.

21. Ibid.

22. Ibid., 142. Variations of this phrase repeat regularly throughout chapter 20.

23. Ibid., chapters 18 and 21.

24. For more information about Daddy Joe, see Larry Tye, *Rising from the Rails: Pullman Porters and the Making of the Black Middle Class* (New York: Henry Holt, 2004). Tye's research, based on numerous interviews and oral histories with former Pullman porters, uncovered legends about this first Pullman porter, whose name was ostensibly lost in a fire, that ranks Daddy Joe at a mythological level nearly equal to that of Paul Bunyan or Hercules.

25. Durham and Jones, *The Negro Cowboys,* chapter 12.

26. William Loren Katz, *The Black West: A Documentary and Pictorial History of the African American Role in the Westward Expansion of the United States* (New York: Doubleday, 2005), chapter 6; also see Katz's Introduction, *The Life and Adventures of Nat Love, Better Known in the Cattle Country as "Deadwood Dick"* by Nat Love (Lincoln: University of Nebraska Press, 1995); Katz, *The Black West,* 150–52.

27. Katz, *The Black West,* chapter 7.

28. Michael K. Johnson, *Black Masculinity and the Frontier Myth in American Literature* (Norman: University of Oklahoma Press, 2002), chapter 3.

29. Love, *The Life and Adventures of Nat Love,* 41

30. Oscar Micheaux, *The Conquest: The Story of a Negro Pioneer* (Lincoln, NE: The Woodruff Press, 1913), accessed 21 November 2010, http://www.archive.org/details/conqueststoryofn00michrich.

31. Richard Slotkin, *Regeneration through Violence: The Mythology of the American Frontier, 1600–1860* (Middletown, CT: Wesleyan University Press, 1973).

32. Love, *The Life and Adventures of Nat Love,* 7.

33. Booker T. Washington, *Up from Slavery* (New York: Doubleday, 1901), 1, accessed 21 November 2010, http://www.bartleby.com/1004/.

34. Frederick Douglass, *Narrative of the Life of Frederick Douglass, an American Slave* (Boston, MA: Anti-Slavery Office, 1847), accessed 21 November 2010, http://www.archive.org/details/douglasfred00dougrich.

35. Love, *The Life and Adventures of Nat Love,* 18.

36. Ibid., 130.

37. Ibid., 133.

38. Ibid.
39. Ibid., 134.
40. Ibid.
41. Ibid., 16–17.
42. Ibid., 11–13, 156.
43. Ibid., 13.

9

From Haiti to Harpers Ferry

The Insurrectionary Tradition in American Literature

COLLEEN C. O'BRIEN

> The mystic spell of Africa is and ever was over all America. It has guided her hardest work, inspired her finest literature, and sung her sweetest songs. Her greatest destiny—unsensed and despised though it be,—is to give back to the first of continents the gifts which Africa of old gave to America's fathers' fathers.
>
> —W. E. B. Du Bois

The opening lines of W. E. B. Du Bois's 1909 biography *John Brown* make a remarkable argument for America's potential to be cosmopolitan—to achieve an intellectual stance of openness to the world, to Africa in particular. These lines are even more remarkable because they reverse the trajectory of "civilizing" influence that the Progressive Party in the United States assumed in its own assimilationist, Eurocentric, and "enlightened" definition of cosmopolitanism. By referring to "her" qualities no less than four times, Du Bois also feminizes "America," a move that seems to challenge the dominant political identity that historian Gail Bederman ascribes to the nation, which began in the aftermath of the Civil War and extended into the first decade of the twentieth century.[1] Essentially, the men of the Anglo-Saxon race in America were the exclusive purveyors of "civilization" in the Americas and had a distinct right, especially after President Theodore Roosevelt extended the Monroe Doctrine in 1904, to disseminate and protect their civilization across national borders. To refer to Roosevelt's nation in terms of "her greatest destiny" and the African origin of her strengths, as Du Bois did, troubled the distinctly masculinist meanings of "Manifest Destiny."

Of course, Africa's gifts to America remain "unsensed and despised" by its leaders. In contrast to a lineage, beginning with "America's fathers' fathers," that ignored Africa's mystic spell, Du Bois offers up the visionary insurgent, John Brown. Rather than following the pattern of Anglo-Saxon masculinity, Brown crosses the color line to participate in its alternative—a black cosmopolitan masculinity inspired by Africa's mystic spell. Du Bois does little to distinguish the mystic spell's effects on the Connecticut-born martyr from its effects on his revolutionary predecessor, Toussaint L'Ouverture. Throughout the biography, Du Bois links John Brown's character and his spirit to Toussaint; both are likewise connected to this "mystic spell of Africa." Thus the foundational moment of freedom in the Western Hemisphere is not the American Revolution, it is the Haitian Revolution. In contrast to the Anglo-Saxon myths of racial purity and white supremacy that undergirded the founding of the republic, Du Bois imagines the republic of Haiti as an origin of democracy in the Americas that might enact its destiny very differently than the United States. As such, the insurrectionary ethos long understood to equate with Americanness became, in Du Bois's reading of L'Ouverture and writing of Brown, one of a cosmopolitanism in which the impulse to freedom exceeded boundaries of nation and race.

For Du Bois, disrupting the longstanding liberal tradition of imagining a unified republic, homogenous in its political views and racial constitution, proved integral to attaining democracy worldwide. Attacking the premise of a homogenous Anglo-American nation from the outset, Du Bois begins John Brown's life story with the words, "the mystic spell of Africa is and ever was over all America." He is eminently concerned, as the term "mystic spell of Africa" suggests, with the colonization of Africa by Europeans as well as Africa's "gifts" to the New World, yet the biography never visits Africa. Rather, it collapses space and time, focusing on the landscape of Harpers Ferry in 1859 as well as the Harpers Ferry that Thomas Jefferson extolled in his consummate literary endeavor to portray the United States as a unified nation—*Notes on the State of Virginia. John Brown* challenges Jefferson's objective in *Notes* by revisiting a scene of racial disruption that deeply troubled Jefferson: the Haitian Revolution. Du Bois, whose own father was Haitian, attaches as much significance to L'Ouverture and the geography of revolutionary Haiti as he does to Brown and Jefferson's "America." Writing the histories of slave insurrections as revolutionary moments, he interweaves the stories of Toussaint, Gabriel Prosser, Denmark Vesey, and Brown because they challenge the illusion of a national culture of freedom—an illusion that justified burgeoning U.S. dominance throughout the world by the twentieth century. Du Bois also invests Toussaint and Brown with a more significant revolutionary spirit than "America's fathers' fathers" could have imagined as he inverts the narratives of progress that credited the likes of Jefferson and, by 1909, William McKinley and Theodore Roosevelt, with civilizing the United States and several "islands of the sea."[2]

However, Du Bois's revolution is more intellectual than insurgent. In addition to inspiring revolution, this mystic spell conjures an insurrectionary tradition in African American literature that extends well back into the nineteenth century and begins in Haiti. In *John Brown,* America's "greatest destiny" is none other than freedom, a gift that the "despised" Africanist presence in the New World yearns to reveal through the additional gifts of literature and song.[3] For America to "give back the gifts" Africa has bestowed upon it would be to fulfill the destiny of freedom, not only in Africa but in the United States and the Caribbean as well. Du Bois considers Haiti as the inspiration for these gifts, the locus of freedom that spurred progress in its larger neighbor rather than a volatile and primitive space awaiting the civilizing effects of Anglo-American culture. For Du Bois, Anglo-masculinity—due to its erasure directed at, or perhaps denial of, Africa's mystic spell—sorely lacked the aesthetic or moral sensibilities that could engender modernity, particularly its promises of universal freedom. Anglo-masculinity, in this equation, is itself quite primitive.

Black Masculine Cosmopolitanism

An element of justice denied also characterizes Anglo-America's "unsensed and despised" debt to Africa, a debt that African American writers had used the "gift of literature" to call in for nearly a century before Du Bois wrote. With the exception of what may have been the first published fiction in an African American periodical, *Freedom's Journal*'s publication of "Teresa, _____ a Haytian Story" in 1827, literary representations of insurgent black cosmopolitanism are overwhelmingly masculine. Two of Brown's closest friends, Frederick Douglass and James McCune Smith, also wrote for black periodicals.[4] Their contributions to the insurrectionary tradition include Smith's 1841 publication, "A

Lecture on the Haytien Revolutions; with a sketch of the character of Toussaint L'Ouverture" and Douglass's 1852 novella, *The Heroic Slave,* a retelling of the Creole rebellion.[5] Antislavery fervor in the 1850s seems to have fanned the flames of insurgent literature, for Martin Delany's 1859 novel, *Blake; or, the Huts of America,* also features a transnational slave rebellion. Forty years later, Sutton Griggs imagined a black nationalist uprising at the outbreak of the Spanish American War in *Imperium in Imperio* (1899); Charles Chesnutt novelized the Wilmington, North Carolina, racial massacre in *The Marrow of Tradition* (1901); and writers for *The Colored American Magazine,* some of whom had attended the first Pan-African conference in 1901, published historical sketches on Toussaint, Brown, Nat Turner, and even Filipino nationalist José Rizal. At the historical moment when the United States accelerated the process of becoming a supremacist, masculinist, and militaristic power, Du Bois and others invoked stories of insurrection challenging the racial, gender, and national basis for U.S. claims to supremacy. Instead, they described the cultural geographies of Africa and the Caribbean as personifying Africa's mystic spell *and* the legacy of Toussaint.

John Brown is as much about this legacy, an intellectual and historical narrative of freedom, as it is about Harpers Ferry. By displacing the significance of the French and American revolutions in favor of what he saw as the greatest revolution—Toussaint's attempts to secure Haiti as the first free nation in the Western Hemisphere—Du Bois revises the history of the New World. The biography juxtaposes the Haitian Revolution, the Jeffersonian era, the radical abolitionist 1850s, and early-twentieth-century imperialism. He first connects the Jeffersonian era with Haiti and with Brown, reminding the reader, "There was hell in Haiti in the red waning of the eighteenth century, in the days when John Brown was born."[6] As David Roediger points out, Du Bois attenuates 1800 as a watershed year in the history of insurrection. The year of Brown's birth also coincided with Prosser's uprising and, as Du Bois so dramatically recounts, "[T]he shudder of Haiti was running through all the Americas."[7] The spell of Africa emanates through Haiti, then Brown's Harpers Ferry, and later in the book, even as far as twentieth-century Japan. This broad geography culminates with an extensive critique of the social Darwinist logic behind the White Man's Burden.

According to Du Bois, Africa's "mystic spell" is consummately cosmopolitan, albeit not in the conventional U.S. definition emphasizing Eurocentricism, because it is connected to a world spirit, yet also grounded materially in local geographic spaces. These geographic locales provide a vernacular and regional sense of identity, of one's home and place of belonging in the world, which can also be called ethnicity. To complete the cosmopolitan persona, spirit and locale triangulate with an embodied presence in the world. For Du Bois, as for his predecessors interested in Toussaint, this presence is distinctly masculine.

Du Bois's redefined cosmopolitanism builds upon a nineteenth-century black intellectual tradition that also attends to the global as well as the vernacular and regional specificity of African American life. The impulse to connect cosmopolitanisms to the vernacular and regional has yielded many useful studies of it in the twenty-first century; Du Bois's early-twentieth-century text proves particularly helpful, however, because it defines ethnicity in terms of the region where one works, either as the laborer who cultivates the soil and produces a way of life from natural resources, or as the artist who renders the landscape artistically. According to the black intellectual tradition that Du Bois draws from and builds upon, the simultaneous experience of an ethnic connection to the local and the worldly inspiration of "Africa's mystic spell" creates a new world cosmopolitan persona that attends simultaneously to labor, to art, and to liberty.

Embodied in the figures of Toussaint and Brown, the new world cosmopolitan persona draws his insurrectionary identity from specific local geographies, although he—and the masculine is intended—remains simultaneously connected to Haiti, the United States, and Africa. Black cosmopolitanism, obviously, does not discriminate on the basis of skin color, nor does it eschew European influence. Brown is cosmopolitan for his engagement with the aesthetic inspiration offered by the natural world, for his spiritual connection to "every human soul," and for a grounding in material reality that enables him to act in accordance with ideal "social doctrines." As *John Brown* attests, the lessons of the Hebrew religion influenced John Brown's spirited understanding of "neighbor[liness]" just as the "social doctrines" of the French Revolution affected his belief in equality. These traditions worked in unison to commit him to a "more just and equal distribution of property" that would usher in "liberty" and alleviate "repression" (225).

Du Bois's cosmopolitanism is different from Euro-American models because of its more inclusive geographic breadth and because of its synergy with, rather than need to dominate, the power of the natural world. Its assertions of masculinity, likewise, are singular because nature is not to be dominated by the insurgent cosmopolitan man—whose own gender, while often asserted in Du Bois's at times masculinist tendencies, occasionally expands to gender feminine the African as the materfamilias. Just as in Du Bois there is none of the people vs. nature binary so prevalent in Euro-American discourse of the turn of the twentieth century, the impulse to dominate others rarely appears—for revolution is the resistance of domination, not its enactment. According to Du Bois, Brown and L'Ouverture were apprised of equality and liberty, not only by Enlightenment philosophers but also and foremost by the spell of Africa, which "came like some great grinding ground swell, . . . like the dark, low whispering of some infinite disembodied voice." Regional locations in the biography inspire this vision of freedom: the geography of Harpers Ferry, like the Alleghenies and the mountains of Haiti, resonate with the "voice of God or the spell of Africa," inspiring great men to act. Notably, the desire for freedom emanates, quake-like, from the earth as a "great grinding ground swell" and reverberates in a "dark low whispering." The earth itself resonates as a voice similar to laborers singing "Go Down, Moses" as they work in the fields. The voice of freedom, dark and whispering, speaks through the landscape.

Figures on a Landscape

In Du Bois's account, Brown's connection to the landscape, the Alleghenies in particular, also ties him to the Great Black Way: the geographical entity of swamps and rivers that fugitive slaves mastered, traversing in their escape to freedom. Brown's connection to the Alleghenies, not only to their beauty and the fertility of their valleys but to the pathway to freedom that they provided, gave birth to his "terrible dream" of insurrection. Du Bois fashions his descriptions of Brown and the Alleghenies much as his nineteenth-century predecessors did, drawing mystical power from depictions of the landscape. Du Bois echoes Delany's sentiments about the heightened consciousness and desire for freedom that the Alleghenies inspire. In a letter to Frederick Douglass, Delany wrote, "The soul may here expand in the magnitude of its nature, and soar to the extent of human susceptibility. Indeed, it is only in the mountains that I can fully appreciate my existence as a man in America, and my own native land." In his 1841 speech, McCune Smith argued that the Haitian landscape fostered Toussaint's purchase on liberty: "a lofty range of mountains thickly serried with primeval forests . . . altars which nature in all ages has consecrated to liberty." He goes on to say: "The mountainous regions of the island, therefore, were an elementary cause of the revolution, since amid their rugged passes slaves had learned that there was such a thing as successful resistance against their masters, and such a thing also as compelling their masters to yield to them their liberty."[8]

Du Bois's similarities to Delany and Smith not only connect him to a black intellectual tradition; they also place him in opposition to the dominant political rhetoric of the nineteenth and early twentieth century, a rhetoric also integrally connected to landscape. As Du Bois located the Haitian landscape at the center of American history, he revised the nationalistic claim to the natural space of the Americas that Anglo-American leaders such as Jefferson and Roosevelt imagined in their own writing. Eric Kaufmann traces the emergence of a hybrid form of Anglo-American identity in the early-twentieth-century United States that justified imperialism, one that fused Jefferson's emphasis on the yeoman farmer who civilizes the sublime landscape and Roosevelt's description of the frontiersman who draws an exceptionally "American" spirit from the untamed West.[9] In many ways, Du Bois's Brown is antithetical to this figure. He cites Franklin Sanborn's 1885 collection of Brown's letters effusively, drawing attention to passages that define Brown's relationship to the landscape of the Alleghenies.

It becomes apparent that the way one relates to the landscape—to the natural world so frequently treated as feminine—also governs one's relationship to other cultures. By selecting passages from Brown's letters that both resonate and contrast with Roosevelt's definition of a frontiersman, Du Bois models a relationship to the wilderness not bent on justifying the domination and conquest, in this case, of Native Americans. Both Sanborn and Du Bois admit that Brown was at first frightened by Indians, but because his "father thought of Indians as neither vermin nor property," this anxiety "soon wore off and he used to hang about them quite as much as was consistent with good manners."[10] Unlike Jefferson or Roosevelt, who relied on the exclusivity of Euro-American racial categories to narrate the ascendance of the yeoman farmer or frontiersman as he enslaved the African and exterminated the Indian, Du Bois's insurrectionary tradition embraces other continents and cultures to garner the revolutionary spirit. *John Brown* critiques the ruggedly masculine figure of the Anglo-American pioneer or frontiersman.[11] Ultimately, Du Bois extends the narrative to the United States in the first decade of the twentieth century and the critique to a condemnation of Anglo-American imperialism throughout the world.

While Du Bois's evocations of landscape have not received adequate critical attention, important critical work has explored his anti-imperialist and transnational politics. Amy Kaplan discusses Du Bois's transnational and insurgent recasting of American history, particularly the way his references to Toussaint challenge the Anglo-American rhetoric of U.S. expansion, which "does not arise from its self-generated compulsion— 'the frontier,' the 'errand into the wilderness,' or 'manifest destiny'— but develops in relation to the imperial and antislavery struggles of the Caribbean revolution."[12] Essentially, Du Bois uses the figure of Toussaint to connect the history of European colonization that the United States purported to oppose, particularly in the aftermath of the Spanish-American War, to national policy at the turn of the twentieth century.[13] As it obtained Louisiana from France, evicted the Spanish from Cuba, and then purchased the Philippines, the country undertook economic ventures very much like those that spurred the French and Spanish colonization of the New World. In contrast to Toussaint's and Brown's claims to the landscape, Du Bois sees Anglo-American claims to new territory not as a naturalistic "errand into the wilderness" to promote civilization and foster a new culture of freedom, but as economic ventures intended to dominate and, if necessary, eradicate the cultures that preceded them. Kaplan traces these associations in the 1920s; it is important to note that *John Brown* performed this critique of imperialism more than a decade earlier and that Du Bois's radical leanings surfaced well before 1920.[14]

Evoking a transnational landscape of resistance to make aesthetic and political claims for a New World identity that contrasts with Anglo-American masculinity becomes a central feature of Du Bois's oeuvre, one that resonates with singular cosmopolitan ideals. In his 1920 collection of essays and fiction, *Darkwater,* the natural environment engenders what Du Bois calls "juxtaposition"; Homi Bhabha describes juxtaposition as a displacement wherein "the domestic norms of discrimination" come into proximity with "'extraterritorial' symbolic and social orders— Nature's sublimity, transnational transitions, and aesthetic transcriptions." The "intolerable in the 'local' lifeworld of racial injustice" projected on a transnational screen illuminates "an imaginative appeal to freedom through *counterfactual* choice—the freedom from humiliation, suffering, racism."[15] Bhabha sees in Du Bois's fiction the only domain of liberty.

Considering Du Bois's descriptions of landscape, however, expands the reader's understanding of what he means by "freedom." This appeal to liberty is not entirely counterfactual, not entirely about freedom from European cultures, because he juxtaposes the ugly and unethical world of imperialist politics with scenes of sublime natural beauty such as "moonlight on Montego Bay." Du Bois not only resists racial injustice but also offers an alternative vision of freedom. Bhabha's focus on the resistant Du Bois overlooks the spiritual Du Bois who connects to his nineteenth-century predecessors, the Du Bois who also finds Africa's mystic spell in that "local lifeworld" and uses its power to create an intellectual stance of openness, a solidarity with the "darker races." As Du Bois unveils the workings of Africa's mystic spell upon the New World, the landscape of the United States in *John Brown* becomes transnational, inviting a cosmopolitan identity in the place of imperialist nationalism. Africa's mystic spell connects people of African descent to a broad geography—to landscapes that symbolize freedom and are cultivated by the work and presence of the darker races.

This position of cosmopolitan "openness," however, is far more complex than Kwame Anthony Appiah's "universalism with difference." Du Bois's vision for justice requires openness to other cultures and a humanistic recognition of equality, yet democracy does not end there. As Russ Castronovo points out, Du Bois's democracy does not come without struggle. We could add that Du Bois's cosmopolitan ideal does not come without struggle, either. Locality, partiality, and the heterogeneous knowledge produced by diverse cultures in disparate spaces contribute to this struggle, and only through the negotiation of those differences, through struggle, can justice be safeguarded. When Du Bois recasts Jefferson's Harpers Ferry, then, he constructs a very different narrative of the United States and its origin and location as a nation than one finds in *Notes*. The narrative project that Castronovo attributes to *Souls of Black Folk* recurs in *John Brown,* one wherein Du Bois "hopes that he can tell 'a tale twice told but seldom written,' which will lead, not to the repetition of the same story over and over, but to different versions rife with the partiality of incompleteness and commitment."[16]

Du Bois's use of landscape to articulate this commitment to justice differs from Jefferson's because he attenuates two different ways of relating to the landscape—through a romantically imagined transcendental mysticism as well as through the embodied, visceral, immanent life of the worker who cultivates the land.[17] As Castronovo also points out, the "natural order" does not only unify; it can at the same time be a site of disruption, because "Du Bois posits racial servitude as the antisublime."[18] Forced labor in *John Brown* forges a different kind of unity with nature, one that inspires violence and struggle as it aspires toward justice. The ability to embrace natural beauty and identify with a landscape, to translate Africa's "mystic spell" into literature and song, also fuels insurrection. The aesthetic sensibility of the insurrectionist and the New World cosmopolitan persona—drawn from the experience of the laborer—merges the sublime and anti-sublime. Contrary to the Anglo-American tradition of depicting national unity as a product of the natural order, Du Bois's natural order leads to righteous rebellion. Violence in service of liberty is just—and also bound with human difference, and thereby arguably privileges blackness.

Toussaint L'Ouverture provides the quintessential symbol of the insurgent and violent potential of the natural order, the right to forge one's relationship to the natural world on one's own terms rather than through the exploitative dictates of another. Thus Jefferson's admission that "I tremble for my country when I recollect that God is just: that his justice cannot sleep for ever," suggests an anxious awareness of a very tenuous illusion of unity.[19] By inserting Toussaint into Jefferson's naturalistic narrative of nation, Du Bois gives voice to a reality that Anglo-Americans had worked assiduously to ignore for at least a hundred years. The face of democracy and revolution, as Eric Sundquist points out, acquired darker-hued tones when, in 1791, Toussaint liberated Haiti. Sundquist states, "Thereafter, especially in the wake of Nat Turner's uprising in 1831 and the emancipation of slaves in British Jamaica in the same year, Haiti came to seem the fearful precursor of black rebellion throughout the New World."[20] While it would take seventeen more years to outlaw the transatlantic slave trade for the United States, L'Ouverture enlivened, for Euro-Americans, the theoretical question of whether the capacity for freedom and blackness could cohabit in one body. For Jefferson, it was important to diffuse such inquiries. Sundquist continues, "San Domingo thus offered both a distilled symbolic impression of the legacy of the American and French Revolutions, [and] a realization of the Rights of Man" that had been suppressed.[21] The Haitian Revolution posed a major threat to Euro-American dominance in the eighteenth century, and its spirit challenged the tenets of racial difference that spurred the development of imperial culture in the United States during the early twentieth century.

The absence of Haiti in the history of the New World is conspicuous. As Sibylle Fisher illustrates, the Caribbean may have affected Europe's understanding of freedom well before those revolutions; the ways that the space of the sugar plantation in particular could deprive its workers of freedom and deny their humanity was antithetical to the purchase on life, liberty, and property that characterized Euro-American subjectivity.[22] Yet from this site of deprivation and denial a brilliant act of imagination blossomed; to imagine Haiti free from French, British, and Spanish domination and to act on that dream by rising up against the Europeans required a very different understanding of freedom. The act of conceptualizing the Haitian Revolution as a foundational political moment of revolutionary antislavery thus makes a radical difference in how we understand the history of the Americas, as it places black and de facto masculine identity at the center of an imperial sphere, not as an abject victim of history but as the driving force of liberty.

That insurrectionary impulse proved inseparable from the natural world that European traditions regularly feminize. In *John Brown's* descriptions of Haiti and Harpers Ferry, the aesthetic quality of the landscape articulates a desire for beauty and a spiritual, rather than economic, sense of connectedness to the increasingly global world—this is Du Bois's construction of freedom. The desire for freedom is more than a reaction to imperial domination; Du Bois mediates the counterfactual construction of freedom *from* oppression with the aesthetic construction of freedom *through* the sublime landscape. The subject apprehends this sublimity spiritually, in an almost animistic connection, but also through labor. The dominant Anglo-American nationalist logic that creates a racially striated and segregated United States comes undone in *John Brown* as the natural beauty of the domestic landscape exudes the transnational spirit of Africa's mystic spell. Constructions of freedom figured through the mystic spell, though counterfactual, also emanate from a material connection to the landscape—a New World identity that is more than a reaction to European power.

In Du Boiss' evocation, the Haitian Revolution and the raid on Harpers Ferry were acts of nature as well as human bravery—of Africa's mystic spell crossing the Atlantic to inspire freedom in a new incarnation. The only free nation in the Western Hemisphere was made up primarily of laborers who claimed an entitlement to the island by virtue of their working relation to the land and its productivity. Although the desire for labor and production—the desire to marshal human and natural resources into a mechanism for garnering capital—characterizes European domination of the enslaved, Du Bois does not permit the historical reality of exploitation and domination to define the Haitian insurgent's relationship to the natural world. Rather than a site of oppression, the natural world provides a space within which Toussaint and his followers could imagine their own culture and sense of being in relationship to nature, not only relationally as a culture of foment and resistance to Europe. An organic connection to nature enables the production of culture untainted by the influence of Europe. In turn, self-definition emerges unconcerned by the constraints and labels of the oppressor.

Despite the fact that Brown was a white man, Du Bois claims that his identification with the landscape of the Great Black Way and his ability to hear the "mystic" voice of Africa calling out for freedom engendered his identification with people of African descent. Or perhaps Brown simply read Douglass and McCune Smith's prose. In Du Bois's rendition, the "dark low whispering" that demanded freedom was part of Africa's mystic spell and infused the Alleghenies with a spirit that inspired Brown to act: "It was the mystic, awful voice of the mountains that lured him to liberty, death and martyrdom within their wildest fastness, and in their bosom he sleeps his last sleep."[23] Brown drew from a connection to the landscape much like McCune Smith and Delany describe to fight for freedom, yet the specter of nationalism might also have led to his demise. The competing cultural nationalism of Anglo-American supremacy could not tolerate Brown's presence, his insurgency, or his claim for universal human equality. In order to maintain the union—to keep the power of white America consolidated—the landscape had to be purified, and Brown purged from it.

The Black Man's Burden

Du Bois goes to great lengths to illustrate how subjectivity among the "darker races" has evolved differently from Anglo-Americans. This difference is not biologically determined or essential, or John Brown could not cross over to Toussaint's side, but it does come from variations in the way the subject apprehends the natural world. For Brown, Delany, and McCune Smith, as for Du Bois, African slaves who interacted with the natural landscape produced a culture of freedom. Although Du Bois, like many of his intellectual forefathers, characterizes Toussaint as intrinsically peaceful and nonviolent, the social construct of slavery invited rebellion to the sublime naturalistic space of Haiti.

It thus makes sense that Du Bois pursued the unfinished project of securing human freedom, a project that the Euro-American imaginations of the founding fathers could not complete, by invoking the memory of Toussaint and recapturing the American landscape. Apparently, Thomas Jefferson did not hear the "dark low whispering" of an African voice emanating from the American landscape as he gazed upon Virginia; he was deaf to African American culture and could not recognize it, any more than he could acknowledge the African American connection to the landscape or African American rights. In marked contrast, *John Brown* envisions Harpers Ferry as a natural and intrinsically black American space, reconnecting African Americans to the landscape in a literary revision of *Notes on Virginia*. He begins with the words "Half-way between Maine and Florida, in the heart of the Alleghenies, a mighty gateway lifts its head and discloses a scene which, a century and a quarter ago, Thomas Jefferson said was 'worth a voyage across the Atlantic.'"[24]

The irony that seeing Harpers Ferry is "worth a voyage across the Atlantic" comes from the difference between Jefferson imagining a European dignitary making a leisurely trip to admire natural beauty and Du Bois recalling the history of the Middle Passage—a very different journey across the Atlantic. However, if Harpers Ferry promises freedom, then the Middle Passage was not in vain, as it conveyed its own gifts. The imagery of Du Bois's Harpers Ferry reckons with Anglo-African cultural contact in the Americas; two rivers come to symbolize this collision. The black cosmopolite "stand[s] on a very high point of land" to view the landscape where the Shenandoah, which has "ranged along the foot of the mountain a hundred miles to find a vent" meets the Potomac, "in quest of a passage also." The encounter between rivers is violent and awesome, "In the moment of their junction they rush together against the mountain, rend it asunder, and pass off to the sea."[25]

The similarity between this landscape and Du Bois's articulation of his own identity in terms of "double-consciousness" eleven years earlier is striking: identity emerges from "two warring ideals in one dark body, whose dogged strength alone keeps it from being torn asunder."[26] The dark body merges the two cultural geographies, African and Anglo-American, just as the mountain merges the two rivers; cultures collide like the rushing rivers and, rather than being torn asunder by the force, the dark body integrates the two—becoming African and American— and flows to the Atlantic, perhaps to return the gifts that Africa gave America's fathers' fathers. In the next stroke, Du Bois pivots away from Jefferson's view of Harpers Ferry. The revolutionary figure who masters the landscape is no longer a founding father, but John Brown. Keeping the aesthetic character of the landscape sublime and imposing, Du Bois points toward the natural beauty and the political significance of the military arsenal in this powerful geographic space: "This is Harpers Ferry and this was the point which John Brown chose for his attack on American slavery. He chose it for many reasons [. . .] he loved beauty [. . .]

He chose Harpers Ferry because a United States arsenal was there [. . .] the foremost and decisive reason was that Harpers Ferry was the safest natural entrance to the Great Black Way."[27]

By referring to the South as the "Great Black Way," the vast Southern landscape Brown hoped would provide an army of insurgents, Du Bois invokes an image of millions of laborers. Equating African Americans with the fertile, rich soil of the Black Belt, Du Bois claims the land tilled by black labor as the rightful place of the people who built the South. In his evocation of the sublime, meanwhile, Du Bois appropriates the discourse of white men like Jefferson, claiming entitlement to the pastoral United States by replacing the image of the yeoman farmer with that of the black slave who should be a farmer and would be a warrior to become so. Similarly, the modern world awaits the synthesis of nature and culture, labor and imagination, that can free it from its shackles.

STILL, JEFFERSON was never able to imagine such a synthesis, and Du Bois intervened in the political and aesthetic conclusions that Jefferson drew from his study of the landscape. *Notes on the State of Virginia* also articulates a plan for African colonization and insists that the slave presence in the United States should be replaced with European immigrants; Jefferson's fear of insurrection, perhaps a reflection of the "hell in Haiti" as well, motivates his emigration plan. Presaging social Darwinist claims of natural racial distinctions as well as the white paranoia and fear of insurrection that will reemerge even after the end of slavery, Jefferson wrote, "Deep rooted prejudices entertained by whites; ten thousand recollections, by the blacks, of the injuries they have sustained; new provocations; the real distinctions which nature has made; and many other circumstances, will divide us into parties, and produce convulsions which will probably never end but in the extermination of the one or the other race."[28]

Du Bois's description of Harpers Ferry as the "entrance to the Great Black Way" crushes Jefferson's vision of a whitened American landscape— for his "race" will not be evicted, forced to emigrate, nor exterminated. It is also as relevant to anti-imperialist interests in 1909 as it was to antislavery in 1859 because it connects the landscape of the United States to the Atlantic world. As the Shenandoah and Potomac merge at Harpers Ferry and "pass off to the sea," their movement toward the Atlantic also points toward another geography of identity across the sea—Africa. Invoking the Black Atlantic as an extension of the Great Black Way, Du

Bois replaces Jefferson's desire for Anglo-American racial purity and a whitened landscape with a transatlantic remapping that points toward Africa rather than Europe. However, Du Bois's radical narrative intervention in the rhetoric of Anglo-American nationalism seems to have left it unscathed—in the twenty-first century, liberal democratic promises of progress justify more violent interventions and more global expansions. Certainly, as he protested imperialism, Du Bois realized that, as Simon Gikandi suggests, the "promise of modernity, the dream of a universal culture based on human values, democracy, and freedom keeps falling on its face." As Du Bois highlights the "irrational forces inherent within the project of modernity itself," he articulates the problem, not only of the twentieth century but of the twenty-first as well.[29]

Notes

1. As Bederman indicates, "During the decades around the turn of the century, Americans were obsessed with the connection between manhood and racial dominance. This obsession was expressed in a profusion of issues, from debates over lynching, to concern about the white man's imperialistic burden overseas, to discussions of child-drearing." See *Manliness and Civilization* (Chicago: University of Chicago Press, 1995), 4.

2. W. E. B. Du Bois, *The Souls of Black Folk* (New York: Vintage Books, 1990), 2.

3. Du Bois, *John Brown,* David R. Roediger, ed. (New York: Modern Library, 2001), 3.

4. Brown was a founding member of the Radical Abolition political party with white reformer Gerrit Smith, Douglass, and McCune Smith; see John Stauffer, *The Black Hearts of Men: Radical Abolitionists and the Transformation of Race* (Cambridge, MA: Harvard University Press, 2001).

5. William Wells Brown included an account of the Haitian Revolution in his L'Ouverture entry of *The Black Man, His Antecedents, His Genius, and His Achievements* (New York: Thomas Hamilton, 1863), and James Theodore Holly also wrote histories of the Haitian Revolution in 1857.

6. Du Bois, *John Brown,* 40.

7. Ibid.

8. Martin Delaney, "Nature Inspired, Spiritual Despair," *The North Star* (24 February 1849). Smith's speech was published in pamphlet form. The extant copy exists in a bound volume that Charles Sumner donated to Harvard University. I thank the staff at the Houghton Library for the opportunity to use this text.

9. Eric P. Kaufmann, *The Rise and Fall of Anglo-America* (Cambridge, MA: Harvard University Press, 2004).

10. Du Bois, *John Brown,* 6; he cites Franklin Benjamin Sanborn.

11. For more on rugged masculinity and the frontier, see Amy Kaplan, "Romancing the Empire: The Embodiment of American Masculinity in the Popular Historical Novel of the 1890s," *American Literary History* 2 (1990): 659–90.

12. Amy Kaplan, *The Anarchy of Empire in the Making of U.S. Culture* (Cambridge, MA: Harvard University Press, 2002), 176.

13. John Trombold discusses Roosevelt's claims that his "civilizing mission" was to spread U.S. multicultural pluralism throughout the world in the name of democracy. The myth of American exceptionalism distinguishes U.S. imperialism from European colonialism, but according to Trombold, Roosevelt saw his challenge differently, as "one of orchestrating plurality within the United States while imposing American dominance abroad"; see "Neo-Roosevelt, or, Why Post-Colonialism Is Premature," *Interventions* 7:2 (2005): 199. Du Bois refutes the U.S. claims to pluralism and racial equality by connecting the "darker races" in the supposedly multicultural and pluralistic United States to those who are clearly oppressed in other parts of the world, including Haiti and the Congo, but also extending to other U.S. imperial spaces.

14. Du Bois's early career coincides with the phase when Hazel V. Carby and Kevin Gaines interpret his ideas as far more conciliatory with white patriarchal culture; see Carby, *Race Men* (Cambridge, MA: Harvard University Press, 1998); Gaines, *Uplifting the Race : Black Leadership, Politics, and Culture in the Twentieth Century* (Chapel Hill: University of North Carolina Press, 1996). In more recent scholarship, Maria Farland has located Du Bois's radicalism in the first decade of the twentieth century; see Farland, "W. E. B. DuBois, Anthropometric Science, and the Limits of Racial Uplift," *American Quarterly* 58:4 (2006): 1017–44.

15. Homi K. Bhabha, "The Black Savant and the Dark Princess," *ESQ* (2006): 139–40.

16. Du Bois, *Souls of Black Folk,* 209; Russ Castronovo, "Within the Veil of Interdisciplinary Knowledge? Jefferson, Du Bois, and the Negation of Politics," *New Literary History* 31 (2000): 781–804.

17. Saidiya Hartman's observations about the development of a racist social structure in the same historical moment revolve largely around the demarcation of the black body as alien and dangerous to the patriarchal order—and landscape—that would govern an increasingly imperialist and masculinist U.S. national identity; see *Scenes of Subjection: Terror, Slavery, and Self-Making in Nineteenth-Century America* (New York: Oxford University Press, 1997), 179.

18. Castronovo, "Within the Veil of Interdisciplinary Knowledge?" 794.

19. Qtd. in ibid., 793.

20. Eric J. Sundquist, *To Wake the Nations: Race in the Making of American Literature* (Cambridge, MA.: Belknap Press of Harvard University Press, 1993), 32.

21. Ibid., 141.

22. Sibylle Fischer, *Modernity Disavowed: Haiti and the Cultures of Slavery in the Age of Revolution* (Durham, NC: Duke University Press, 2004).

23. Du Bois, *John Brown,* 23.

24. Ibid., 163.

25. Ibid.

26. Du Bois, *Souls of Black Folk,* 2.

27. Du Bois, *John Brown,* 163.

28. Thomas Jefferson, "From *Notes on the State of Virginia,*" in *Classical Black Nationalism,* Wilson Jeremiah Moses, ed. (New York: New York University Press, 1996), 46. Wilson Moses points out other resonances of Jefferson in Du Bois's work, particularly

in the metaphor of the veil; see *The Golden Age of Black Nationalism* (New York: Oxford University Press, 1978), 167. Jefferson described "that immovable veil of black which covers all the emotions of the other race." In contrast to Jefferson's use of the veil metaphor to describe an utter absence of the healthy passions that motivated and invigorated the Anglo-American, the passions engendered by the mystic spell of Africa seem quite similar to those hidden behind Du Bois's veil.

29. Simon Gikandi, "Race and Cosmopolitanism," *American Literary History* 14:3 (2002): 596, 602.

10

The Political Is Personal

Black Family Manhood and the Social Science of
E. Franklin Frazier, 1930–1945

MALINDA ALAINE LINDQUIST

The history of the family is frequently read as the history of women, mothers, and children. Writing against the ideology of separate spheres and moving toward the reality of women's presence and prominence in the public sphere has, in the course of two generations, fundamentally contested narratives privileging the domestication of women. Gender studies have not, however, to the same degree, inspired the examination of men in the family. A growing historical scholarship does exist, from Robert Griswold's *Fatherhood in America* to Shawn Johansen's *Family Man,* but the discussion of the raced nature and racial implications of husbandhood and fatherhood are frequently muted.[1] With the exception of a series of studies examining the marriage and courtship of specific, usually highly accomplished, African American couples and families, and the new work on black sexualities, the scholarship on black families still primarily focuses on women.[2]

To date, the most robust literature on black family men and the dilemmas of husbands and fathers in the African American community has been produced by literary scholars, cultural critics, and social scientists.[3] The historical scholarship on black family men focuses largely on the nineteenth century and interracial relationships.[4] And yet it is in the twentieth century that the qualifications of the black family man and questions about his presence and absence have generated some of the most vigorous and sustained national debates. These debates peaked, first, in the wake of Daniel Patrick Moynihan's *The Negro Family: The Case for National Action* (1965) and, again, in 1995 with Louis Farrakhan's Million Man March.[5] Both the Moynihan Report and the march drew generously, if imperfectly, upon the scholarship of African American intellectuals, from Edward Franklin Frazier's *The Negro Family in the United States* (1939)[6] to Jawanza Kunjufu's *Countering the Conspiracy to Destroy Black Boy,* respectively.[7] Notwithstanding their attempts to start a national conversation and set a broad agenda, the Moynihan Report's and the Million Man March's emphasis on black boys' needs for strong black fathers as male role models are most useful for what they reveal about the social scientific assumptions of the sixties and their cooption by black nationalists in the nineties. At the same time, each has managed both to obscure black scholars' nuanced work and the broad vision of black family manhood prevailing at mid-century.

Most early black social scientists dwelt briefly on male bonding and father-son psychologies, instead focusing on family men as patriarchal cultural producers, interracial proletariats, and democratic role models.[8] Moreover, relationships between fathers and daughters and husbands and wives garnered the most sustained attention. While contemporary crises in the African American community are depicted as hinging fundamentally on the problems of black boys and the father-son relationship,[9] what this formulation hides is the extent to which the meaning of the black family man has narrowed and evolved from a vital constructive historical force to a political and economic model for democratic living to a series of apolitical personal and interpersonal relationships between fathers and sons.

Throughout the twentieth century, the black family man has been cast as a vital but shrouded figure in the African American struggle. But it is only since the Civil Rights and Voting Rights Acts that he has been called upon to arrest the problems of racism, discrimination, and inequality by showing his sons how to be hardworking men, hands-on fathers, and loving husbands. Ironically, we must turn to the era of jim crow to catch a glimmer of a broader, potentially more progressive, and fundamentally more political vision of the black family man. This should come as no surprise, since during the latter half of the twentieth century at just that moment when African Americans stepped up their struggle for full citizenship rights, the family was increasingly identified as the most important institution in personality formation, community development, and racial advancement. That is to say, when blacks were most fervently asserting the need for institutional and structural changes on a national scale, intellectuals like Moynihan claimed that no change in the status of African Americans was possible without fundamentally transforming the black family, whose "vicious" "tangle of pathology" was circular and largely self-sustaining. Moynihan and others came to this conclusion at least partially through the work of black scholars who stressed the role and power of the family. Still, black scholars rarely lost sight of the overwhelming power of racism, economic inequality, and political discrimination in shaping family fortunes and potentials.[10]

In the decades following the freedom movement and up through the Million Man March, connections between the family and the social, economic, and racial forces determining its shape have deteriorated and been replaced by the idea that families ought to be strong enough to transcend these forces. African Americans were among the popularizers of this theory, but the genesis of this idea came to life in the wake of the disillusionment caused by the half gains and lost promises of the rights movements.[11] As full integration failed to materialize and the hope for equal access and opportunity hit up against the reality of continuing subordination, social scientists argued that African American parents needed to raise children impervious to the gap between American ideals and American racism. These scholars did not doubt that black families were largely limited by their second-class status, but they still counseled them to protect their children in anyway possible. One popular mid-century method focused on the development of strong individual personalities capable of withstanding the frustrations caused by the persistence of prejudice.[12] Others counseled parents and schools to raise dissatisfied youth with activist mentalities who would carry the struggle forward.[13] African American scholars' emphasis on family fortification as both a stabilizing force and a defense mechanism, however, has been displaced by a theory of the family that makes it the most important institution with the ability to overcome race problems singularly and of its own accord.[14] It is this late-twentieth-century worldview that has managed simultaneously to make the black family man responsible for solving the race problem and to ensure his failure by suggesting that most of this work can be confined and resolved within the domestic sphere.

At the same time, the purview and the vision of the black family man have shrunk to a series of reproductive, interpersonal, and economic relationships with no larger political or social vision.[15] By making the domestication of black men the central front of the struggle, the extent to which the power of the family man historically lay in his ability to move between the private and the public sphere, family and community, and affection and politics has nearly vanished. At mid-century the black family man was characterized as a freedom fighter, patriot, community pioneer, man of distinction, or cutting-edge member of an interracial proletarian social movement. Moreover, E. Franklin Frazier depicted the most innovative black families as ones in which family men and women learned important lessons from each other. Fathers were encouraged to build affectional and sympathetic ties as modeled by devoted mothers and mothers were encouraged to claim an equal footing in the family through their labor (wage and unwaged) and by fostering a working-class consciousness in their children. The late-twentieth- and early-twenty-first-century notion that fathers need to be heroes to their endangered, embattled, and embittered sons clearly has a certain provincial self-help appeal and partially resonates with Frazier's early emphasis on family pride and late emphasis on male role modeling. In an era of continuing racial disparities and entrenched segregation, however, Frazier was suspect of any theories of family manhood that lacked a broader political, social, or economic perspective and focused on highlighting the differences between mothers and fathers as opposed to building strong, progressive families around a community of shared interests.

Today we take for granted the importance of fathers as moral, economic, and psychological resources, leaders, and role models in the family and gloss over how fatherhood has been reinvented and reimagined over the course of the twentieth century. We inculcate a confused and even dueling notion of fatherhood as, on the one hand, a biological reality and an organic product of nature, and, on the other hand, requiring nurture through public and private, local and national fatherhood initiatives.[16] As a nation, we remain of two minds on the matter, certain that biology binds father and child and simultaneously confident that social forces, policies, and commentators can and must strengthen these potentially tenuous natural bonds.

Writing eight decades ago, the acclaimed African American sociologist E. Franklin Frazier (1894–1962) was not compelled to straddle this divide. He argued that while males were biologically connected to their children, fatherhood was not solely or even primarily a product of biology. Whereas females, according to Frazier, were transformed into mothers through the act of reproduction, sentiment, and nurture, males were transformed into fathers, not only through reproduction but, even more importantly, via cultural and historical traditions; labor, class-consciousness, and political vision; and only much later through psychological bonds. According to Frazier, family men were manufactured and manly production, not simply biological reproduction, established men's interest and authority in the family and made them fathers. Whereas motherhood was described as a natural, organic state for women, fatherhood was a cultural, economic, social, political, and creative process.[17] Its malleability also left it open to reform. As a sociologist, Frazier set for himself the task of examining, historicizing, challenging, and transforming the role of the black family man.

Frazier is most remembered for his work on the black family. Earning his doctorate from the University of Chicago in 1931, his sociological career spanned four decades in which time he authored seven books, four on the black family, and over a hundred articles. Incredibly prolific, Frazier, like most black scholars of his generation, remained a segregated scholar, spending his career in underfunded historically black colleges and universities at Morehouse (1922–27), Fisk (1929–34), and Howard (1934–59, where he chaired the Department of Sociology).[18] Still, his accomplishments were highly respected and his colleagues elected him president of the American Sociological Society in 1948.[19] Writing and publishing throughout the era of jim crow, primarily between 1922 and 1961, Frazier identified the family as a vital source of racial development, a vehicle of assimilation and acculturation, and the "final frontier" in the race relation's cycle. Family was the foundation upon which communities were built; it was where traditions were grown, assimilated, and acculturated, and fathers, according to Frazier, played a major role, if not the major role, in this process. Without the fathers' gifts, first, of a tradition of distinction; second, of economic stability, working-class values, and interracial political solidarity; and, third, of male role modeling, no reasonable racial accommodation could be achieved.

Unwrapping the notion of "the family" and looking beneath its surface, we find that for Frazier the family constituted a means of expressing his concerns about and interest in family manhood, culture, and class. At work on a group biography of eminent sociologists at midcentury, Howard Odum, the famous University of North Carolina sociologist, solicited an intellectual autobiographical statement from Frazier, who identified race relations and the family as his primary areas of research. Frazier elaborated, "I have been interested in studying such purely sociological problems as the development of the interest of the male in the family, the establishment of masculine authority and discipline in the family life, and the influence of family traditions on the stability of the family and the behavior of its members."[20] Moreover, the family and paternal authority were not static concepts but dynamic constructs. Their meaning and importance evolved as he matured as a scholar, reflecting both social and economic change as well as the intellectual currents of the mid-twentieth century. Thus, Frazier's corpus offers the historian an opportunity to reconstruct and expose the evolving significance of family manhood and the changing definitions and requirements of black fatherhood and husbandhood in the mid-twentieth century before Moynihan and the Million Man March moved the father-son relationship to the center of discussions about the black family. Moreover, I suggest that the feminist slogan "the personal is political" finds its counterpoint—the political is personal—in Frazier's theory of family manhood, a theory that simultaneously posits the significance of the family man, while refusing to concede his political orientation. Instead, it is through men's values and politics that we can best understand their role in the family.

Frazier was not the only scholar to emphasize the importance of masculinity in his work. Gender and manhood, in particular, figured prominently in the work of a number of black social scientists from W. E. B. Du Bois, George Edmund Haynes, and Oliver Cox to Horace Cayton and St. Clair Drake. Each of these scholars took for granted that "exceptional men," "talented men," "intelligent men," "best men," and "Race Men" were to play the decisive role in the struggle for African American advancement and equality.[21] While the emphasis on exceptionalism, especially intellectual, economic, or political distinction, in the public sphere in conjunction with the gendered division of labor implicitly encouraged these scholars to accentuate men's leadership in the community and in institution building, most recognized, even if they did not equally value, the role men played in the family. Yet, for scholars like Frazier, who asserted that the family was "the basic social group through which changes in status [we]re mediated and accommodations to the urban environment [we]re made," the family man's importance grew exponentially.[22]

Frazier's sense of black manhood stood in contrast with many of his contemporaries: Du Bois's Talented Tenth, the highly educated, cultural missionaries to the masses; Cayton's and Drake's Race Man, who earned his status by aggressively vindicating African Americans in a hostile white world; and the Marginal Man, whose bicultural experience and world-view facilitated and propelled his mobility between both racial worlds allowing him to act as a conduit of information and values. Instead, Frazier emphasized the significant role black men played in the family. He deemed paternal authority in the private sphere as inseparable from masculine "distinction" in the public sphere and masculine "distinction" in the public sphere as vital to the growth and proliferation of stable black families.

Like many of his contemporaries, Frazier's early work suggested that manhood was limited to the most "intelligent," "energetic," and "talented" black men. Examining the family in light of its historical context, he argued that the roots of the institutional black family could be traced to the free, patriarchal, and frequently artisanal "founding fathers" and "fountain heads" of antebellum "family lines." However, as Frazier witnessed the displacement of patriarchal family traditions by bourgeois lifestyles following decades of migration and urbanization, he clarified that the "mark of distinction," which turned ordinary men into "founding fathers" and created a proud "self-concept" and "family consciousness," was not gained through idle wealth but through constructive labor. The stability of the contemporary twentieth-century family, he argued, rested on a firm paternal working-class foundation.[23] This shift in perspective led to the democratization and working-class orientation of Frazier's theory of the modern family man. Whereas Du Bois, Drake, and Cayton largely espoused middle-class ideals of black family manhood, Frazier maintained that as more black men entered the urban industrial economy or self-identified as members of the working class, as expressed through their lifestyle, family values, labor activism, and politics, their working-class consciousness would create a vital and viable family manhood. The working-class orientation required to generate modern family manhood is conveyed perfectly in one of Frazier's favorite and oft-cited family life history documents. His source described the working-class family man and his legacy in the proudest of terms, writing:

> So it was very early that we acquired a deep and abiding respect for the people of the working class because we were and are part and parcel of them. We were taught early by both our parents to respect personality as it showed itself through constructive labor. The men who worked for Dad, the mechanics as well as the laborers, we thought of as constructive forces in the community. It was probably because of these ideas that we regarded with pride all the male members of the family.[24]

While emphasizing the political and classed nature of family manhood, Frazier's theory also created new divisions among African Americans. He celebrated the masculinity of the industrial proletariat of the 1930s and 1940s and castigated both the estranged, wandering individuated masses and the feminized, society-driven black bourgeois.

Using family manhood to reinterpret class and occupational divisions within the community, Frazier equally deployed black fatherhood as a discursive tool to challenge white oppression in the sciences, regarding the slave trade, and on the question of segregation. Frazier's specific sociological emphasis on questions of "masculine authority," "discipline," "tradition," and male development directly challenged the paternalist tendencies in white sociology that infantilized and cast African Americans as immature dependents, hereditary outcasts, or backward, underdeveloped African savages.[25] Rather, he emphasized the extent to which the transatlantic slave trade, emancipation, migration, and urbanization eroded "social controls" that undermined masculine development and destabilized and demoralized families. His analysis of these transformations both took into account black agency and initiative, while also holding white Americans responsible for the continuous erosion and disruption of black family life. Thus, black family manhood was not merely a historical construct whose meaning changed over the course of three decades; it was equally a relational and highly political concept both at the level of practical politics and as an abstraction.

Culture, Class, Psychology, and the Politics of Family Manhood

Through E. Franklin Frazier's scholarship we can trace the evolution of family manhood from a cultural to an economic to a psychological construct. Moreover, to understand Frazier's 1950 call for black fathers to "provide the model or image of the values which should shape their [children's, especially their son's] personalities" requires an awareness of Frazier's broader vision of family manhood as expressed in his series of family studies.[26] His four book-length family studies—*The Negro Family in Chicago* (1932), *The Free Negro Family* (1932), *The Negro Family in the United States* (1939), and *Black Bourgeois* (1957)—offer a powerful prism through which the intellectual history of the black family man can be recounted. Moreover, together they historicize and help to differentiate between the nature of contemporary apolitical theories of the family man and Frazier's early-twentieth-century emphasis on identifying and cultivating a politics of family manhood.

Coinciding with and in response to the raging debates about the cultural basis of race and the race problem in the 1920s and 1930s, Frazier's 1931 dissertation, "The Negro Family in Chicago," published the following year under the same title as his first book, focused primarily on the cultural and historical aspects of paternal authority. Published that same year, *The Free Negro Family* (1932) expanded on Frazier's thesis, which traced the cultural germ of stable black family life back to free black families and more specifically to a set of founding family fathers whose talents (artisanal, agricultural, religious) and embrace of a democratic politics, love of freedom, and independent and rebel spirit, permeated the family culture, reinforced social controls that stabilized their families, and created traditions that sustained future generations. In both early studies, Frazier contested arguments that traced the demoralization of black families to Africa, slavery, or racial immaturity asserting that black family disorganization and the excessive masculine freedom of single men were the products of the black families' loss of paternal authority, memory, and tradition.

Reflecting post–World War I occupational stratification as well as the economic anguish of the Great Depression, *The Negro Family in the United States* (1939), Frazier's third monograph, captures the evolution of black fatherhood from a cultural to primarily an economic product and philosophy. Here he narrated an explicitly gendered natural history of the black family that moved from slave to matriarchal to patriarchal and, finally, to the emergence of middle-class and proletarian families. Approaching patriarchy primarily as a historic pre-urban family form that stabilized the first institutional black families and helped sustain their family lineages, he suggested that in modern America, a land of corporate wealth and capitalist exploitation, the rebirth of family manhood and stable black families was contingent on the industrial integration of black men and their development of a working-class consciousness. Finally, with the Cold War era publication of *Black Bourgeoisie* (1957) and in the midst of rampant fears about the softening of American men, Frazier stepped up his denunciations of middle-class family manhood. As the fifties witnessed the increasing confluence of sociology and psychology, Frazier identified the absence of paternal authority among the middle classes as a psychological and a developmental disorder. The black middle class suffered inferiority complexes, the stunted development of their sons, and the feminization, and potentially the homosexualization, of their men. In the wake of what he understood to be the dilution of the political orientation of black family manhood among a flailing black elite, his promotion of the father-son relationship was both affectional and political.

Questions of morality, culture, and manliness stood at the center of Frazier's first major study of the black family, *The Negro Family in Chicago* (1932). Responding to a bevy of scholars from Du Bois to Howard Odum to Jerome Dowd, Frazier fundamentally contested the connections drawn between unstable black families and their African heritage. Rather, he consistently asserted that demoralization and disorganization were natural, even necessary civilizational processes that black families were going through. To make this point, he put equal effort into arguing strenuously against the homogenization of black family life, demonstrating that both demoralization and stabilization were active and ongoing processes. Documenting rampant dependency, desertion, illegitimacy, juvenile delinquency, and an excess of single men in the inner zones of black Chicago, he also established that most of these problems disappeared in the outer zones where married men predominated. Graphically displaying a geography of irresponsible, isolated nonfamily men and responsible family men, he asserted that family manhood was largely a product of a paternal heritage of distinction and civic engagement. Identifying a lack of culture, traditions, and social controls as key to the proliferation of single, unattached men in the central city, he traced the preponderance of married men in the outer zones to a heritage of paternal family traditions.

On the one hand, Frazier's Chicago study offered a gendered geography of stable family life, correlating an excess of single men in the central city to demoralization and the increase in married men on the urban peripheries to stabilization. On the other hand, Frazier was equally, if not most concerned with a family's paternal heritage when differentiating between stable and disorganized families. Actual husbands and fathers mattered, but what mattered even more, according to Frazier, were their fathers and their father's fathers. Family manhood was a generational concept that was based on and inseparable from a broader engagement in public service, racial advancement, community building, resistance to subordination, and a spirit of independence. The family man, according to Frazier, was engaged in civic life as opposed to the hordes of individuated single men who lacked patriarchal origins, a family life, and productive community connections.

While social and economic status differentiated Chicago's stable families from the demoralized Southern migrant families and unattached masses, Frazier maintained what really separated these two groups was culture. By culture he meant "family tradition" and "the extent to which the culture of one generation was transmitted to the succeeding generation."[27] Culture and family tradition were gendered constructs for Frazier. The key to stable and dynamic black families and communities as far as he was concerned was a vigorous paternal heritage. In the penultimate chapter of *The Negro Family in Chicago,* which overlapped significantly with the thesis of his second book, *The Free Negro Family* (1932), Frazier contended that family traditions were grown by men, in this case founding fathers, and proliferated and strengthened through the act of remembering.

Specifically, Frazier traced these patriarchal family traditions back to a number of "founding fathers," "fountain heads," and "family lines" that gained distinction owing to a record of military service; to the pioneering efforts of ancestors; or to educated or highly skilled forefathers. Tracing stable black family life primarily back to the free black patriarchs of the antebellum period, Frazier also asserted that some important family lines and traditions were also derived from and attributable to the largely male, fugitive and manumitted, slaves who escaped to freedom; talented and skilled slaves, who purchased their freedom; and house slaves, whose culture was obtained not through the emulation of their masters, but based upon an "acquaintance with the larger world" afforded by their privileged position in slavery.[28] He argued that stable families essentially shared a tradition, a positive "self-concept," "pride," and "family consciousness" as a result of a father's, grandfather's, or great grandfather's services, successes, and distinctions. Whereas unstable families lived a "casual," "precarious," "fragmentary" existence with no deep roots and fading memories, stable families were "full of memories," memories of active civic engagement, service, and accomplishment. These memories bound families to both their pasts and their futures and played a central role in community building. Frazier credited the "ideals and conceptions" growing out of these traditions with "determin[ing] whether one will marry or remain single, have children or maintain a certain standard of life, endure an unhappy married life for the sake of his social status or change mates for the fulfillment of a career."[29]

Whereas rural traditions and sympathetic bonds had stabilized families prior to migration, the loss of controls, the shallow nature and lack of transferability of rural traditions to city life allowed migration, continuous mobility, and urbanization to destabilize and demoralize families.[30] Yet, the fundamental problem, according to Frazier, was that "these families possessed no family traditions to bind the generations together and give continuity to life."[31] Migration and urbanization were and would continue to be disorganizing forces, but he wrote, "the extent of disorganization will depend upon the fund of social tradition which will become the basis for the reorganization of life on a more intelligent and more efficient basis."[32] Family men of distinction were the essential glue that stabilized families and bound one generation to the next. Frazier's concept of family manhood was multigenerational and deeply psychological in its orientation. Contemporary black men could aspire to make a "mark of distinction," and he saw cities like Chicago as offering numerous opportunities for such manly expressions, but even here he focused more on the generational implications of making such a "mark" as opposed to the immediate impact such successes might bring to one's family. He concluded it was these distinctions that would determine men's roles in the community and that would make them "the fountainhead of the family tradition."[33]

Frazier's concept of tradition emphasized the "memory" of the father and "knowledge" of the father as a key factor in family stability. Moreover, family manhood was defined more as a generational responsibility and a geographical construct than as a series of actual relationships between family members. Still, if any family ties were privileged, it is fair to say that the father-daughter relationship was a cornerstone of black fatherhood as Frazier understood it in the 1920s and 1930s. A major thesis of his Chicago study was that disorganization, expressed in terms of illegitimacy and desertion, was a direct consequence of the absence of paternal memory and authority. Even here he made a generational argument when he claimed the fundamental source and consequence of illegitimacy was that it literally cut off access to one's paternal heritage and memory. Illegitimacy and desertion were conceived primarily as cultural problems proliferating in the absence of father knowledge, instead of as the product of social and economic deprivation. Attributing illegitimacy to the disorganization women experienced in their natal families, the proof he returned to again and again was the fact that many unwed mothers had no "knowledge" of their own father or "knew nothing" of him but his name.[34] It was not that the unwed mother was harmed by their father's or mate's inability to provide for them financially or even emotionally, but that in not knowing their fathers they were demoralized and crippled by a lack of family traditions and culture, vital social controls that would have protected their chastity. Moreover, Frazier identified mothers and young women as the greatest victims of paternal memory loss. By the end of his career, the primary victims of unfulfilled family manhood were black boys who did not have fathers either to help them bridge the divide between the private and public sphere or to infuse them with a political orientation ground in a virile paternal heritage and robust, interracial, proletarian activism. Before Frazier turned his attention to the crisis of black boys, however, the patriarchal culture of family manhood was partially eclipsed and complimented by a theory of the economic origins and political responsibilities of the black family man in an industrial society.

Working-Class Fatherhood

By the end of the 1930s, the ravages of the Great Depression, in conjunction with Frazier's loss of faith in middle-class politics grew, and his focus shifted appreciably toward a class analysis of black family disorganization. While not ignoring class, *The Negro Family in Chicago* (1932) downplayed its importance and emphasized the acquisition of culture through the black patriarch and transmitted to future generations as a solution to demoralization. *The Negro Family in the United States* (1939), on the other hand, argued that cultural forms were a product of one's class values as opposed to patriarchal traditions spearheaded by founding fathers. Frazier also paid more attention both to the division of labor, the Great Depression, discrimination in the labor market, and segregation.[35] Moreover, masculine authority and family stability were less a matter of father memory or the father-daughter relationship and increasingly a product of an interracial proletarian politics, the rebalancing of the spousal relationship, and the simultaneous democratization of family life. Frazier's emphasis on class politics was in many ways in line with the theories and politics generated by other young Howard University scholars in the 1930s, like Abram Harris and Ralph Bunche, but Frazier extended this argument to the family and offered a gendered, historical narrative for an emerging black proletariat that placed the working-class black family man at its center.[36]

Frazier's new vision of working-class black manhood and fatherhood was powerfully captured in two artistic interpretations of his award-winning study, *The Negro Family in the United States*. In the linoleum cuts incorporated throughout the text and in his description of a set of dioramas commissioned for the 1940 American Negro Exposition held in Chicago, Frazier traced racial progress to the development of working-class paternal authority in the family. The absence of the father from the family was equated with the absence of authority and economic, cultural, institutional, and political vitality. In the presence of the father, the family formed a coherent social group with a common set of interests and all sorts of racial development were possible.

The first linoleum cut depicts black bodies probably though not necessarily male laboring strenuously in a field. "In the House of the Master" makes it clear that the control of a black labor force, not family formation, was the primary purpose of slavery. The central figure in the second linoleum cut, "In the House of the Mother," is a black mother surrounded by two small girls and two other women fill the background. The black man is absent from this family group. Capturing Frazier's theory that the maternal family was the original family group, the naturalization of motherhood and maternal bonds is further exemplified by the naturescape that enfolds this all-female clan. Frazier frequently asserted that the matriarchal family was a strong, resilient, and nurturing family type in simple rural areas, but the linoleum cut's allusions to female sexuality and the absence of any signs of development is equally evocative of how Frazier conceived of matriarchy as stable but fundamentally undeveloped.

A black father with a hoe, the evidence of his labor and economic self-sufficiency, is the central figure in the third linoleum cut, "In the House of the Father." He is larger than his wife, who stands behind him nursing their youngest child, and a very small girl stands to his right. The "In the House of the Father" diorama commissioned for the American Negro Exposition was even more explicit about how the incorporation of the black patriarchal father into the family transformed the African American community. A male farmer attended by his wife and children were in the foreground, and a rich institutional life blossoms in his midst. The appearance of this individual black family man was equated with modernity and wrought far-reaching consequences extending beyond the confines of his family. Describing the diorama for the artists, Frazier stated, that since the black man "is a pioneer in building up the institutional life of the Negro[,] . . . this scene should include a picture of the school house and the church in a rural setting as well as the Negro cabin."[37] The presence, labor, and civic engagement of the father fundamentally changed family and community dynamics.[38] Maternal dominance was reigned in as wives submitted to their husbands and paternal authority and self-sufficiency in the family translated into institutional advances in the larger community. Expanding on the themes originally raised in his first two books, Frazier dramatized the extent to which patriarchy was based on the subordination of women, especially the husband's right to control his wife's labor, as well as on the acquisition of property, and a man's ability to distinguish himself. The actual sequence of events fluctuated, but together these three events, according to Frazier, solidified men's authority and interest in the family and created the necessary tradition that stabilized family life from one generation to the next. Patriarchal family stability was also inseparable from institution building since, on the one hand, founding fathers were frequently responsible for these feats and, on the other hand, the institutions they built, such as black churches, set out and were set up to reinscribe the authority of the family man.

Another linoleum cut, "In the City of Destruction," leaves behind the rural world and transports the viewer to a cityscape as we follow the northern and western paths of nearly two million Southern black migrants. Dilapidated tenements cloud the horizon, oddly shaped geometric symbols of industry crowd the middle ground, and a dead body is highlighted in the foreground. The viewer's eye is drawn to the ambiguously gendered, solitary figure standing with his or her arms raised prostrate with fear and despair. The overall effect is one of disarray, disorder, resignation, defeat, and most important utter alienation. The family is absent from the scene, the city has clearly ravaged it. Frazier was an advocate of migration and urbanization, two forces that he believed would eventually improve the quality of African American manhood and family life, but in the short term the migration and urbanization of an undereducated people led to the dissolution of families, tearing asunder many of the rural matriarchal and patriarchal families that had been able to survive in the South.[39]

Still another linoleum cut, "In the City of Rebirth," contrasts with "Destruction," presenting a world that is calm, orderly, and precise. A state building hovering in the background indicates African Americans' political awakening and the central figures are men, the forbearers of the new class traditions that will stabilize African American families and fundamentally transform their status through a culture of civic, political, and labor activism. In the foreground, a well-dressed scholar sits at his desk writing and over his right shoulder a skilled artisan is busy constructing the structures and institutions of urban life. With his square in hand, he symbolically measures and is a measure of racial and family progress.[40] The family itself is strikingly absent from this last image.

In its absence, however, it is clear that these perfect specimens of skilled black family manhood are both the products and disseminators of a new masculine authority, which economically, politically, and culturally stabilizes the family and makes modern, democratic institution building possible. Frazier's sociohistorical theory of the black family was inextricably connected to the paternal authority that only gainfully employed skilled black men could marshal. What is reborn in the city are families headed by skilled black men, men whose success, virility, and working-class consciousness make the formation of healthy modern African American families and communities possible. The emphasis on the power of patriarchal memories has been replaced with an emphasis on the class-based paternal authority and politics of the modern black male worker.

According to Frazier, patriarchy was a historical family form, and its memory alone was of less service to modern urban black families than it had been in the past. In fact, he compared some of the remnants of these "old families" to an "animated museum," suggesting how out of place the patriarchal family was.[41] Rather, he forecasted the mid-century reconstitution of paternal authority through the integration of black men into organized industrial occupations. As the "old families" disappeared or intermarried with members of the emerging brown middle class, he maintained that the old division between the black upper class and the black masses was no longer an accurate or even a relevant description of the community. Rather, he described the appearance of occupational classes as the "most significant differentiation" African Americans experienced in the post–Civil War era.[42] These new classes created two new family types—the brown middle class and the black proletariat. Whereas family culture was originally the product of the traditions created by the accomplishments of individual patriarchs and projected downward through the generations and sustained through memory, the transfer of property and heirlooms, and patriarchal institutions, now family cultures were bound to where and how black family men earned their living and the class values and civic orientation inculcated. The democratic proletarian family represented the new heights of civilization and a wellspring of paternal authority based in large measure on the father's embrace of an interracial proletarian politics, the rebalancing of authority between men and women in the family (with women losing some and men gaining an equal measure without reinscribing patriarchal domination), and the subsequent democratization of the family. The brown middle class, however, was plagued by an assortment of gender dysfunctions and conservative racial and class politics that were largely the product of the middle-class family man's inability to embrace on appropriate class identity and civic mentality.

Frazier was confident that the entrance of black workers into industry was transforming African Americans' status, restoring paternal authority, and invigorating African American husbandhood and fatherhood. He correlated manly industrial work and the proletarian family with the rebirth of "masculine authority."[43] Grouping black workers into four categories—skilled, semi-skilled, laborers, and domestic servants—he argued that although most black men were workers, each category of workers had not yet developed a working-class consciousness. In the case of industrial and organized black workers, he wrote, their "working-class consciousness has been influenced by their experience in industrial struggles, including, of course, cooperation with white workers."[44] He also explored the struggle that these workers faced, not only to "prove" their "discipline" to their white employers and coworkers, but also in terms of the challenges they faced in the African American community, due to the "middle-class outlook" promoted in black schools and churches. While this group continued to face real obstacles in housing and the labor market, he maintained that as their class values coalesced and the labor movement integrated, an empowered, interracial proletariat would see no need to resort to racism.

Frazier further defined the rewards of working-class consciousness quite clearly, deeming these men the new models of black family manhood. It is in the households of working-class family men that he identified the roots of a new modern masculine authority. Mothers and wives were economically dependent, but "occup[ied] position[s] of authority and [were] not completely subordinate[d] to masculine authority." Frazier explained that "the authority of the father in the family has been strengthened, and the wife has lost some of her authority in family matters." The father gained authority and the mother gained support. Frazier was also more hopeful about the children of the black proletariat. While a significant portion of working-class children were neglected as a consequence of "economic and social factors," he deemed them, on the whole, less spoiled than middle-class children and essentially manlier. According to Frazier, the well-organized proletarian family produced "a spirit of democracy." Moreover, unlike the uncompetitive, insecure, spoiled boys of the middle class, the children of the proletariat often developed "a spirit of self-reliance."[45] Frazier concluded, "As the Negro has become an industrial worker and received adequate compensation, the father has become the chief breadwinner and assumed a responsible place in his family."[46] Put another way, the economic and the political were personal.

Frazier's portrait of the feminine brown middle class offered a stark contrast to the masculine black proletariat. While Frazier asserted that both classes were still in their initial stages of growth, he traced the brown middle class's lack of viable father figures to their "naïve profession of faith in individual thrift and individual enterprise in a world that was rapidly entering a period of corporate wealth."[47] Their economic philosophy infused them with the "psychology of the modern businessman" and encouraged their embrace of conservative economic and political outlooks. Unlike the black proletariat, the brown middle class tended toward Republicanism, opposed socialized medicine, were unable to identify and sympathize with the plight of the Scottsboro boys, and were invested in segregation since it allowed them to "monopolize the Negro market." Frazier exhorted: "They prefer the overvaluation of their achievements and position behind the walls of segregation to a democratic order that would result in economic and social devaluation of themselves." Not wanting to leave the readers with any doubt about the black middle class's failure to realize a modern family manhood, Frazier likened the middle class's security in segregation to a "mulatto woman . . . who, enjoying a position in the Negro group far beyond her social and personal worth, views with the fiercest antagonism the competition of white women."[48] Lacking a working-class consciousness, Frazier described a brown middle class whose values were organized around "standards of consumptions" and emulations of whiteness, which increased criminality as black men attempted to consume at a rate beyond their limited economic means and encouraged a focus on "social life" and frivolity.[49] While middle-class incomes allowed portions of the brown middle class to purchase homes, a major indicator of family stability, Frazier maintained that incomes without the appropriate cultural and political values could lead just as quickly to family instability and disorganization. Identifying a small portion of the brown middle class as "equalitarian" and counseling "salaried workers" to adopt a working-class consciousness, Frazier's overall estimation of middle-class black men and the families they produced was less than optimistic.

According to Frazier, middle-class marriages suffered significant gender dysfunctions, and the few children they raised were characterized by their "softness" and "unfit[ness] for life in a world of competition." Economically dependent wives were forced to "show strict regard for conventional standards of conduct," while their husbands "enjoyed considerable freedom and in some cases may even have outside affairs." In other cases, these same wives were "dominant," making their husbands "slave to her whims and extravagances." Conversely, economically independent wives "submitted to extreme domination by their husbands."[50] These distorted gender roles and role reversals were symptomatic of families without the leadership and common set of interests fostered by working-class-oriented family men. Furthermore, Frazier found the children socialized by middle-class families spoiled and poisoned by the cult of conspicuous consumption that was practiced in the home and preached in black colleges. Meager class traditions were making them "soft" and unmanning their sons, who, Frazier explained, were "often as spoiled as their sisters."[51] Their sons, he attested, were competent only to secure incomes in philanthropy, through the state, or in a segregated economy.

In *Black Bourgeois* (1957) Frazier took these arguments to the next level. While Robert Ezra Park of the Chicago School of Sociology described African Americans as "the lady of the races" (1918) and the *Moynihan Report* (1965) popularized the idea that poor black women were to blame for the emasculation of black men, in *Black Bourgeoisie* Frazier suggested that if we restrict our observation to middle-class males then blacks truly were the "the lady among the races."[52] While the Moynihan Report highlighted a cycle of lower-class black emasculation, Frazier depicted a cycle of middle-class emasculation and worse yet homosexualization as a consequence of segregation-inspired inferiority complexes. Their resulting inferiority complex encouraged middle-class black men to seek compensation through a sort of feminine consumption or sexualization rather than via working-class masculine production or protest.

Throughout the 1950s, Frazier's repulsion with the middle class was balanced with his continuing concerns about unstable families at the lower end of the economic spectrum where fathers were literally, not figuratively, absent. Their absence was troubling to Frazier for a variety of reasons, which Frazier laid out in an essay written in anticipation of the Midcentury White House Conference on Children. Here Frazier revisited the importance of paternal heritage;[53] he wedded it to men's "limited economic opportunities in industrial occupations" and repackaged it as a call for "the male to serve as a model for the children, especially male offspring."[54] Frazier, however, described the primary problem in these terms: black children were "handicapped [...] in their relations to the institutions in the community."[55] There was no relationship between their private values in the home and their public values in the community. This bridge, spanning the political and the personal, was one that Frazier determined black family men were responsible for and capable of building once they developed a working-class consciousness. This was the bridge that Frazier's own father built for him, he stated as much when attributing his own "militant character" to "the example and indoctrination of his father," and this was the bridge that he sought to repair.[56]

The black father, in both his absence and his presence, stands at the center of Frazier's sociological corpus. Posthumously Frazier's name has become associated both with the black matriarchy/patriarchy debates, fueled by the Moynihan report in the 1960s, and the underclass debates of the late twentieth century. In the years following his death in 1962, Frazier has been accused of castigating black matriarchs and promoting the installation of black patriarchs by a number of historians, sociologists, and feminist scholars, who have accepted Moynihan's distortions of Frazier's family studies rather than returning to the original text. However, when read in light of his long scholarly career and the debates of the mid-twentieth century, it is quite clear that Frazier believed that matriarchy and patriarchy were historical concepts with no particular baring on contemporary issues in the modern black family. Anthony Platt, Cloves Semmes, and Robert Hill have begun the work of recuperating Frazier's voice in his own words as opposed to reifying Moynihan's very selective reading of well over forty years of scholarship on the black family.[57] This essay is a part of that project. The point is not to absolve Frazier of all charges of sexism. Feminist scholars, like Melinda Chateauvert and Joy James[58], are right to note and problematize masculinist visions of social change that marginalize women and reinscribe racist, heterosexist, and middle-class ideologies. However, the now all too common tendency to reduce and dehistoricize the richness of Frazier's scholarship down to the singular problem of matriarchy as defined by Moynihan, is troublesome. First, Frazier never characterized the challenges of black family life in such narrow terms. And, second, and more importantly, misreading Frazier encourages scholars to miss the very complex portraits and amazing resilience of black family life (that grew out of the love and the political, social, and economic ambitions of black mothers and fathers) so powerfully documented by Frazier's scholarship.

Rather than attempting to trace the conservative and highly inflammatory "politics" of the black family to an erroneous reading of Frazier's corpus, we might, in returning to his work and his words, actually identify a progressive, masculinist vision of the black family, which problematizes both maternal and paternal dominance and asserts that the strongest families are infused with an egalitarian or democratic, not authoritarian, spirit. Frazier was not the only witness to these dramatic transformations in gender norms, but he was one of a few scholars who captured these changes in the African American community. The same year *Black Bourgeoisie* hit the bookstores, a short essay entitled "A Century of Declining Paternal Authority" was published. The author, an English scholar, J. M. Mogey charted a similar transformation in the meaning of paternal authority, from an authoritarian social control for the family and society to an emphasis on the social role of the father in the family. Whereas the economist Frederic Le Play (1855) had asserted that familial and societal stability were a product of the absolute legal and customary right of the father over his wife and children, Mogey suggested that contemporary family and societal "stability rests upon a new base, the redefinition of the father role."[59] Frazier would surely have agreed with Mogey about both the continuing redefinition of family manhood and the modern challenges it posed. Frazier's story, however, was as much a declension narrative as it was a story of masculine rebirth revitalized through its commitment to and active participation in the extension of democratic, interracial, proletarian values through the family man. These values sustained Frazier's vision of modern family manhood and bridged the divide between the public and private sphere, and between the political and the personal.

Notes

1. Robert Griswold, *Fatherhood in America: A History* (New York: Basic Books, 1993); and Shawn Johansen, *Family Man* (New York: Routledge, 2001).

2. For marriage and courtship, see Eleanor Alexander, *Lyrics of Sunshine and Shadow: The Tragic Courtship and Marriage of Paul Laurence Dunbar and Alice Ruth Moore: A History of Love and Violence among the African American Elite* (New York: New York University Press, 2001); Adele Alexander, *Homelands and Waterways: The American Journey of the Bond Family, 1846–1926* (New York: Pantheon, 1999); Richard Hobbs, *The Cayton Family Legacy: An African American Family* (Seattle: University of Washington Press, 2002); and Douglass Hales, *A Southern Family in White & Black: The Cuneys of Texas* (College Station: Texas A&M University Press, 2003). New work on black sexualities includes Melinda Chateauvert, "Framing Sexual Citizenship: Reconsidering the Discourse on African American Families," *Journal of African American History* 93:2 (Spring 2008): 198–222; Lisa Thompson, *Beyond the Black Lady: Sexuality and the New African American Middle Class* (Urbana: University of Illinois Press, 2009); Michele Mitchell, *Righteous Propagation: African Americans and the Politics of Racial Destiny after Reconstruc-*

tion (Chapel Hill: University of North Carolina Press, 2004); and Siobhan Somerville, *Queering the Color Line: Race and the Invention of Homosexuality in American Culture* (Durham, NC: Duke University Press, 2000). For recent scholarship on black families, see Carol Bleser, *In Joy and in Sorrow: Women, Family, and Marriage in the Victorian South, 1830–1900* (New York: Oxford University Press, 1991); Bart Landry, *Black Working Wives: Pioneers of the American Family Revolution* (Berkeley: University of California Press, 2000); and Melissa Walker and Rebecca Sharpless, *Work, Family, and Faith: Rural Southern Women in the Twentieth Century* (Columbia: University of Missouri Press, 2006).

3. Maurice Wallace, *Constructing the Black Masculine: Identity and Ideality in African American Men's Literature and Culture, 1775–1995* (Durham, NC: Duke University Press, 2002); David Dudley, *My Father's Shadow: Intergenerational Conflict in African American Men's Autobiography* (Philadelphia: University of Pennsylvania Press, 1991); bell hooks, *We Real Cool: Black Men and Masculinity* (New York: Routledge, 2004); Athena Mutua, *Progressive Black Masculinities* (New York: Routledge, 2006); Michael Connor and Joseph White, *Black Fathers: An Invisible Presence in America* (Mahwah, NJ: Lawrence Erlbaum Associates, 2006); Cynthia Daniels, *Lost Fathers: The Politics of Fatherlessness in America* (New York: St. Martin's Press, 1998); Jennifer Hamer, *What It Means to Be Daddy: Fatherhood for Black Men Living Away from the Families* (New York: Columbia University Press, 2001); Richard Majors and Jacob Gordon, *The American Black Male: His Present Status and His Future* (New York: Nelson-Hall Publishers, 1994); Robert Staples, *Black Masculinity: The Black Male's Role in American Society* (New York: Black Scholar's Press, 1982); and David Marriott, *On Black Men* (Edinburgh, Scotland: Edinburgh University Press, 2000).

4. Elizabeth Regosin, *Voices of Emancipation: Understanding Slavery, the Civil War, and Reconstruction through the U.S. Pension Bureau Files* (New York: New York University Press, 2008); Rebecca Fraser, *Courtship and Love among the Enslaved in North Carolina: Love & Marriage in Early African America* (Jackson: University of Mississippi Press, 2007); Laura Edwards, *Gendered Strife and Confusion: The Politics of Reconstruction* (Chicago: University of Illinois Press, 1997); Werner Sollors, *Interracialism: Black-White Intermarriage in American History, Literature, and Law* (New York: Oxford University Press, 2000); and Martha Hodes, *Sex, Love, Race: Crossing Boundaries in North American History* (New York: New York University Press, 1999).

5. United States Department of Labor, Office of Policy Planning and Research, *The Negro Family: The Case for National Action* (Washington, DC: U.S. Government Printing Office, 1965); hereafter Moynihan Report.

6. E. Franklin Frazier, *The Negro Family in the United States* (Chicago: University of Chicago Press, 1939). Charles A. Valentine, *Culture and Poverty: Critique and Counter-Proposals* (Chicago: University of Chicago Press, 1968); Paula Giddings, *When and Where I Enter: The Impact of Black Women on Race and Sex in America* (New York: Bantam Books, 1984); and Anthony Platt, *E. Franklin Frazier Reconsidered* (New Brunswick, NJ: Rutgers University Press, 1991).

7. Jawanza Kunjufu, *Countering the Conspiracy to Destroy Black Boys,* vols. 1–4 (New York: African American Images, 1985–86).

8. W. E. B. Du Bois and Kelly Miller also promoted a more scientific approach to black family planning that was open to the use of eugenics in building better mar-

riages and creating stronger children. See Kelly Miller, "Eugenics of the Negro Race," *Scientific Monthly* 5:1 (July 1917): 57–59; and Daylanne English, *Unnatural Selections: Eugenics in American Modern and the Harlem Renaissance* (Chapel Hill: University of North Carolina Press, 2004).

9. Connor and White, *Black Fathers: An Invisible Presence in America*.

10. Charles S. Johnson, "The Problems and Needs of the Negro Adolescent in View of His Minority Racial Status: A Critical Summary," *Journal of Negro Education* 9:3 (July 1940): 346.

11. William Robinson, "Integration's Delay and Frustration Tolerance," *Journal of Negro Education* 28:4 (Autumn 1959): 472–75. Robinson asserted that "frustration tolerance" might provide African Americans with a sort of psychological immunity. He put it in these terms: "In the Negro home and community the child develops a resistance against the internalization of attitudes of racial inferiority, while seeking for a realization of the desirable values found in the total cultural pattern of American life" (474).

12. Lester Granger, "Problems and Needs of Negro Adolescent Workers," *Journal of Negro Education* 9:3 (July 1940): 321. He stressed, for example, "that the individual himself can be helped to withstand and repel hostile social forces by developing sufficient strength within himself and among sustaining influences in his community" (321). See also Herman Canady, "The Social Psychology of Youth," *Journal of Negro Education* 17:2 (Spring 1948): 120–23; Ruth Taylor, "Health Problems and Needs of Negro Children," *Journal of Negro Education* 19:3 (Summer 1950): 283. On "frustration-tolerance" see Walter G. Daniel, "The Responsibility of Education for the Preparation of Children and Youth to Live in a Multi-Racial Society," *Journal of Negro Education* 19:3 (Summer 1950): 388–98.

13. James Bayton, "The Guidance Dilemma: With Special Reference to the Guidance of Negro Youth," *Journal of Negro Education* 18:4 (Autumn 1949): 465–73; and Howard Hale Long, "Improving the Morale of Negro Youth and Children," *Journal of Negro Education* 19:3 (Summer 1950): 412–19.

14. Thomas Pettigrew, *A Profile of the Negro American* (Princeton, NJ: D. Van Nostrand Co, 1964), 22, 23, 25.

15. At this point, it might be instructive to differentiate between my argument and Melinda Chateauvert's. We both agree that "the negro family" and "the black family" became powerful and obstructive political fault lines at the legislative peak of the Civil Rights Movements of the 1960s. But this politicization of "the black family" went hand in hand with the domestication and depoliticization of black family manhood. Chateauvert demonstrates the political consequences of perceived personal failures, but in the case of Frazier, I am asserting that he understood family manhood as a simultaneously personal and political construct to begin with. Frazier increasingly linked family disorganization to family men's failure to fulfill their political responsibilities and obligations. While black women faced political censure for their sexual decisions, Frazier argued that political failings just as frequently undermined black family life. See Chateauvert, "Framing Sexual Citizenship," 198–99, 205–9.

16. See University of Medicine and Dentistry of New Jersey Department of Urban and Community Affairs, *Crisis of the Minority Male* (1989); California State Commission on the Status of African American Males, *Opportunity or Chaos: A Generation in*

Peril—A Preliminary Report on the Status of African-American Males in California (Sacramento, CA: Assembly Publications Office, 1992); California State Commission on the Status of African American Males, *African American Males: The Struggle for Equality* (Sacramento, CA: Assembly Publications Office, October 1996); North Carolina Department of Public Instruction, *African American Male Task Force Report* (1992); Lois W. Abramczyk and Jean Ross, eds., *Nurturing the Black Adolescent Male in the Family Context: A Public Health Responsibility* (Columbia, SC: College of Social Work, University of South Carolina, 1992); African American Males Task Force, *Educating African American Males: A Dream Deferred* (Milwaukee, WI: Milwaukee Public Schools, 1990); Bobby William Austin, ed., *Repairing the Breach: Key Ways to Support Family Life, Reclaim Our Streets, and Rebuild Civil Society in America's Communities: Report of the National Task Force on African-American Men and Boys* (Dillon, CO: Alpine Guild Inc., 1996); Ohio Office of Black Affairs, *Ohio's African American Males: A Call to Action* (1990); The Urban Institute, *Nurturing Young Black Males: Programs That Work* (1996); and Richard Majors and Susan Weiner, *Programs That Serve African American Male Youth* (Washington, DC: The Urban Institute, 1995).

17. While many feminists, from Joyce Ladner and Paula Giddings to Dorothy Roberts, have identified Frazier as originating the idea that most black families were matriarchal and pathological, Frazier never made any such assertions. Rather, he argued that the primary and most natural family bond was between the mother, regardless of her race, and her children (except in the case of the white slaveholding family where he asserted that the children of white slaveholders formed their strongest attachments with the enslaved, black surrogate mothers). Moreover, when Frazier used the term "matriarchate," he did so to designate a pre-urban mother- or grandmother-centered family group. The term was frequently geographically and historically specific. Central to Frazier's sociological research was actually how and why fatherhood developed. There is no doubt that his perpetuation of the notion that motherhood was static and natural in comparison to a virile and dynamic fatherhood bespoke a sexism common for his time and invoked the masculinism that deeply informed his sociological worldview; but that is a far cry from the assertion, frequently ascribed to Frazier, that most black families were matriarchal and thus pathological on these specifically misogynist grounds. See Joyce Ladner, *Tomorrow's Tomorrow: The Black Woman* (Garden City, NY: Anchor Books, 1972), 15–17; Dorothy Roberts, *Killing the Black Body: Race, Reproduction, and the Meaning of Liberty* (New York: Pantheon, 1997), 15–16; and, most importantly, Clovis Semmes, "E. Franklin Frazier's Theory of the Black Family: Vindication and Sociological Insight," *Journal of Sociology and Social Welfare* 28:2 (June 2001): 3–21, for an insightful assessment of the many ways in which Frazier's work has been misinterpreted and misrepresented by a variety of scholars across disciplines.

18. For more on the experiences of segregated social scientists like Frazier, see Francille Wilson, *The Segregated Scholars: Black Social Scientists and the Creation of Black Labor Studies* (Richmond: University of Virginia Press, 2006).

19. "A Lecture Series in Honor of Edward Franklin Frazier," E. Frazier Collection 131-1-1, Moorland-Spingarn Research Center, Howard University.

20. Howard Odum quoting Frazier in *American Sociology: The Story of Sociology in the United States through 1950,* 238. Howard Odum requested this statement in January 1948.

21. "The Talented Tenth," in *The Negro Problem* (Miami: Mnemosyne Publishing, 1969 [New York: Pratt and Co, 1903]); St. Clair Drake and Horace Cayton, *Black Metropolis: The Study of Negro Life in a Northern City* (Chicago: University of Chicago Press, 1945, repr. 1993); and Everett Stonequist, *The Marginal Man: A Study of Personality and Culture Conflict* (Chicago: Charles Scribner's Sons, 1937).

22. Frazier, *The Negro Family in Chicago* (Chicago: University of Chicago Press, 1932).

23. Frazier primarily used the term "patriarchy" to describe the highest stage of development for the pre-urban black family. He used the term "paternal authority" more broadly to describe the cultural, social, and economic power of male-headed households.

24. Frazier, *The Negro Family in Chicago,* 284; also in *The Negro Family in the United States,* 454.

25. Jerome Dowd, *The Negro in American Life* (New York, 1926); W. D. Weatherford, *The Negro from Africa to America* (New York: Julian Messner, 1924); Howard Odum, *Social and Mental Traits of the Negro* (New York, 1910); William Pickett, *The Negro Problem* (New York: Columbia University, 1909); Frederick Hoffman, *Race Traits and Tendencies of the American Negro* (New York: Macmillan, published for The American Economic Association, 1896); William Thomas, *The American Negro: What He Has, What He Is, and What He May Become* (New York: Macmillan, 1901).

26. E. Franklin Frazier, "Problems and Needs of Negro Children and Youth Resulting from Family Disorganization," *Journal of Negro Education* 19:3 (Summer 1950): 274.

27. Frazier, *The Negro Family in Chicago,* 260.

28. Ibid., 270.

29. Ibid., 289.

30. For a fascinating critique of black social scientists' attempts to curtail and problematize black migration, see Marlon Ross, *Manning the Race: Reforming Black Men in the Jim Crow Era* (New York: New York University Press, 2004).

31. Frazier, *The Negro Family in Chicago,* 298.

32. Ibid., 299.

33. Ibid., 287.

34. Ibid., 187–88.

35. E. Franklin Frazier, *The Negro Family in the United States* (Notre Dame, IN: University of Notre Dame Press, 2001), 488.

36. For more on this generation of scholars and their politics at Howard University, see Jonathan Scott Holloway, *Confronting the Veil: Abram Harris, Jr., E. Franklin Frazier, and Ralph Bunche* (Chapel Hill: University of North Carolina Press, 2002).

37. "American Negro Exposition, July 4 to September 2, 1940," Frazier Collection, 131-22-32.

38. Oliver Cox argued that African Americans married earlier because they arrived at cultural maturity earlier due to their limited racial status and their higher rates of employment. Oliver Cox, "Employment, Education, and Marriage of Young Negro Adults," *Journal of Negro Education* 10:1 (January 1941): 39–42; and Oliver Cox, "Farm Tenancy and Marital Status, With Special Emphasis upon Negro Marriage," *Social Forces* 19:1 (October 1940): 81, 84.

39. Oliver Cox, "Sex Ratio and Marital Status Among Negroes," *American Sociological Review* 5:6 (December 1940): 937–947, 941, 942.

40. Frazier, *The Negro Family in the United States,* 2, 88, 162, 270, 392.

41. Ibid., 414.

42. Frazier, "Occupational Classes among Negroes in Cities," *American Journal of Sociology* 35:5 (March 1930): 718–38. Frazier broke African Americans into eight occupational groups—professional service, public service, trade, clerical, skilled workers, semi-skilled workers, domestic and personal service, and laborers.

43. Frazier, *The Negro Family in the United States,* 461.

44. Ibid., 453.

45. Ibid., 469.

46. Ibid., 487.

47. Ibid., 420.

48. Ibid., 436–37.

49. Charles S. Johnson, on the other hand, documented the extent to which poor rural African Americans were equally limited by their emulation of the "backward or narrow or stagnant white element of the culture and thus offer[ed] no advantage." See Johnson, "The Education of the Negro Child," *American Sociological Review* 1:2 (April 1936): 266. For a wonderful example of the generational tensions over the meaning of middle-class status in the early twentieth century, see Martin Summers, *Manliness and Its Discontents: The Black Middle Class and the Transformation of Masculinity, 1900–1930* (Chapel Hill: University of North Carolina Press, 2004).

50. Frazier, *The Negro Family in the United States,* 438, 439

51. Ibid., 443, 445.

52. Frazier, *Black Bourgeoisie,* 220–21. In the original handwritten text, Frazier referred to black men in general, but as he edited, he narrowed his critique to focus on middle-class men specifically. "Black Bourgeoisie, unsorted drafts," Frazier Collection, Moorland-Spingarn Research Collection, Howard University.

53. E. Franklin Frazier, "Problems and Needs of Negro Children and Youth Resulting from Family Disorganization," *Journal of Negro Education* 19:3 (Summer 1950): 269–77.

54. Ibid., 272n6.

55. Ibid., 276.

56. Arthur Davis, "E. Franklin Frazier (1894–1962): A Profile," *Journal of Negro Education* 31:4 (Autumn 1962): 429–35, 430.

57. Anthony Platt, *E. Franklin Frazier Reconsidered;* Cloves Semmes, "E. Franklin Frazier's Theory;" and Robert Hill, *Research on the African-American Family: A Holistic Perspective* (Westport, CT: Auburn House, 1993), 7–8.

58. Joy James, *Transcending the Talented Tenth: Black Leaders and American Intellectuals* (New York: Routledge, 1997).

59. J. M. Mogey, "A Century of Declining Paternal Authority," *Marriage and Family Living* 19:3 (August 1957): 239, 234–39. Note that Mogey read his paper at the Annual Meeting of the American Sociological Society in Washington, DC, in 1955.

Postscript

Black Masculinity and New Precedents

RICHÉ RICHARDSON

The notion of national manhood that consolidated in the late eighteenth century as the republic itself emerged prioritized elite white men in its definition and coalesced against the ideological backdrop of an Enlightenment philosophical discourse that defined black people as inferior and incapable of rationality. Manhood in the United States has never been imagined as an interracial fraternity, nor has the office of the presidency, any more than the nation has ever truly actualized its great potential to be a true interracial democracy. Even some radical black liberation activists of the 1960s, for example, who frequently invoked the ubiquity of "the man" to describe how white men dominated the nation's power structure and the centrality of whiteness in defining manhood—and notwithstanding the masculinism and misogyny that tinged aspects of this ideology and its failure to provide a fuller critique of patriarchy—were keenly instinctive in apprehending and referencing the hegemony of this raced, sexed, classed, and gendered system. With great accuracy, they articulated the ways in which it excluded and devalued black men and regarded them as unequal. As this volume illustrates, black men, since the antebellum era, have been perceived as alien from and fundamentally incompatible with the dominant and inherently hierarchical national model of manhood, a model in relation to which ideals of freedom, humanity, democracy, and citizenship have been historically constituted. The election of Barack Obama as president of the United States on November 4, 2008—a mixed-race man who identifies as black and African American and is descended from a black Kenyan father and a white American mother from the state of Kansas—shattered the conventional racial (and arguably racist) fantasy of manhood in the national imaginary as white. To be sure, President Obama has set a new precedent by also unsettling the conventional definition of "presidentialism" in this nation.[1]

One cannot overlook this history, including the purist and racialist perceptions of the presidency as "white" that have been deeply entrenched in the consciousness of many citizens in the United States, in thinking, for example, about why some contemporary neoconservative grassroots political movements such as the Birthers have been so invested in constructing a narrative of Obama as "foreign" and in questioning the constitutionality of his presidency. Similarly, it is important to consider why their close compatriots in the public sphere, the Tea Partiers, as they have theatrically enacted dress dating back to periods such as the American Revolution and the Civil War, have simultaneously disseminated an unremitting barrage of propagandistic visual images of the president that make him over as Adolph Hitler to associate him with fascism, portray him as a naked "native," and cast him lynched in effigy.

The span of years to which this new critical volume draws us back, especially the Reconstruction era of the late nineteenth century, during which gross caricatures of blackness began to circulate—caricatures that authors such as Charles Chesnutt confronted in fiction—is a necessary framework to draw on for understanding these perverse images that have circulated so unapologetically in the public sphere of politics in recent times, along with the new forms of nativism that inflect them. The anecdote mentioned in this volume's opening pages about Judge Joseph Mills's recounting of how he mistook Frederick Douglass for a president in a dialogue with Abraham Lincoln illustrates some of the competing and contradictory models of black manhood that were operative during the antebellum era. It confirmed the potential among white men to think progressively and inclusively to the point of admiring and embracing a black man like Frederick Douglass who was eloquent, commanding and visually iconic in the public sphere sincerely as a "man" and a "brother," to invoke the famous slogan of abolitionism set forth in the plea, "Am I

Not a Man and a Brother?" However, it also attests to the titillating allure of an image of the president in blackface within this exclusive white male fraternity, an image that rested, incidentally, in the continuum with a range of other minstrel images of blackness of the time, images that had currency on liberal political circuits during the nineteenth century.

The efforts of Obama's detractors to invalidate his presidency by constructing grotesque images of his body function as a form of neo-minstrelsy whose racism is intrinsic and undeniable and cannot be ratio-nalized or camouflaged as a form of free speech. The byproduct is a scripting of him in a continuum with the perverse and notorious archive of caricatures that portrayed black politicians of the Reconstruction era as unintelligent and incapable of leadership, who were imagined as bed-fellows of Reconstruction's white Carpetbaggers and Scalawags. This new concerted and calculated partisan script of Obama in the public sphere, I believe, is fundamentally distinct from those intramural assertive criticisms of him that have been staged as a form of "tough love" and that have been counterbalanced, say, by donations to his campaign and attendance at his historic presidential inauguration.

Some of the earliest critical studies of "maleness," "manhood," and "masculinity" tended to repeat and mirror the exclusions in the nation's conventional definitions of these various terms by focusing exclusively on white middle-class men as a category of analysis and presuming their experiences as normative and representative, just as work in women's studies, which helped to pave the way to some of the new ways of think-ing about male subjectivity and new epistemologies on gender and sexu-ality that have emerged over the past several decades, frequently excluded black women and other women of color. Work that underscored the importance of thinking about race in the construction of masculinity set new precedents in studies of masculinity. Critical work on topics such as "black masculinity" and "black manhood" has proliferated over the past several decades, to the point that it represents a thriving subfield in and of itself. The many graduate and undergraduate courses that have emerged in this bourgeoning field of study in recent years, and the aca-demic conferences of national scope that have been devoted to it, illus-trate that it is a viable area for teaching, research, and study and attracts diverse audiences.

The essays in *Fathers, Preachers, Rebels, Men* make an important contri-bution to the dialogues on black masculinity and chart some new direc-tions for the interdisciplinary field of study that in recent years has been shaping up as "critical black masculinities." It reveals how black manhood has been shaped dialectically in varying historical moments by a diverse range of identities and clarifies how they have impacted its complex processes of formation. It registers the role of blackness in shaping notions of manhood at the national level, and further unsettles the myth of a pure white manhood. It demonstrates the utility of black manhood as a concept to "think with" in light of processes of gender formation given its broad cultural reach. Even the diverse group of scholars who have contributed essays to this volume—white and black, male and female—reveals that the critical interest in black masculinity and manhood as topics is widespread, and for analytical purposes in fields such as gender studies, is broad, and even increasingly universal.

Given the fascination with President Obama in a range of cultural contexts in the United States and abroad, the history related to his revolutionary campaign that gained momentum through new technological innovations, his election as the nation's first black president, and the debates about his approaches to policymaking, a figure like him presents a great opportunity and also poses new challenges for scholarship on black manhood and masculinity. His speeches and books and his iconic construction in the public and popular spheres are already the subject of growing fascination in scholarship and in teaching. This anthology registers awareness of this important paradigm shift that has come in the nation's public sphere with the election of the first black man in history as president and, notably, is one of the earliest comprehensive studies of black masculinity published in the wake of this moment. It sets a range of new precedents of its own through its interdisciplinary and comparative methodology in a text on black masculinity.

Its basic organization recalls aspects of "call and response" in the African American musical tradition. That is to say, one quality that makes this volume distinct is a structure that pairs a range of topics or figures and puts them into dialogue from chapter to chapter. Such a structure forces the members of the audience to think with more focus than we might ordinarily, for example, about distinctions between the experiences of enslaved black men and free ones, and black men in the North and the South. Chapters that juxtapose Thomas Nast and Charles Chesnutt highlight the complex relationships of white men and black men to the politics of visual representation in areas such as magazine illustration during the politically charged years after slavery. Similarly, it is useful that several chapters in this rich volume, such as the one by Julius Bailey, draw attention to black female subjectivity in the process of analyzing male subjects. In the course of dialoguing about how figures such as the black itinerant preacher helped to expand and diversify notions of black manhood during the nineteenth century, he adds to our insights about the experiences of some of the best known black women in this sacred league, such as Jarena Lee and Zilpha Elaw. Such layers embedded in the volume help to move us beyond the "separate spheres" approaches to gender during the nineteenth century that, as critics in American literature argue, have long cast a shadow over studies of gender during the period.[2] At the same time, this dimension underscores the indispensability of comparative approaches to gender when analyzing not only black masculinity but also black male and female identities.

For a long time in academic discourses, and particularly in areas such as literature and history, the experience of slavery has served as the primary framework for documenting and interpreting the black experience during the antebellum era, a perspective that has obscured the experiences of free blacks in the black population, even as their condition was volatile, provisional, and of necessity conditioned and circumscribed by the ubiquity of the slave system in society. This study moves beyond the former premise and heralds newer methodologies of comparativism that have impacted the historiography on slavery in recent years, which have drawn attention to the diversity in black communities by acknowledging the broad range of subject positions that black men occupied during the antebellum era, from being enslaved and categorized as property to being free and literate. The presumption that blacks were unlettered during the antebellum era and that the white master class mainly produced the written records of slavery that have been valued for archival research and study is unsettled in the diaries of William Johnson, a free black man who owned slaves. As his writings reveal, at times he adapted and relied on the protocols of paternalism in his relationships with his black male slaves. Furthermore, this section makes clear how the barber shop, which has long been recognized and analyzed as a public sphere in black masculine contexts in the contemporary era, established this function during the antebellum era. Similarly, this study shows that in spite of their subordinated position, black men who were slaves typically have been dissociated from notions of honor. However, it reveals how they internalized aspects of the culture of poor white men to formulate notions of masculine honor and invested energy in protecting and defending it among themselves, even through forms of violence. *Fathers, Preachers, Rebels, Men* also breaks new ground by expanding the understanding of the methods that black men in the antebellum era used for resistance beyond the forms of violent confrontation that have been romanticized in relation to figures such as Frederick Douglass. This is a critical revelation that invites us to consider more of the ways in which black women may have claimed agency within the slave system, that went beyond the quieter and subtler strategies of resistance that critics associate with them in light of their feminine gender and status as mothers that tended to make them less individualistic and more bound to family and community. In general, the volume is richly historicized. The meticulous archival work on which its essays draw, along with their exacting and eclectic methodologies, make this volume a model one in the field on this topic. The harmony that draws these essays into running and sometimes overlapping dialogues from chapter to chapter—dialogues that are detailed and highly integrative—is another admirable quality. Their seamlessness is all the more remarkable and noteworthy given this volume's interdisciplinary orientation.

The widespread critical fascination with black women that emerged during the 1980s in scholarship shows us that new markets of consumption and exchange, even in academia, can mirror and extend the exploits of the old forms of black objectification, consumption, and specularity that coincided with the rise of modernism.[3] It is telling that just as black women became the subject of growing scholarly interest in academia, young, single, poor, and unemployed black mothers in the nation's "inner cities" were simultaneously being pathologized in the nation's public sphere as "welfare queens" by conservative Republicans invested in reducing government spending. This background is important to consider in a university system that increasingly has been corporatized during the first decade of this new millennium. Similarly, it is crucial that the growing critical fascination with black men not obscure aspects of their lived reality in society or the ways in which they are so frequently stereotyped and misrepresented in the contexts such as the public sphere and popular culture. Black men have become the emphasis of more and more critical discussion in academic contexts at precisely the same time that statistics reveal that they encounter the highest levels of unemployment in the labor market in decades, some of the lowest enrollments in the nation's colleges and universities, high rates of infection from HIV/ AIDS, increased forms of surveillance such as racial profiling, and mass incarceration within the nation's corporatized prison industrial complex. Study of archives related to black masculinity, including some of the key literary, historical, and visual narratives, is inevitably shadowed by the reality of black men's continuing marginality in some of the nation's institutions, including academia.

To put it another way, even as black men are studied more and more frequently in academia, in the real world, black men, along with other men of color, are not necessarily prioritized in recruitment and hiring processes in academic departments, and they typically have very few opportunities for tenure, promotion, and administrative leadership within academic institutions. Even though it is important, of course, to avoid the pitfall of positioning them as "native informants" and reinscribing essentialist identity politics, it *is* significant that the work of so many black male scholars has been foundational in shaping this field. It is work that has been at the forefront in formulating questions about black masculinity in relation to areas such as law, sexuality, popular culture, art, sports, and politics, and that has approached the topic with an understanding of the value of considering the intersectionality of factors such as race, gender, class, sexuality, nationality, and region. As the field itself has become more and more diverse, black men's voices have continued to make unique and important contributions to critical dialogues. This field will be enhanced, I suspect, by yet more comparative work that looks at black masculine formations in relation to a more diverse spectrum of racial and ethnic contexts, and in global and transnational perspective. In general, it is exciting that the field itself, in terms of its major researchers, is increasingly reflecting the growing racial and ethnic diversity that characterizes U.S. society, even as the prevailing ideology of the United States as a "post-racial" society given the election of Barack Obama registers as a cruel fiction, especially when we consider the bitter and racially charged contestations regarding his policies and the glaring disrespect for his presidency that is apparent in some reactionary political sectors.

In January 2010, the devastating earthquake in Haiti and the catastrophe left in its wake drew an outpouring of support from around the globe. This tragedy has increased interest in the history of Haiti, the first black democracy established in the Western Hemisphere. One of this volume's penultimate essays, which compares and contrasts U.S.- and Caribbean-based forms of resistance through the models offered by John Brown and Toussaint L'Ouverture, makes a valuable contribution to the scholarship on Haiti, a nation, as Susan Buck-Morss has recently shown in her groundbreaking philosophical scholarship on Hegel and Haiti, that is useful to think with to help unsettle notions of "universal history."[4]

When I was serving as a Cultural Envoy to the U.S. Embassy under the auspices of a grant from the U.S. Department of State, and hosted for a week in the "Speaker Series," it was sobering that as I was speaking to a group of high school seniors in the banlieues in Saint-Denis and discussed black male leaders and the upcoming presidential inauguration in the U.S, and as I underscored the importance of situating Obama and Martin Luther King in relation to Frederick Douglass, several black male students from Africa and the Caribbean stopped me and asked me who Douglass was; they had never heard of him. On the spot, I gave an overview of his slave narrative and history, along with other figures with whom they had no familiarity, such as Olaudah Equiano. This moment underscored for me that as much as we may value and understand certain histories related to black masculinity, we cannot presume that they are shared, even throughout the African diaspora. It also underscored the value of comparative and transnational approaches in studies of black masculinity. Similarly, the multi-ethnic group of nineteen teens who interviewed me at the Bondy Blog—the first media outlet to report on the unrest in the banlieues in the fall of 2005—admired the election of a black President Obama in the United States, but doubted that an "Obama" was conceivable in a context such as France, given its history. I mentioned prominent historical figures such as Toussaint L'Ouverture, Alexandre Dumas, Aime Cesaire, Leopold Senghor, and Frantz Fanon to remind them of the historical legacies of black masculine leadership and achievement in Francophone contexts to help them imagine and think toward a future that might include leaders at the national level who look more like they do, and who might someday occupy the position of the presidency in France, which has been defined across time by legacies ranging from those of Napoleon Bonaparte to Jacque Chirac. It is crucial that in doing this work on black masculinity, we conceptualize the field in the broadest and most inclusive sense and understand its potential to inspire people, give them hope, and potentially transform their lives. I know that I have deeply appreciated how the work in this field has helped to transform mine.

This volume comes at an important time and is a gift to the field of black masculinity studies. It opens up more interpretive possibilities for black masculinity, even as it challenges many things that we thought we know about it. From essay to essay, it challenges, enlightens, inspires, and teaches all at once. It has opened the door to many more exciting possibilities.

Notes

1. Dana Nelson, *National Manhood: Capitalist Citizenship and the Imagined Fraternity of White Men* (Durham, NC: Duke University Press, 1998), ix. In this important study, Nelson defines "national manhood" as "an ideology that has worked powerfully since the Constitutional era to link a fraternal articulation of white manhood to civic identity." Furthermore, this study reveals how the concept of presidentialism has played a central and even foundational role in shaping this raced and gendered ideology.

2. See "No More Separate Spheres!" a special issue of *American Literature* coedited by Cathy N. Davidson, Mary C. Fuller, and Joseph F. Aranda, *American Literature* 70 (September 1998). The anthology that builds upon the volume is *No More Separate Spheres! A Next Wave American Studies Reader,* Cathy N. Davidson, Jessamyn Hatcher, Linda K. Kerber, and Judith Fetterley, eds. (Durham, NC: Duke University Press, 2002).

3. For further engagement of this problem related to scholarship on black women, see, for example, Ann DuCille, "The Occult of True Black Womanhood: Critical Demeanor and Black Feminist Studies," *Signs* 19 (1994): 591–629.

4. Here, I reference Susan Buck-Morss's short and masterful critical study entitled *Hegel, Haiti, and Universal History* (Pittsburgh: University of Pittsburgh Press, 2009), which is the outgrowth of an earlier article published in the journal *Critical Inquiry.*

Selected Bibliography

Appleby, Joyce. *Inheriting the Revolution: The First Generation of Americans.* Cambridge, MA: Harvard University Press, 2000.

Ayers, Edward L. *Vengeance and Justice: Crime and Punishment in the 19th-Century American South.* New York: Oxford University Press, 1984.

Bacon, Jacqueline. *Freedom's Journal: The First African American Newspaper.* Lanham, MD: Lexington Books, 2007.

Bailey, Julius H. *Around the Family Altar: Domesticity in the African Methodist Episcopal Church, 1865–1900.* Gainesville: University Press of Florida, 2005.

Bakken, Gordon and Brenda Farrington, eds. *Racial Encounters in the Multi-Cultural West: The American West,* vol. 2. New York: Garland, 2001.

Bay, Mia. *The White Image in the Black Mind: African American Ideas about White People, 1830–1925.* New York: Oxford University Press, 2000.

Bean, Annamarie, James V. Hatch, and Brooks McNamara, eds. *Inside the Minstrel Mask: Readings in Nineteenth-Century Blackface Minstrelsy.* Middletown, CT: Wesleyan University Press, 1996.

Bederman, Gail. *Manliness and Civilization: A Cultural History of Gender and Race in the United States, 1880–1917.* Chicago: University of Chicago Press, 1995.

Bell, Howard, ed. *Minutes of the Proceedings of the National Negro Conventions, 1830–1864.* New York: Arno Press, 1969.

Bethel, Elizabeth Rauh. *The Roots of African-American Identity: Memory and History in Free Antebellum Communities.* New York: St. Martin's Press, 1997.

Black, Daniel P. *Dismantling Black Manhood: An Historical and Literary Analysis of the Legacy of Slavery.* New York: Garland, 1997.

Blassingame, John W. *The Slave Community: Plantation Life in the Antebellum South.* New York: Oxford University Press, 1972.

Bleser, Carol, ed. *In Joy & in Sorrow: Women, Family, and Marriage in the Victorian South, 1830–1890.* New York: Oxford University Press, 1991.

Blount, Marcellus and George P. Cunningham. *Representing Black Men.* New York: Routledge, 1996.

Boskin, Joseph. *Sambo: The Rise and Demise of an American Jester.* New York: Oxford University Press, 1986.

Brown, Joshua. *Beyond the Lines: Pictorial Reporting, Everyday Life, and the Crisis of Gilded Age America.* Berkeley: University of California Press, 2002.

Brown, Kathleen. *Good Wives, Nasty Wenches, and Anxious Patriarchs: Gender, Race, and Power in Colonial Virginia.* Williamsburg, VA: Published for the Institute of Early American History and Culture by the University of North Carolina Press, 1996.

Brown, William Wells. *The Black Man, His Antecedents, His Genius, and His Achievements.* New York: Thomas Hamilton, 1863.

Bruce, Dickson D. Jr. *Violence and Culture in the Antebellum South.* Austin: University of Texas Press, 1979.

Carby, Hazel. *Race Men: The W. E. B. Du Bois Lectures.* Cambridge, MA: Harvard University Press, 1998.

Caster, Peter. *Prisons, Race, and Masculinity in Twentieth-Century U.S. Literature and Film.* Columbus: The Ohio State University Press, 2008.

Clinton, Catherine and Michele Gillespie, eds. *The Devil's Lane: Sex and Race in the Early South.* New York: Oxford University Press, 1997.

Clinton, Catherine and Nina Silber, eds. *Divided Houses: Gender and the Civil War.* New York: Oxford University Press, 1992.

Connor, Michael and Joseph White. *Black Fathers: An Invisible Presence in America.* Mahwah, NJ: Lawrence Erlbaum, 2006.

Daniels, Cynthia. *Lost Fathers: The Politics of Fatherlessness in America.* New York: St. Martin's Press, 1998.

Dann, Martin E. *The Black Press, 1827–1890: The Quest for a National Identity.* New York: G. P. Putnam's Sons, 1971.

Davidson, James West. *'They Say': Ida B. Wells and the Reconstruction of Race.* New York: Oxford University Press, 2007.

Davis, James F. *Who Is Black? One Nation's Definition.* University Park: Pennsylvania State University Press, 1991.

Davis, Jane. *The White Image in the Black Mind: A Study of African American Literature.* Westport, CT: Greenwood Press, 2000.

Dorsey, Bruce. *Reforming Men and Women: Gender in the Antebellum City.* Ithaca, NY: Cornell University Press, 2002.

Douglass, Frederick. *The Life and Times of Frederick Douglass.* London: Christian Age Office, 1882.

———. *My Bondage and My Freedom.* New York and Auburn: Miller, Orton, & Co., 1857.

———. *Narrative of the Life of Frederick Douglass, an American Slave, Written by Himself.* David W. Blight, ed. Boston: Bedford/St. Martin's, 1993.

Du Bois, W. E. B. *The Philadelphia Negro: A Social Study.* Boston: Ginn & Co., 1899.

———. *The Souls of Black Folk.* New York: Vintage, 1990.

Dudley, David. *My Father's Shadow: Intergenerational Conflict in African American Men's Autobiography.* Philadelphia: University of Pennsylvania Press, 1991.

Durham, Philip and Everett L. Jones. *The Negro Cowboys.* Lincoln: University of Nebraska Press, 1983.

Edwards, Laura. *Gendered Strife and Confusion: The Politics of Reconstruction.* Chicago: University of Illinois Press, 1997.

Elkins, Stanley. *Slavery: A Problem in American Institutional and Intellectual Life.* Chicago: University of Chicago Press, 1976.

Fahs, Alice. *The Imagined Civil War: Popular Literature of the North and South, 1861–1865.* Chapel Hill: University of North Carolina Press, 2001.

Fischer, Sibylle. *Modernity Disavowed: Haiti and the Cultures of Slavery in the Age of Revolution.* Durham, NC: Duke University Press, 2004.

Foley, Barbara. *Specters of 1919: Class and Nation in the Making of the New Negro.* Urbana: University of Illinois Press, 2003.

Foner, Eric. *Free Soil, Free Labor, Free Men: The Ideology of the Republican Party before the Civil War.* 2nd ed. New York: Oxford University Press, 1995.

———. *Politics and Ideology in the Age of the Civil War.* New York: Oxford University Press, 1981.

———. *Reconstruction: America's Unfinished Revolution, 1863–1877.* New York: Harper & Row, 1988.

Forret, Jeff. *Race Relations at the Margins: Slaves and Poor Whites in the Antebellum Southern Countryside.* Baton Rouge: Louisiana State University Press, 2006.

Foster, Francis Smith. *Witnessing Slavery: The Development of Ante-Bellum Slave Narratives.* Westport, CT: Greenwood Press, 1979.

Fox-Genovese, Elizabeth. *Within the Plantation Household: Black and White Women of the Old South.* Chapel Hill: University of North Carolina Press, 1988.

Franklin, H. Bruce. *Prison Literature in America: The Victim as Criminal and Artist.* New York: Oxford University Press, 1989.

Franklin, John Hope and Loren Schweninger. *In Search of the Promised Land: A Slave Family in the Old South.* New York: Oxford University Press, 2006.

Fraser, Rebecca J. *Courtship and Love among the Enslaved in North Carolina; Love & Marriage in Early African America.* Jackson: University Press of Mississippi, 2007.

Frazier, E. Franklin. *Black Bourgeoisie.* New York: Free Press, 1957, 1990.

———. *The Negro Family in the United States.* Notre Dame, IN: University of Notre Dame Press, 2001. First published 1939 by University of Chicago Press.

Frederickson, George M. *The Black Image in the White Mind: The Debate on Afro-American Character and Destiny, 1817–1914.* New York: Harper & Row, 1971.

Frey, Sylvia. *Water from the Rock: Black Resistance in a Revolutionary Age.* Princeton, NJ: Princeton University Press, 1991.

Friend, Craig Thompson and Lorri Glover, eds. *Southern Manhood: Perspectives on Masculinity in the Old South.* Athens: University of Georgia Press, 2004.

Gaines, Kevin. *Uplifting the Race: Black Leadership, Politics, and Culture in the Twentieth Century.* Chapel Hill: University of North Carolina Press, 1996.

Gaspar, David Barry and Darlene Clark Hine, eds. *More than Chattel: Black Women and Slavery in the Americas.* Bloomington: Indiana University Press, 1996.

Gates, Henry Louis Jr. *Figures in Black: Words, Signs, and the "Racial" Self.* New York: Oxford University Press, 1987.

Gates, Henry Louis Jr. and William L. Andrews, eds. *Pioneers of the Black Atlantic: Five Slave Narratives.* New York: Basic Civitas Books, 1998.

Genovese, Eugene. *Roll, Jordan, Roll: The World the Slaves Made.* New York: Vintage, 1976.

Gerster, Patrick and Nicholas Cords, eds. *Myth and Southern History, vol. 1: The Old South.* Urbana: University of Illinois Press, 1989.

———. *Myth and Southern History, vol. 2: The New South.* Urbana: University of Illinois Press, 1989.

Gillman, Susan and Alys Eve Weinbaum, eds. *Next to the Color Line: Gender, Sexuality, and W. E. B. Du Bois.* Minneapolis: University of Minnesota Press, 2007.

Gilmore, Glenda Elizabeth. *Gender and Jim Crow: Women and the Politics of White Supremacy in North Carolina, 1896–1920.* Chapel Hill: University of North Carolina Press, 1996.

Gilmore, Paul. *The Genuine Article: Race, Mass Culture, and American Literary Manhood.* Durham, NC: Duke University Press, 2001.

Gilroy, Paul. *'There Ain't No Black in the Union Jack': The Cultural Politics of Race and Nation.* Chicago: University of Chicago Press, 1991.

Goldsby, Jacquelyn. *A Spectacular Secret: Lynching in American Life and Literature.* Chicago: University of Chicago Press, 2006.

Green, Tara T., ed. *From Plantation to the Prison: African American Confinement Literature.* Macon, GA: Mercer University Press, 2007.

Greenberg, Kenneth S. *Honor & Slavery: Lies, Duels, Noses, Masks, Dressing as a Woman, Gifts, Strangers, Humanitarianism, Death, Slave Rebellions, the Proslavery Argument, Baseball, Hunting, and Gambling in the Old South.* Princeton, NJ: Princeton University Press, 1996.

Greene, J. Lee. *Blacks in Eden: The African American Novel's First Century.* Charlottesville: University Press of Virginia, 1996.

Griswold, Robert. *Fatherhood in America: A History.* New York: Basic Books, 1993.

Gross, Ariela J. *Double Character: Slavery and Mastery in the Antebellum Southern Courtroom.* Princeton, NJ: Princeton University Press, 2000.

Gutman, Herbert. *The Black Family in Slavery and Freedom, 1750–1925.* New York: Random House, 1976.

Hamer, Jennifer. *What It Means to Be Daddy: Fatherhood for Black Men Living Away from Their Families.* New York: Columbia University Press, 2001.

Harding, Vincent. *There Is a River: The Black Struggle for Freedom in America.* New York: Harcourt, 1981.

Harper, Phillip Brian. *Are We Not Men? Masculine Anxiety and the Problem of African-American Identity.* New York: Oxford University Press, 1996.

Harris, Leslie. *In the Shadow of Slavery: African Americans in New York City, 1626–1863.* Chicago: University of Chicago Press, 2003.

Harris, Trudier. *Exorcising Blackness: Historical and Literary Lynching and Burning Rituals.* Bloomington: Indiana University Press, 1984.

Harrold, Stanley. *The Rise of Aggressive Abolitionism: Addresses to the Slaves.* Lexington: University Press of Kentucky, 2004.

Hartman, Saidiya. *Scenes of Subjection: Terror, Slavery, and Self-Making in Nineteenth-Century America*. New York: Oxford University Press, 1997.

Henri, Florette. *Black Migration: Movement North, 1900–1920*. New York: Anchor/Doubleday, 1975.

Hine, Darlene Clark and Earnestine Jenkins, eds. *A Question of Manhood: A Reader in U.S. Black Men's History and Masculinity*, vols. 1 and 2. Bloomington: Indiana University Press, 1999.

Hodes, Martha. *Sex, Love, Race: Crossing Boundaries in North American History*. New York: New York University Press, 1999.

hooks, bell. *Black Looks: Race and Representation*. Boston: South End Press, 1992.

———. *We Real Cool: Black Men and Masculinity*. New York: Routledge, 2003.

Horton, James Oliver. *Free People of Color: Inside the African American Community*. Washington, DC, and London: Smithsonian Institution Press, 1993.

Hunter, Tera W. *To 'Joy My Freedom: Southern Black Women's Lives and Labors after the Civil War*. Cambridge, MA: Harvard University Press, 1997.

Iliffe, John. *Honour in African History*. New York: Cambridge University Press, 2005.

Jackson, Jesse Jr., with Frank E. Watkins. *A More Perfect Union: Advancing New American Rights*. New York: Welcome Rain Publishers, 2001.

Jackson, Ronald L. *Scripting the Black Masculine Body: Identity, Discourse, and Racial Politics in Popular Media*. Albany: State University of New York Press, 2006.

Johansen, Shawn. *Family Man*. New York: Routledge, 2001.

Johnson, Lyman L. and Sonya Lipsett-Rivera, eds. *The Faces of Honor: Sex, Shame, and Violence in Colonial Latin America*. Albuquerque: University of New Mexico Press, 1998.

Johnson, Michael K. *Black Masculinity and the Frontier Myth in American Literature*. Norman: University of Oklahoma Press, 2002.

Johnson, Michael P., ed. *Reading the American Past: Selected Historical Documents*, vol. 1. Boston: Bedford/St. Martin's, 2005.

Jones, Jacqueline. *Labor of Love, Labor of Sorrow: Black Women, Work, and the Family from Slavery to the Present*. New York: Basic Books, 1985.

Jordan, Winthop D. *White over Black: American Attitudes toward the Negro, 1550–1812*. Williamsburg, VA: Published for the Institute of Early American History and Culture by the University of North Carolina Press, 1968.

Kaplan, Amy. *The Social Construction of American Realism*. Chicago: University of Chicago Press, 1988.

Katz, William Loren. *The Black West: A Documentary and Pictorial History of the African American Role in the Westward Expansion of the United States*. New York: Doubleday, 2005.

Kelley, Robin. *Race Rebels: Culture, Politics, and the Black Working Class*. New York: Free Press, 1994.

Kunjufu, Jawanza. *Countering the Conspiracy to Destroy Black Boys*, vols. 1–4. New York: African American Images, 1985–86.

Lebsock, Suzanne. *The Free Women of Petersburg: Status and Culture in a Southern Town, 1784–1860*. New York: W. W. Norton, 1984.

Lemann, Nicholas. *Redemption: The Last Battle of the Civil War*. New York: Farrar, Straus & Giroux, 2007.

Levernz, David. *Manhood and the American Renaissance.* Ithaca, NY: Cornell University Press, 1989.

Levine, Lawrence W. *Black Culture and Black Consciousness: Afro-American Folk Thought from Slavery to Freedom.* New York: Oxford University Press, 1977.

Levine, Robert S. *Martin Delany, Frederick Douglass, and the Politics of Representative Identity.* Chapel Hill: University of North Carolina Press, 1997.

Levy, Eugene. *James Weldon Johnson: Black Leader, Black Voice.* Chicago: University of Chicago Press, 1976.

Lewis, David Levering. *W. E. B. Du Bois: Biography of a Race, 1868–1919.* New York: Henry Holt, 1993.

———. *When Harlem Was in Vogue.* New York: Oxford University Press, 1982.

Litwack, Leon F. *Been in the Storm So Long: The Aftermath of Slavery.* New York: Alfred A. Knopf, 1979.

Logan, Rayford Whittingham. *The Betrayal of the Negro, from Rutherford B. Hayes to Woodrow Wilson.* New York: Da Capo Press, 1997.

Loggins, Vernon. *The Negro Author, His Development in America.* New York: Columbia University Press, 1931.

Lott, Eric. *Love and Theft: Blackface Minstrelsy and the American Working Class.* New York: Oxford University Press, 1995.

Love, Nat. *The Life and Adventures of Nat Love, Better Known in the Cattle Country as "Deadwood Dick"* (Los Angeles, CA: Wayside Press, 1907), accessed 21 November 2010, http://docsouth.unc.edu/neh/natlove/natlove.html.

Lyons, Clare. *Sex among the Rabble: An Intimate History of Gender & Power in the Age of Revolution, Philadelphia, 1730–1830.* Chapel Hill: University of North Carolina Press, 2006.

Mahar, William J. *Behind the Burnt Cork Mask: Early Blackface Minstrelsy and Antebellum American Popular Culture.* Urbana: University of Illinois Press, 1998.

Majors, Richard and Jacob Gordon. *The American Black Male: His Present Status and His Future.* New York: Nelson-Hall, 1994.

Majors, Richard and Janet Mancini Billson. *Cool Pose: The Dilemmas of Black Manhood in America.* New York: Simon & Schuster, 1992.

Marriott, David. *On Black Men.* Edinburgh, UK: Edinburgh University Press, 2000.

McCaskill, Barbara and Caroline Gebhard, eds. *Post-Bellum, Pre-Harlem: African American Literature and Culture.* New York: New York University Press, 2006.

McFeely, William S. *Frederick Douglass.* New York: W. W. Norton, 1991.

McHenry, Elizabeth. *Forgotten Readers: Recovering the Lost History of African American Literary Societies.* Durham, NC: Duke University Press, 2002.

McKay, Nellie Y., with Marcy Knopf. *The Sleeper Wakes: Harlem Renaissance Stories by Women.* New Brunswick, NJ: Rutgers University Press, 1993.

McPherson, James. *The Abolitionist Legacy.* Princeton, NJ: Princeton University Press, 1976.

———. *Marching toward Freedom: Blacks in the Civil War, 1861–1865.* New York: Facts on File, 1965.

McWilliams, Dean. *Charles W. Chesnutt and the Fictions of Race.* Athens: University of Georgia Press, 2002.

Meer, Sarah. *Uncle Tom Mania: Slavery, Minstrelsy, and Transatlantic Culture in the 1850s.* Athens: University of Georgia Press, 2005.

Millichamp, Joseph R. *Dixie Limited: Railroads, Culture, and the Southern Renaissance.* Lexington: University Press of Kentucky, 2002.

Minnick, Lisa Cohen. *Dialect and Dichotomy: Literary Representations of African American Speech.* Tuscaloosa: University of Alabama Press, 2004.

Mitchell, Michelle. *Righteous Propagation: African Americans and the Politics of Racial Destiny after Reconstruction.* Chapel Hill: University of North Carolina Press, 2004.

Moore, Winfred B. Jr., Joseph F. Tripp, and Lyon G. Tyler Jr., eds. *Developing Dixie: Modernization in a Traditional Society.* Westport, CT: Greenwood Press, 1988.

Morgan, Edmund S. *American Slavery, American Freedom: The Ordeal of Colonial Virginia.* New York: W. W. Norton, 1975.

Moses, Wilson Jeremiah. *Black Messiahs and Uncle Toms: Social and Literary Manipulations of a Religious Myth.* University Park: Pennsylvania State University Press, 1993.

———. *The Golden Age of Black Nationalism.* New York: Oxford University Press, 1978.

———, ed. *Classical Black Nationalism: From the American Revolution to Marcus Garvey.* New York: New York University Press, 1996.

Murray, Roland. *Our Living Manhood: Literature, Black Power, and Masculine Ideology.* Philadelphia: University of Pennsylvania Press, 2007.

Mutua, Athena. *Progressive Black Masculinities.* New York: Routledge, 2006.

Nelson, Dana D. *National Manhood: Capitalist Citizenship and the Imagined Fraternity of White Men.* Durham, NC: Duke University Press, 1998.

Oshinsky, David M. *"Worse than Slavery": Parchman Farm and the Ordeal of Jim Crow Justice.* New York: Free Press Paperbacks, 1997.

Page, Thomas Nelson. *The Negro: The Southerner's Problem.* New York: Charles Scribner's Sons, 1904.

Patterson, Orlando. *Slavery and Social Death: A Comparative Study.* Cambridge, MA: Harvard University Press, 1982.

Penningroth, Dylan C. *The Claims of Kinfolk: African American Property and Community in the Nineteenth-Century South.* Chapel Hill: University of North Carolina Press, 2003.

Phillips, Ulrich B. *American Negro Slavery.* Charleston, SC: BiblioBazaar, 2006.

Pieterse, Jan Nederveen. *White on Black: Images of Africa and Blacks in Western Popular Culture.* New Haven, CT: Yale University Press, 1995.

Pinar, William F. *The Gender of Racial Politics and Violence in America: Lynching, Prison Rape, & the Crisis of Masculinity.* New York: Peter Lang, 2001.

Prather, H. Leon. *We Have Taken a City: The Wilmington Racial Massacre and Coup of 1898.* Rutherford, NJ: Fairleigh Dickinson University Press, 1984.

Rael, Patrick. *Black Identity and Black Protest in the Antebellum North.* Chapel Hill: University of North Carolina Press, 2002.

Regosin, Elizabeth. *Voices of Emancipation: Understanding Slavery, the Civil War, and Reconstruction through the U.S. Pension Bureau Files.* New York: New York University Press, 2008.

Reid-Pharr, Robert. *Once You Go Black: Choice, Desire, and the Black American Intellectual.* New York: New York University Press, 2007.

Richardson, Riché. *Black Masculinity and the U.S. South*. Athens: University of Georgia Press, 2007.

Ross, Marlon B. *Manning the Race: Reforming Black Men in the Jim Crow Era*. New York: New York University Press, 2004.

Rothman, Joshua D. *Notorious in the Neighborhood: Sex and Families across the Color Line in Virginia, 1787–1861*. Chapel Hill: University of North Carolina Press, 2003.

Rotundo, E. Anthony. *American Manhood: Transformations in Masculinity from the Revolution to the Modern Era*. New York: Basic Books, 1993.

Ryan, Mary P. *Cradle of the Middle Class: The Family in Oneida County, New York, 1790–1865*. Cambridge: Cambridge University Press, 1981.

Savage, Kirk. *Standing Soldiers, Kneeling Slaves: Race, War, and Monument in Nineteenth-Century America*. Princeton, NJ: Princeton University Press, 1997.

Sidbury, James. *Becoming African in America: Race and Nation in the Early Black Atlantic*. New York: Oxford University Press, 2007.

Sielke, Sabine. *Reading Rape: The Rhetoric of Sexual Violence in American Literature and Culture, 1790–1990*. Princeton, NJ: Princeton University Press, 2002.

Silver, Andrew. *Minstrelsy and Murder: The Crisis of Southern Humor, 1835–1925*. Baton Rouge: Louisiana State University Press, 2006.

Smith, Felipe. *American Body Politics: Race, Gender, and Black Literary Renaissance*. Athens: University of Georgia Press, 1998.

Smith, Shawn Michelle. *Photography on the Color Line: W. E. B. Du Bois, Race, and Visual Culture*. Durham, NC: Duke University Press, 2004.

Sollors, Werner. *Interracialism: Black-White Intermarriage in American History, Literature, and Law*. New York: Oxford University Press, 2000.

———. *Neither Black nor White yet Both: Thematic Explorations of Interracial Literature*. Cambridge, MA: Harvard University Press, 1999.

Southern, Eileen. *The Music of Black Americans: A History*. 3rd ed. New York: W. W. Norton, 1997.

Spillers, Hortense. *Comparative American Identities: Race, Sex, and Nationality in the Modern Text*. New York: Routledge, 1991.

Stampp, Kenneth M. *The Peculiar Institution: Slavery in the Ante-Bellum South*. New York: Vintage, 1989.

Staples, Robert. *Black Masculinity: The Black Male's Role in American Society*. New York: Black Scholar's Press, 1982.

Stauffer, John. *The Black Hearts of Men: Radical Abolitionists and the Transformation of Race*. Cambridge, MA, and London: Harvard University Press, 2004.

Stecopoulos, Harry and Michael Uebel. *Race and the Subject of Masculinities*. Durham, NC: Duke University Press, 1997.

Sterling, Dorothy. *We Are Your Sisters: Black Women in the Nineteenth Century*. New York: W. W. Norton, 1984.

Stevenson, Brenda E. *Life in Black and White: Family and Community in the Slave South*. New York: Oxford University Press, 1996.

Stowe, Harriet Beecher. *Uncle Tom's Cabin; Or, Life Among the Lowly*. Boston: John P. Jewett & Co, 1855.

Summers, Martin Anthony. *Manliness and Its Discontents: The Black Middle Class and the*

Transformation of Masculinity, 1900–1930. Chapel Hill: University of North Carolina Press, 2004.

Sundquist, Eric J. *To Wake the Nations: Race in the Making of American Literature.* Cambridge, MA: Belknap Press of Harvard University Press, 1993.

Takaki, Ronald T. *Violence in the Black Imagination: Essays and Documents.* New York: Oxford University Press, 1993.

Tate, Gayle. *Unknown Tongues: Black Women's Political Activism in the Antebellum Era, 1830–1860.* East Lansing: Michigan State University Press, 2003.

Taylor, William B. *Drinking, Homicide, and Rebellion in Colonial Mexican Villages.* Palo Alto, CA: Stanford University Press, 1979.

Terborg-Penn, Rosalyn. *African American Women in the Struggle for the Vote, 1850–1920.* Bloomington: Indiana University Press, 1998.

Tye, Larry. *Rising from the Rails: Pullman Porters and the Making of the Black Middle Class.* New York: Henry Holt, 2004.

United States Department of Labor, Office of Policy Planning and Research. *The Negro Family: The Case for National Action.* Washington, DC: U.S. Government Printing Office, 1965.

Urwin, Gregory J. W., ed. *Black Flag over Dixie: Racial Atrocities and Reprisals in the Civil War.* Carbondale: Southern Illinois University Press, 2004.

Walker, Clarence E. *A Rock in a Weary Land: The African Methodist Episcopal Church during the Civil War and Reconstruction.* Baton Rouge: Louisiana State University Press, 1982.

Wallace, Maurice O. *Constructing the Black Masculine: Identity and Ideality in African American Men's Literature and Culture, 1775–1995.* Durham, NC: Duke University Press, 2002.

Wallace, Michelle. *Black Macho and the Myth of the Superwoman.* New York: Warner, 1978.

Wang, Xi. *The Trial of Democracy: Black Suffrage & Northern Republicans, 1860–1910.* Athens: University of Georgia Press, 1997.

Washington, Mary Helen. *Invented Lives: Narratives of Black Women, 1860–1960.* New York: Doubleday, 1987.

Wells, Ida B. *Southern Horrors and Other Writings: The Anti-Lynching Campaign of Ida B. Wells, 1892–1900.* Jacqueline Jones Royster, ed. Boston: Bedford/St. Martin's, 1997.

Wheatley, Phillis. *Poems on Various Subjects, Religious and Moral.* New York: Cosimo Classics, 2005.

White, Deborah Gray. *Ar'n't I a Woman? Female Slaves in the Plantation South.* New York: W. W. Norton, 1985.

———. *Too Heavy a Load: Black Women in Defense of Themselves, 1894–1994.* New York: W. W. Norton, 1999.

Wiggins, David K. and Patrick B. Miller. *The Unlevel Playing Field: A Documentary History of the African American Experience in Sport.* Urbana: University of Illinois Press, 2003.

Williamson, Joel. *The Crucible of Race: Black-White Relations in the American South since Emancipation.* New York: Oxford University Press, 1984.

————. *New People: Miscegenation and Mulattoes in the United States.* Baton Rouge: Louisiana State University Press, 1995.

Wills, David W. and Richard Newman, eds. *Black Apostles at Home and Abroad: Afro-Americans and the Christian Mission from the Revolution to Reconstruction.* Boston: G. K. Hall, 1982.

Wilson, David. *Inventing Black-on-Black Violence: Discourse, Space, and Representation.* Syracuse, NY: Syracuse University Press, 2005.

Wilson, Francille Rusan. *The Segregated Scholars: Black Social Scientists and the Creation of Black Labor Studies.* Richmond: University Press of Virginia, 2006.

Wilson, Sondra Kathryn, ed. *In Search of Democracy: The NAACP Writings of James Weldon Johnson, Walter White, and Roy Wilkins (1920–1977).* New York: Oxford University Press, 1999.

Winch, Julie. *Philadelphia's Black Elite: Activism, Accommodation, and the Struggle for Autonomy, 1787–1848.* Philadelphia, PA: Temple University Press, 1988.

————, ed. *The Elite of Our People: Joseph Willson's Sketches of Black Upper-Class Life in Antebellum Philadelphia.* University Park: Pennsylvania State University Press, 2000.

Wonham, Henry B. *Playing the Races: Ethnic Caricature and American Literary Realism.* New York: Oxford University Press, 2004.

Woodward, C. Vann. *The Strange Career of Jim Crow.* New York: Oxford University Press, 1974.

Wright, Richard. *Native Son.* Restored text edition. New York: Perennial Classics, 1998.

Wyatt-Brown, Bertram. *The Shaping of Southern Culture: Honor, Grace, and War, 1760s–1880s.* Chapel Hill: University of North Carolina Press, 2001.

————. *Southern Honor: Ethics and Behavior in the Old South.* New York: Oxford University Press, 1982.

Yellin, Jean Fagan and John C. Van Horne, eds. *The Abolitionist Sisterhood: Women's Political Culture in Antebellum America.* Ithaca, NY: Cornell University Press, 1994.

Young, R. J. *Antebellum Black Activists: Race, Gender, Self.* New York: Garland, 1996.

Contributors

JULIUS H. BAILEY is Associate Professor of Religious Studies at the University of Redlands in California. His book, *Around the Family Altar: Domesticity in the AME Church, 1865–1900* (University Press of Florida, 2005), examines African American familial religious life in the home.

ERICA L. BALL is Assistant Professor in the American Studies Department at California State University, Fullerton. She is writing a book on the cultural politics of African Americans in the antebellum North titled *To Live an Antislavery Life: Personal Politics and the Antebellum Black Middle Class.*

TIMOTHY R. BUCKNER is Associate Professor of History at Troy University in Alabama. He studies African American community and identity in antebellum Mississippi.

PETER CASTER is Associate Professor of Literature and Department Chair at the University of South Carolina Upstate. He is the author of *Prisons, Race, and Masculinity in Twentieth-Century U.S. Literature and Film* (The Ohio State University Press, 2008).

SIMONE C. DRAKE is Assistant Professor of English in the Department of African American and African Studies at The Ohio State University. She has published numerous articles on race and gender in literature, film, and culture.

JEFF FORRET is Associate Professor of History at Lamar University in Beaumont, Texas. He is the author of *Race Relations at the Margins: Slaves and Poor Whites in the Antebellum Southern Countryside* (Louisiana State University Press, 2006) and the forthcoming American slavery volume in Facts on File's *Issues and Controversies in American History* series (Facts on File, 2011). He is currently writing a book on violence among slaves in the antebellum South.

CHARITY FOX is an Assistant Professor in the School of Communications Design at the University of Baltimore. Her research and teaching focus on American cultural history, literature, film, television, and popular culture. She is currently working on a study of American mercenary figures in nineteenth- and twentieth-century popular culture narratives.

FIONA DEANS HALLORAN is Assistant Professor of American History at Eastern Kentucky University. Her manuscript *The Power of the Pencil: Thomas Nast and American Political Art* is under contract with the University of North Carolina Press.

MALINDA ALAINE LINDQUIST is Assistant Professor in the History Department at the University of Minnesota, Twin Cities. She studies the intellectual history of the social science of black masculinity from the turn of the century to the 1960s.

COLLEEN C. O'BRIEN is Assistant Professor of Literature at the University of South Carolina Upstate. She studies race, gender, and the political imagination in American writing and has published numerous articles in the *African American Review, African Studies Review, American Quarterly,* and other journals.

RICHÉ RICHARDSON is Associate Professor at Cornell University in the Africana Studies and Research Center. She is the author of *Black Masculinity and the U.S. South* (University of Georgia Press, 2007) and a series editor for the University of Georgia Press.

Index

Black Performance and Cultural Criticism

Valerie Lee and E. Patrick Johnson, Series Editors

The Black Performance and Cultural Criticism series includes monographs that draw on interdisciplinary methods to analyze, critique, and theorize black cultural production. Books in the series take as their object of intellectual inquiry the performances produced on the stage and on the page, stretching the boundaries of both black performance and literary criticism.

PS
374
.M37
F38
2011